AGAINST ALL ODDS

Published by SuccessBooks®, Lake Mary, FL.

SuccessBooks® is a registered trademark.

ISBN: 979-8-9892734-4-7
LCCN: 2024908337

This publication is designed to provide accurate and authoritative information with regard to the subject matter covered. It is sold with the understanding that the publisher is not engaged in rendering legal, accounting, or other professional advice. If legal advice or other expert assistance is required, the services of a competent professional should be sought. The opinions expressed by the authors in this book are not endorsed by SuccessBooks® and are the sole responsibility of the author rendering the opinion.

Scripture quotations marked CSB have been taken from the Christian Standard Bible®, Copyright © 2017 by Holman Bible Publishers. Used by permission. Christian Standard Bible® and CSB® are federally registered trademarks of Holman Bible Publishers.

Scripture quotations marked NKJV are taken from the New King James Version®. Copyright © 1982 by Thomas Nelson. Used by permission. All rights reserved.

Most SuccessBooks® titles are available at special quantity discounts for bulk purchases for sales promotions, premiums, fundraising, and educational use. Special versions or book excerpts can also be created to fit specific needs.

For more information, please write:

SuccessBooks®
3415 W. Lake Mary Blvd. #950370
Lake Mary, FL 32746
or call 1.877.261.4930

Visit us online at www.CelebrityPressPublishing.com.

AGAINST ALL ODDS

SUCCESS
BOOKS®
Lake Mary, FL

CONTENTS

CHAPTER 1

A JOURNEY BACK TO YOU

Learning to Love Yourself

———————

By Lisa Nichols

L ove is such a big word. I think it often gets overused. We say we love things like, "Oh, I love that movie. Or, "Oh, I love those jeans." Or, "Oh, I love him." Sometimes it gets so good, you think it's love in the moment.

Love is a sacred experience, but love for other people can be born only from a love that we first have with ourselves.

One of the best and most difficult journeys I ever took was the journey to fall back in love with Lisa, and I didn't know that journey would cost so much.

I was in South Africa, and I was rocking my 'fro, and this woman stood up and said, "Sistah, how do you wear your hair like that?"

"How do I get my Afro like this? I'm in Africa! Isn't an Afro normal for us? I'm wearing my hair like this because I was coming home."

She said, "No, I am wearing an Afro; *you* are wearing a *crown*."

I thought about it for a moment: "Oh, I get it."

I said to her, in front of five hundred people, "While wearing my natural hair is the easiest style to manage, getting to the point where I was comfortable enough to wear my hair natural was the longest journey I ever took—because it was the journey back to me."

And so what happens when we take a journey back to our core self? It starts by finding a way to reconnect, finding what we lost. In our busyness being busy, we can disconnect our body from our heart. Sometimes the longest journey to take is the one from our head and our heart.

I remember a time when I didn't fully love Lisa. I didn't see anyone beautiful that looked like Lisa on television. I didn't see any Miss Americas rocking mocha skin, full lips, round hips, and curly hair. So I had a hard time embracing my own beauty—my internal beauty and my external beauty.

I look at my life today and I think, "Wow, I'm blown away by the blessings I get to live out every day. It's exciting to travel the world, to run my mouth on stage and autograph things, to be a global student at the feet of leaders, dignitaries, kings and queens." But this was a long road that couldn't start until I fell in love with me.

The part of *The Secret* that everyone appeared to love was when I spoke about loving yourself before you could love anyone else. And here I am, all these years later, writing about the same topic because it is still relevant.

Until you can love your life where it is now, all aspects—your bank account *now*, your weight *now*—until you can love yourself as you are now, the next best version of your life cannot emerge. When you can love the existing version of who you are and the path you are on, then and only then can you touch the better best version of yourself. It wasn't until I fell in love with the Lisa at 224 pounds that the fitter, leaner, stronger Lisa of today could emerge.

We often wait until something gets better, or until our circumstances change, before we begin our journey of transformation. Like when that thing outside of our control changes, then we decide, "*Now* I'll play full out."

But the future version of you is saying, "Please play full out now. Don't wait for others. The better best version of yourself needs you to be all in *right now*."

———•———

I navigated through being over 220 pounds for nineteen years. And that caused me to compromise in the area of romantic love.

Though I had confidence in my ability to inspire people, I didn't have confidence in my ability to attract my ideal mate. Love had always been so difficult for me.

I met a wonderful man during a trip to Kingston, Jamaica, in 2012. My last night there was his first night. In the lobby of the Pegasus Hotel in Kingston, while I was talking to a colleague, a man passed me. The way he tells it, it took him a few minutes to muster up the nerve to come over to talk to me. We ended up sitting in that lobby and talking for eleven and a half hours, until the sun rose the next morning, and I literally had to run to go catch my flight.

"Lisa, can we stay in contact?"

I politely said, "Sure," but in my head I discounted why I should stay in contact with him. After all, with him being six feet, six inches, extremely athletic, and a public figure in his country, with his Caribbean flavor, I told myself he must be a player. He must already have a woman, and he simply wants me to be his extra sweetheart. Though he had shared he had two kids, I told myself he's probably married with nine kids. I convinced myself that I was too busy to possibly play any of his games.

I left for home, and he immediately began to communicate with me by texting one of three messages:

"Hi"

"Thinking of you"

"How's your son Jelani?"

But I was successfully convinced by my own antics, unsubstantiated by anything he had said or done. Every time I saw a message on my phone from him saying, "Hi," in my head I'd think, "Oh, that's the player. That's the guy who just wants me to be his 'extra.'" Sometimes I even decided not to reply to him at all, thinking, "He doesn't care. He'll eventually go away." I had a thousand reasons for why not now. And every one of those reasons made absolute sense to me even if it was created out of fear or shame.

Months passed, then years, and I found myself in and out of disappointing relationships.

One night, eight years after meeting him, I was in the shower, and I cried out to God, "Just send me a consistent man!" I got out of the shower, and my phone pinged. It was him, this guy I'd met one time so long ago, sending over another "Hi."

Out of curiosity, I began to scroll through my texts. My mouth dropped; I was shocked by what I saw. This gentleman had reached out to me every month, once a month, for close to a decade.

At this realization my heart started to race and I got butter-flies in my stomach. A thought struck me: "Oh my God. Was he serious all those years ago? Was he really interested?"

It was eleven o'clock at night in California, which made it way too early to call him in the Bahamas. So I waited. I spent all that time reading every message he'd sent me. Even though I could see there were months that had gone by that I hadn't replied, his next message never had a negative energy. Still, "Hi. How are you? I was thinking of you. How's Jelani?"

At 3 a.m. promptly I called his phone. He answered the phone with these words: "Are you OK?"

I said, "Yes, I am. Why do you ask?"

"Because I haven't heard your voice in eight years."

All of my eloquence, all of my charisma completely left the room, and a seventh grader's voice stuttered out, "Y-you, you've been texting me for eight years."

He gave a one-word response, "Yep."

Thrown back into 1979 when I attended Foshay Junior High, I said, "D-do you…still like me?"

Another one-word answer. "Yep."

Then the stakes got higher, and I got even more nervous to ask my next question. "Are-are, are you…single?" I kind of knew the answer.

His response was a little longer this time. "For you, I will be."

I knew what that meant, so with zero grace, and absolutely no eloquence, like a schoolgirl handing him a note that said, "Check the box, yes or no," I asked the next question: "D-do, do you…want…to date…me?" immediately followed by me holding my breath.

The articulate, powerful, dynamic speaker had left the room.

And after what felt like a thirty-minute pause, but what was actually only thirty seconds, he said, "I would absolutely love to date you."

Only then did I start to breathe again.

In his defense, he explained, "You made me wait for eight years; I could make you wait for thirty seconds."

When we started our long-distance dating, I was so excited to show him a recent picture of me so he could see how I had transformed from the woman he'd met eight years prior. Now there was ninety-three pounds less of me to love!

I expected all of these different responses from him. But when I sent him the pictures, he said, "Well, I'm happy for you. But remember, I chose you the way I chose you. And when I answered your question, it was not to your size. It was to the spirit you have."

The biggest barrier between me and finding love, in my head, was my weight. What I learned was that I just had to be willing to give myself a chance. The same chance that I was willing to give myself to get off government assistance, I had to give myself to find love, to be loved—to be worthy of love. I had to be willing to give myself a chance after making every single mistake I think a woman could make.

I had to believe that when I doubt my value, doubt my worthiness, I still deserved love.

That my past didn't equal my future.

That I deserved to be chosen by this amazing, breathtaking, almost unbelievable man. Not in spite of my past, but because of my past!

I later asked him, "Why'd you keep messaging me? Why not just stop at some point and move on?"

"Because I decided until I felt the way I felt during our conversation with another woman, I'd wait for you."

That was a really great reminder that even while working on areas of my own insecurities and imperfections, I was still worth loving.

———•———

One of the best decisions I ever made was to take the journey to fall back in love with Lisa. To not just stand *in* my story but instead to stand *on* my story. To use all of my hard times (or perceived failures) as fuel. The journey included turning my crawl into my walk, and my walk into my run, and my run into my soar. And today, I soar through the world teaching people how to turn the unfathomable into the possible. And one of the most exciting parts about my day is when my phone pings and I see "Hi, Mrs. Lisa Nichols-Hall."

And I promptly respond to my husband.

About Lisa

Lisa Nichols is one of the world's most requested speakers, as well as a media personality and corporate CEO whose global platform reaches over 170 countries and serves over 80 million people. Lisa's social media reach is over 2.4 million followers. As founder and chief executive officer of Motivating the Masses Inc., Lisa has helped develop workshops and programs that have transformed thousands of businesses and the lives of entrepreneurs. As a result of her training, her students become unforgettable speakers, best-selling authors, and six- and seven-figure entrepreneurs.

Lisa's extraordinary story of transforming her own life from public assistance to leading a multimillion-dollar enterprise is the inspiration behind her bold mission to teach others that it is possible to do the same. Today, fans worldwide revere Lisa for her mastery of teaching people how to accomplish unfathomable goals and tap into their limitless potential.

CHAPTER 2

THE POSSIBILITY OF NEW BEGINNINGS

By Jude Monteserrato

L et's play hooky," I teased, a lighthearted jest punctuating our morning ritual of getting ready to leave for work.

"We're going away in two weeks. It will be here before we know it," John reassured.

"Yeah, I know."

In the heart of the bustling city, amid the everyday rush and routine, life often paints its most vivid moments with strokes of ordinary detail. It was a morning like any other, the sun spilling its warmth across the streets of Brooklyn. As I bantered with John, preparing for our daily pilgrimage to work, little did I know that this ordinary Tuesday would etch itself into the annals of history, forever altering the tapestry of our lives.

We proceeded as always, headed into the city on the Express Bus. Exiting the bus, I tripped and fell onto my knees.

"Are you OK? Do you want to go to the hospital?" he said.

I'm petite but, of course, a tough New Yorker.

"I'm good. I'm fine. Don't worry about me," I said, "but my knees freakin' hurt!"

I was with John for fifteen years, and we lived together for ten. Though not legally married, he was my husband to me and the love of my life. We were living in Bay Ridge, Brooklyn. I worked for American Express in the World Financial Center, across the street from the World Trade Center, where John worked.

"I love you."

"I love you too."

With a kiss and hug, our paths diverged. I turned and saw him waiting for the elevator. Our eyes met. "I just love him," I thought with a smile. John was on his way up to the 105th floor, working for Cantor Fitzgerald.

The morning air crackled with anticipation, the city awakening to the rhythm of its heartbeat. My morning routine included my tea and muffin, powering on my computer to check emails, and going about my early start. I picked up my phone to call John and say my knees were OK when a thunderous roar shattered our morning tranquility.

"My God. What the hell? It's not raining. It's beautiful and sunny out," I said.

It made no sense.

A woman by the window said, "Something just hit the trade center."

"May I have your attention, please? What's going on is unclear, so please remain at your desk. Everything is going to be OK. Please just stay at your desk. Again, please remain at your desk."

"There's no way I'm staying at my desk," I said to myself.

The elevators were shut down. I climbed down forty-five flights of stairs, walked out of my building, walked across the street, looked up at the World Trade Center, and froze. I was frozen. I saw the flames, the plane hanging out of the building. The chaos and smoke filled the air, and the noise was overwhelming. But strangely, amid the clamor, I heard everything and nothing at all. Years later I would understand I was in shock.

A woman I worked with on the same floor was like my guardian angel that day. She said, "We gotta go. He's going to be OK. We have to go." I turned, and then the second plane hit the South Tower.

We still did not understand that we were under attack. Utter mayhem ensued. A sea of humanity scattered, each individual fleeing in their own direction. Thousands cried in anguish, their voices mingling with the moment's chaos.

"Come on! Let's get out of here!" she asserted in desperate determination. "We'll go to the pier and get on the ferry to New Jersey!"

"I can't stay here. I have to stay with these two women. I don't know what I'm doing," I thought.

Without further hesitation we ran among the thousands on the street and miraculously made it to the dock station. We were among the first on the ferry.

After exiting the ferry, we were going to take the train, and the woman insisted, "Just come home with me."

"No, let me get to my sister's house. At least I'm with my family there, and I'll figure out how to return to Brooklyn later," I said. I asked the train conductor which train I needed to get to Old Bridge, New Jersey, but I struggled to comprehend his instructions despite his repeated attempts.

"Your husband is going to be fine," she kept telling me, seeing the fear and anxiety over me as I wondered where John was.

The silence was deafening on the train. Everyone was in shock. As the train came out of the tunnel, we looked across the water to the unbelievable horror of the trade centers crumbling. Clouds of smoke filled the air above the skyline.

There was a gentleman next to me who said, "Are you OK? Do you know somebody?" I paused and shook my head. I couldn't utter a word. There we sat in a brief sense of consolation through the unspoken language of shared anguish. Each glance and gesture is a testament to the resilience of the human spirit.

When we got off the train, something surreal happened. Workers were busy on rooftops, going about their day as if nothing had changed. They were in a different world, completely unaware of what had happened. I was witnessing two different realities at once.

We arrived at her house, and I tried to reach my sister. I needed to tell her where I was.

"Do you want anything?" the woman asked.

"Do you have cigarettes? That's all I want. I want a cigarette." I had quit smoking just about ten years before that, but if there was ever a day to smoke, this was it.

"We don't smoke, but we keep cigarettes here for our friends. Here's a pack."

My sister finally came to get me and held another pack, though she knew I'd quit. We went to her house, and she tried to reassure me John was OK. I wanted to believe her, but deep down I knew he didn't make it out. I'd seen the horror with my eyes, but I couldn't accept it.

I stayed at my sister's house, surrounded by family and friends, hoping to hear from John. Days passed, but there was no word. Profound silence filled the space, echoing the void that John's absence left behind. After a few days, I said I wanted to go home, and my sister drove me. Walking in, I felt numb. Back then, answering machines were a thing, and ours blinked with dozens of messages. His voice was the only one I longed to hear.

John played basketball on Tuesday nights. His clothes, neatly arranged by the door, awaited his return from work in the city. Months passed before I could bear to move them.

Despite the support of friends and family, I faced the daunting task of healing alone. With no children to distract me, I struggled to find my footing. Days blurred into nights as I neglected my well-being, lost in the throes of grief.

Fourteen Months Later

It was November 2002. I woke up feeling like I had a hangover, even though I hadn't been drinking the night before. I looked at myself in the mirror and saw lifeless eyes staring back at me. That's when I told myself, "It's time to change. It's time to start healing. It's time to truly live again."

While I never drank alone at home, I found myself reaching for alcohol and cigarettes at every gathering with friends. I wasn't quite an alcoholic, but I began developing some dependency on them to avoid facing my issues. It was my way of escaping, of not knowing what else to do.

Years back I underwent a bilateral mastectomy due to Hodgkin's disease. John supported me throughout the decision-making process and accompanied me to every doctor's appointment except this one, when I went to my annual checkup alone. My treatment doctor, whom I trusted and respected, looked me in the eye and said, "You need to prioritize your well-being. I strongly suggest you see a psychiatrist."

There I sat in a psychiatrist's office with my arms crossed.

"You're showing signs of PTSD. You're losing weight. You're not sleeping," the psychiatrist remarked. "I recommend you take this medication."

Feeling uneasy, I hesitated and told him, "I'm not going down that path."

The doctor asked, "Well, what will you do then?"

I replied, "I do not know. Taking medication will only mask the pain. I need to face it head-on, not hide it."

Though it was a slow process, I turned to therapy, which played a small role in nudging me forward, step by painful step. Then, in early 2003, after nearly eighteen months of grappling with loss, I made the difficult decision to leave American Express. I needed time to heal to carve out a new path forward. I never returned to the financial center or set foot in that building after the attacks.

Mindset Will Matter

Before the pain and trauma, I radiated with vitality. Life was vibrant, brimming with possibilities. Despite our corporate jobs, we embraced every moment—traveling, dining at exquisite restaurants, reveling in the city's heartbeat.

In 1989, when Hodgkin's disease struck—a stark reminder of mortality at age twenty-eight—my doctor's words echoed in my mind, a beacon of hope amid the uncertainty. "Your mindset will matter," he said. "Be positive. You're going to get better." Armed with determination, I embarked on the journey toward healing.

Those words stayed with me. I couldn't articulate it, but looking back, I believe something divine was at play. Whether it was God or a force greater than me, I felt it guiding me, working on my behalf. I was a shell, a robot going through the motions. It felt like just passing time, even when I was with family and friends, sharing drinks or meals. I wandered from house to house, seeking any sense of comfort with family and friends but feeling utterly lost.

Nevertheless, I clung to my doctor's words: "Your mindset will matter. Be positive. You're going to get better." Those words were a lifeline, guiding me through the darkest of days.

FINDING YOGA

I was surprised when I felt the urge to start practicing yoga in January 2003. "Yoga? Really?" I thought. This was about the same time I quit my job, intending to focus on healing.

Starting yoga helped me connect with myself spiritually. It prompted me to ponder life's big questions: "Who am I? Why am I here? Where am I going?" It led me to introspection.

I wore all black or dark blue to yoga class, hiding in the corner with my hood up to avoid being noticed. As I focused on the instructor's teachings, I noticed something—I stopped replaying the painful "if only" scenarios in my head. The awareness grew that yoga was helping me take care of myself, a realization that evolved gradually.

Despite my initial resistance to flying, I went to Vegas with my friends. Due to a snowstorm in New York, the trip was extended to three weeks in Mexico. "Nothing is waiting for me back home," I reasoned. During this trip, and because of the awareness caused by yoga, I quit smoking and became a vegetarian.

You don't get over it, but you can live again.

Healing isn't about forgetting; it's about living again. In the realm of grief I've learned not to say, "Move on," or demand, "Get over it." Using the shards of a shattered heart, the slow process of stitching begins. Scars linger, tender to memory's touch. Grief is like wandering in a nocturnal wilderness, unfolding gradually. Progress emerges with each step, the path behind illuminated by the dawn's gentle light.

ACCEPTANCE

I deliberately chose to stay home alone on New Year's Eve of 2003 into 2004. I wanted to practice meditation, yoga, and journaling as the new year dawned. Despite others' questioning, I felt at peace with my decision. It marked a turning point in my journey toward acceptance and understanding.

On New Year's Day, I awoke without the weight of a hangover. A new chapter began. With a trip to Southeast Asia to study Thai massage on the horizon, I embraced various healing practices. That night, as I poured my thoughts onto the pages of my journal, I realized that John may no longer be with me physically, but he resides forever in my heart.

It took two years and four months to embrace acceptance—a pivotal milestone in healing finally.

A NEW ADVENTURE AWAITS

In January 2004 I embarked on a transformative journey to Thailand. Despite venturing with strangers, I found solace in the unfamiliar. Visiting my family in the Philippines added to my sense of self-discovery. Gradually, I rediscovered my independence, reclaiming lost vibrancy.

Ed was one of the group members we met in Seattle to travel and study in Thailand. Our flights were delayed because of the ice and snow, and it was now 04:00 a.m.

"Hi, my name is Ed Cardinal."

"Hello, my name is Judy." (I went by Judy at the time.)

As we explored Thai massage together in Thailand, an

unexpected connection blossomed. Although I initially resisted the idea of a relationship, Ed's genuine presence warmed my heart. Our friendship evolved despite my initial reservations. Over dinner I shared my truth—John's memory remained deeply etched in my life. Ed's understanding and patience marked the beginning of a special bond.

Long-distance dating with Ed brought profound changes. Leaving New York behind in 2006, I embraced growth and renewal in Rhode Island. John's loss catalyzed soul-searching and resilience, and Ed is my husband today.

While I wouldn't wish the pain I endured on anyone, I've come to appreciate the growth it sparked within me. It's a complex dynamic where adversity becomes a catalyst for personal development. Despite the initial turmoil, hardships have a way of transforming into unexpected blessings.

Everyone has their timeline.

It took me years to reach this point, to openly share my journey from darkness to light. As a yoga instructor in Rhode Island, I find fulfillment in guiding others toward healing, even as they may often remain unaware of my struggles. Slowly I began to open up, sharing my story with those who needed it most.

Grief follows no timetable, and pain is a universal experience. It's a journey unique to each individual, with its twists and turns. Grief knows no logic. We all have our way of coping. The essence lies in preserving the memory of the departed within your heart as life unfolds.

But here's the silver lining: you can emerge from the darkness. Life can be vibrant again, even after tragedy strikes. Each loss and story is different, but the possibility of thriving remains. Today, I stand as living proof that a vibrant life can emerge from even the darkest seasons. It's a journey of resilience, finding joy amid sorrow, and embracing the possibility of new beginnings.

About Jude

Embark on a transformative journey with Jude Monteserrato, a seasoned yoga instructor boasting over two thousand hours of training and extensive expertise in yoga therapy. Jude's commitment is to guide individuals who have experienced loss, navigating the challenges of grief toward a thriving life. She utilizes yoga, meditation, and nutritional guidance to foster balance in physical, mental, emotional, and spiritual realms.

Driven by the unwavering passion for yoga, Jude began her yoga teacher training in 2006, discovering her profound calling—to share the magic and sacredness of the practice with those yearning for a fulfilled life. Former co-owner of a studio until December 2021, Jude has been a beacon in the world of alignment-based yoga and meditation, conducting workshops, leading numerous yoga teacher trainings, and extending her reach to corporate offices, support groups for grief and cancer, and meditation sessions at Osher Lifelong Learning Institute (OLLI) in Rhode Island.

Jude's expertise extends beyond yoga into the area of natural cooking as a certified chef from the Natural Gourmet Institute in New York City.

Currently crafting her memoir, Jude delves into her journey through transforming the deep darkness, sadness, and trauma after losing the love of her life, John, while witnessing the tragic events of that fateful day, 9/11/01, to thriving in life again.

Throughout 2024 Jude will participate in a yearlong Certified Transformational Trainer Program under the guidance of Lisa Nichols and Sean Smith.

Featured in publications such as *More* magazine, *Urban Wellness* magazine, and a local Rhode Island newspaper, her story resonates widely. She has also graced the airwaves, appearing on the *Cardinal Points* radio show and the *Cardinal Way for Men* podcast.

Jude possesses a philanthropic heart that took her to Cambodia in 2009, where she raised $20,000 for the Cambodian Children's Fund through a yoga community challenge. Additionally, she initiated a collection of almost one thousand shoes for Soles4Souls, showcasing her genuine passion to extend a helping hand.

Explore the vibrant facets of Jude's life beyond yoga, where she finds joy in hiking, biking, walking, cooking, and reading. Her love for the beach, quality time with her husband, Ed, and their beautiful dog, Angel, adds a delightful dimension to her existence.

Curious to delve deeper into Jude's world? Visit www.judemonteserrato.com to connect, explore, and embark on your own journey toward holistic well-being under her guidance.

CHAPTER 3

THE POWER OF CONNECTION

Navigating Your Teen's Depression

By Kristina Saelee

My daughter was fourteen the night she disappeared. She'd asked some friends to spend the night, and then they all wanted to go to the movie theater. It was late, but I agreed. I watched them all walk into the theater before driving away.

When I came back to pick them up, none of the girls were there. I searched the lobby, the parking lot, and every room in the theater. They weren't anywhere. I called and re-called my daughter and her friends, but no one answered.

With every passing minute, every square inch searched that didn't turn up any sign of them, my heart raced faster. In a panic I called all the friends' parents. I called my daughter's father. We were divorced, but he was soon by my side helping me search. My sons arrived too, and everyone scoured the dark neighborhood streets. Searching. Hoping. Worrying.

Finally, after what felt like weeks, I got a call from one of the friends' moms. The girls were back at my apartment. Everyone was safe.

Except my daughter. She wasn't there.

I raced back to the apartment to figure out what had happened. After talking to my daughter's friends, I learned they'd taken a ride from some boys at the theater and gone to a big house party. My daughter had been extremely drunk and refused to leave with her friends.

I imagined my little girl intoxicated and alone in a strange house. Every possible scenario ran through my head.

After I called the police, the girls took me to the party house. When I arrived, it was empty. Discarded liquor bottles littered the floor, and the smell of weed was everywhere. Once again, I searched. Behind every bedroom and bathroom door, I feared discovering the worst.

But she wasn't anywhere.

In the woods outside the home, my ex-husband and I found the boy who lived at the house. He was stumbling drunk. We got him inside and turned him on his side. Through thick, confused speech, he told us my daughter had left the party with another group of boys.

Through social media we ended up contacting them and convincing them to bring her home. They dropped her off at a school parking lot, alone and drunk, at 4:00 a.m. With a mixture of immense relief, gratitude, and frustration, her dad and brothers picked her up and brought her home.

When she walked in the door, all I could do was hug her. I was so grateful she was safe. And alive. I sent her to bed, saying we'd talk more in the morning.

When she woke, the regret, embarrassment, and shame set in. Thinking she'd disappointed everyone and having already struggled with depression for a couple of years, she found some anti-anxiety medication in the house—and took the entire bottle.

It took time, but eventually she told me what she'd done. After calling poison control, an ambulance rushed her to the ER. There was a flurry of activity at the hospital before it was clear she was going to live.

In the ensuing quiet I looked at my daughter lying in her hospital bed. She seemed impossibly young and small. I knew that must have been how I'd looked to my mother all those years ago when I was lying in my own hospital bed after an intentional overdose.

MY DEPRESSION JOURNEY

I was raised by a mother who was bipolar and struggled intensely with mania and depression. Perhaps because of that I was always drawn to psychology. By ten I was reading dense clinical psychology textbooks.

My own depression began around twelve, manifesting as intense, persistent fatigue. I couldn't get up and go to school, which meant I missed a lot of class time. While other kids played hooky and hung out at the mall, I was in bed. Incapable of getting up. Sleeping all day.

With no support from the school system, I ended up dropping out. My parents also got divorced when I was fourteen, making it a particularly difficult time.

I ended up moving out on my own at fourteen, living with some friends' families before eventually getting an apartment with a roommate. Then the depression became so bad that I couldn't work to support myself. I moved back in with my mom, but everything continued to feel dark and heavy. I couldn't function. Life felt unbearable.

After trying different psychiatrists and every medication imaginable, still nothing worked. With every attempted and failed prescription, I felt more hopeless. I was certain nothing was ever going to get better. Eventually, I closed my door, lined up my medication bottles, and emptied each one.

My mom found me unconscious in the morning and rushed me to the hospital. Somehow I lived. I was in the hospital for a week, trying impossibly to explain that I didn't want to die. I just wanted the pain to end.

And then, shortly after being released, I discovered I was pregnant. Becoming a mom at seventeen was difficult, but it gave me a purpose and a reason to live.

I continued to struggle through my twenties, but the depression was more manageable. I tried going to college, but anxiety and panic attacks made that impossible. At every turn I literally felt like I was going to have a heart attack.

After a lifetime of attempted medications, I was prescribed another option. And like a miracle, it worked. I knew I had been depressed, but on this medication I finally felt the stark, wonderful contrast of happiness.

Medication isn't the answer for everyone, but for me, it gave me my life back.

MY DAUGHTER'S DEPRESSION JOURNEY

Knowing my mother is bipolar and knowing there's a genetic component, I understood there was a good chance at least one of my four biological children would go through this journey as well.

My daughter is my third child, and she began struggling at about the same age as I did.

She had been a national gymnast for ten years, but by her early teens she was starting to feel burned out and wanted to walk away. When she was fourteen, she quit.

It was an incredibly hard decision for her to make, and in many ways she lost her identity in that choice. Gymnastics had been her whole world. She didn't have a social life beyond it, and she struggled to know who or what she was outside of it.

By sixteen she was really struggling. She couldn't function. Her suicidal ideations were mounting. Whenever she attempted to go to school, she ended up calling and begging me to pick her up.

With my training as a behavior specialist and a parent coach, I had skills to help and support her. We also had a very close relationship, which meant she could be open about what she was feeling and thinking. And even with all those resources, I was terrified. Uncertain. Afraid to leave her alone for even one minute.

We tried counseling and different medications. We tried alternative schooling options. Nothing worked. Her risky behavior escalated, culminating in that night of her disappearance. I knew she was drinking. I knew she was getting high and driving. I knew there were nights she didn't come home. This strained our relationship, and I lived in a constant state of fear and worry.

After a lot of intensive counseling and therapy and me using every skill I had ever learned in my professional training, my daughter started to improve. She earned her GED and eventually went on to college. Today, she's doing amazing.

Everyone's depression journey is different. Your teen's progress might not look like you expect, but with unwavering support and love, they can find their way back.

Finding Light in the Darkness of Depression

When I look at my daughter today and how well she's doing, I feel overwhelming pride. Not only did she find her way through, but she's committed to sharing her story in the hopes it helps provide guidance, insight, and hope to others who are struggling.

As her mother and a fellow survivor of depression, I see my daughter as an inspiring pillar of strength.

If you're the parent of a struggling teen, here are just some of the strategies that carried us through.

Use a multiprong approach.

Getting better doesn't often happen after one strategy. It takes everything working together. Getting my daughter well required an entire team and support network.

When your teen is struggling, it means finding a good therapist, exploring different counseling options, figuring out educational alternatives, trying different medications, and teaching your teen healthy coping strategies.

Many teens in this position turn to unproductive coping mechanisms. Screen addiction. Alcohol. Drugs. Unsafe sexuality. Self-harm. These are all forms of coping. The job of the support network is replacing those unhealthy, unhelpful coping strategies with positive, productive ones.

Depression is a difficult, scary, stressful situation. As a parent, it's not on you alone to fix it. It takes a network of qualified help. You're there as the foundation of unconditional love and support.

Notice risky behaviors.

If you suspect your teen is depressed, pay attention to those risky behaviors. Look for sudden alcohol or drug use, vaping, unhealthy sexual practices, increased screen addiction, or self-harm.

Even something like a sudden disinterest in or refusal to attend school can be a major indicator of depression or anxiety.

Be aware of these behaviors, and open the dialogue as soon as you notice them.

Start with a powerful connection.

Your relationship with your teen is at the core of recovery.

When teens struggle with depression, it's not uncommon for them to self-isolate, push away, get irritable, and engage in extremely dangerous behaviors. This obviously makes having a healthy relationship with them difficult and puts a strain on that bond. But nurturing your relationship, especially through this difficult time, is critical.

When the relationship is sound and present, your teen knows they can communicate with you and open up. They're more receptive to your suggestions of help and support. At my request my daughter tried a dialectical behavior therapy (DBT) group. After a few sessions she knew it wasn't for her, but she was willing to try. She acknowledged recovery was a process, and she was open to being an active participant in it.

Even with the extra support of therapists, school counselors, and doctors, your role as a supportive parent is pivotal. Through problem-solving skills, collaboration, open communication, and family meetings, you and your family can navigate a way through this dark period.

I understand firsthand how challenging it is to battle depression. When your teen is struggling, I also know how terrifying it is and how ill-equipped you can feel to handle the magnitude of that challenge. When your teen is telling you they want to take their life, you're worried to death for them. But in that moment, know that they feel safe enough to talk to you about those feelings. Celebrate being there to support them, love them, and get them the necessary help.

Navigating your teen's depression is scary, but having a teen go through it silently and without your knowledge is even scarier.

Get specialized help.

I was trained as a positive discipline educator. I taught others how to be simultaneously kind and firm. I had all the tools, training, and credentials at my disposal, and I *still* felt helpless and lost trying to support my daughter.

Therapy is undoubtedly helpful, but many family therapists aren't equipped with the specific skills to help parents navigate this situation.

Even though I was a parent coach myself, I enlisted the help of another parent coach to help me work through this situation. This specialized help gave me additional insight and tools to foster, nurture, and grow that strong connection with my daughter.

In life's most challenging situations, never be afraid to ask for or to receive the specific, trained, specialized help you need.

Self-regulate emotions.

When a teen struggles deeply with depression, it leads to many intense, high-emotional situations. Begin your work with yourself. Learn to self-regulate your own emotions in those times of extreme distress.

Once you've learned those skills, you're better equipped to teach your teen how to self-regulate and de-escalate those stressful, tense, heated moments.

Advocate for your teen's safety.

If your teen's a danger to themselves, become an advocate for their safety. You don't have to do it alone, and the onus of getting them better isn't on you, but be a part of putting together an appropriate safety plan.

This could include finding the right therapist, considering

medication, considering medication alternatives, putting a 504 plan or IEP in place for school, and removing medications or dangerous objects from the house.

No two people's depression journeys are the same, but ensure there's a support network wherever the teen is spending time.

It *can* get better.

Depression is a lifelong journey. You're never 100 percent cured, but it can become manageable. You can learn the tools and implement the strategies to live a successful, rewarding, happy life.

In the middle of depression, it feels impossible to see a way out, but that's a temporary space. With support and work there is light on the other side.

You (and your teen) aren't alone.

My daughter and I are so passionate about telling our stories because we want people to know they're never alone. There is support. There are options. There's *always* hope.

Even when it feels like it's never going to get better, it can. My mom got better. I got better. My daughter got better. We're living happy, amazing, fulfilling lives because we had support.

Yes, it was dark, but even though we couldn't see in that moment, we could feel the hands holding ours and guiding us toward light.

AFTER THE DARKNESS

I've been a parent coach for about ten years, and now I specialize in helping parents of teens struggling with depression.

When my daughter began struggling, I was already certified in positive discipline. I had all the tools. I ran parenting workshops, but I realized none of those books, workshops, or trainings prepared me for the reality of raising a teen with depression.

So I set out to create a program that addressed that need.

No words can describe the worry you feel as a parent when your teen is struggling. When you're unsure what they're capable of.

When you're searching the dark streets at night for them or don't know what you'll find behind that next bedroom door.

Helping my daughter through her depression was one of the hardest things I've ever done, but I'm so proud to be using those hard-earned lessons to help others learn to connect with, support, and advocate for their teens struggling with depression. To be in the business of teaching others the lifesaving skills of practicing resiliency, overcoming challenges, and *never* letting go of hope.

About Kristina

Kristina Saelee, a dedicated parent coach and the visionary of emPOWERed Parenting, is on a mission to empower parents of teenagers grappling with depression. Her renowned program equips parents with the essential tools to effectively connect with, support, and advocate for their struggling teens during challenging times.

With a bachelor of social work (BSW) degree under her belt, Kristina possesses a solid foundation in social work principles that inform her holistic and compassionate approach to helping families navigate mental health struggles. She seamlessly combines her roles as a writer, speaker, parent coach, and family and youth therapist to provide comprehensive support to parents seeking guidance in handling their teens' mental health issues.

Kristina's expertise shines through in her personalized coaching sessions, where she offers tailored strategies and emotional support to parents who find themselves at a loss when dealing with their teen's depression. Her deep understanding of adolescent psychology and family dynamics enables her to create a safe space for parents to express their concerns, fears, and hopes for their children's well-being.

As a writer, Kristina shares her insights and guidance through thought-provoking articles, blog posts, and educational resources, reaching a wider audience beyond her coaching practice. Her engaging speaking engagements at workshops, conferences, and community events have inspired countless parents to approach teen depression with empathy, patience, and resilience.

In her role as a family and youth therapist, Kristina leverages evidence-based therapeutic techniques and compassionate counseling to guide families toward healing and growth. She empowers parents to strengthen their relationships with their teens, foster open communication, and build a supportive environment that promotes positive mental health outcomes.

Through emPOWERed Parenting, Kristina has created a transformative program that goes beyond traditional parenting advice, offering practical strategies and emotional support tailored to the unique needs of families dealing with teen depression. With Kristina's guidance parents are equipped to navigate the complexities of supporting their teens on their journey to mental wellness, fostering stronger connections and brighter futures for their families.

Kristina is a mother to five children, ages fifteen through twenty-seven. She is a foster parent and hosts foreign exchange students. In her spare time she enjoys traveling and curling up with a good book.

Learn more at www.empoweredparenting.family.

CHAPTER 4

A PATH FOR HEALING AND SELF-DISCOVERY

By Marie McDole

The glare of car lights and thunderous semitrucks drowned the sound of the racing heartbeat within me. My desperate cries for my friend Joe blended with the chaos; I was unsure if they were reaching his ears. In that frantic moment, Joe and I, driven by some reckless pursuit on a stretch of I-95, hoisted ourselves over a cold cement wall and landed with a thud in a train yard. Little did I know this impulsive escapade would become a pivotal encounter, etching its impact on the canvas of my life for years to come.

Ah, the question that has echoed through the corridors of my past like a haunting melody: How did I get here? It's more than a mere inquiry; it's the punctuation mark in a narrative laced with one questionable decision after another. It persisted not just during my runaway escapades but far beyond the days when I finally hung up my running shoes. That particular night, the answer to that poignant question wove into the fabric of a stolen car.

Against better wisdom, we dared to dream of a journey from Lancaster, Pennsylvania, to Parts Unknown, Florida—in a stolen car, mind you. No money in our pockets, just young and blind audacity propelling us forward. It's clear we weren't exactly candidates for Mensa. After all, I was only seventeen years old.

That night unfolded into a gritty tale of pseudo-slumber beneath the cold embrace of a train, the residue of a failed attempt to slip away from the clutches of Baltimore in yet another pilfered vehicle.

The next day read like a chapter from the *Thieves' Triathlon* playbook: a heart-thumping symphony of running from the police, a rendezvous with the depths of a storm drain, and aimless wandering through the labyrinth of an unfamiliar city.

After our escapade, we stumbled onto the shores of safer, saner ground. As fate would have it, two benevolent souls, busy picking up cans on the roadside, extended a hand.

"You two look like you could use some help," one of them said.

"Yes," we replied, then answered a few other questions they asked to understand our situation. Incredibly, they offered to help us.

"OK, wait here. We'll get our truck and pick you up."

Away they walked with their aluminum haul as we found a spot to wait safely. In the blink of an eye, we found ourselves nestled in the back of a modest white pickup truck, cruising toward an unexpected haven.

We arrived at a modest home, unsure of what to expect. Our mysterious benefactors led us to a woman whose heart overflowed with compassion. From the confines of her home she not only nourished and clothed the needy in her community but, inexplicably, saw something in two runaways like us. Perhaps it was the desperation etched on our faces or the vulnerability we wore like a badge of dishonor. Joe pleaded for her to spare us from the clutches of law enforcement and found an empathetic ear in this unexpected savior. The tapestry of generosity extended another mile as she opened her home, offered us clean clothes, and even equipped us with bus tokens the next day's dawn.

Imagine my astonishment; I stood there, rendered speechless. This angel of mercy, this unsung hero, rich in compassion, would resonate through the annals of my memory. The bus tokens weren't just tokens; they were tickets to redemption, guiding us back to Pennsylvania on a Greyhound bus. In the face of her overwhelming generosity, all I could muster was gratitude and a silent acknowledgment of the inexplicable kindness that had woven its way into the chaotic story of our escapades.

We were breathless and anxious at the city bus stop, the looming fear that we had missed our ride hanging heavy in the air. Like a twist of fate, a benevolent cab driver pulled up.

"Can I offer you a ride?" said the kind woman.

She offered us a *free* ride to the station! Up to this point my connection with the religion of my upbringing was on hiatus, but a profound belief in a Power greater than me stirred within me. That conviction lingers, shaping my perspective on those events and anchoring them to the perennial question that echoes through my life: "How did I get here?" It's as if those moments were stitched with threads from the divine, leaving me to unravel their deeper meaning.

Those escapades as a runaway didn't magically transform me into an overnight "saint-sation." No, the pattern persisted—I fled the confines of home as a teenager only to find myself sprinting through the intricate maze of adulthood.

What was I running from? The question lingered, haunting me like a relentless specter. The unflinching answer stared back at me— *myself.* I sought refuge in the shadows of lies and the embrace of strangers' sheets. My shame and inadequacies were drowned in bottles of booze and a repertoire of self-destructive behaviors that cast a looming shadow over my existence. In moments of sobriety I'd cast a searching gaze around me, and the resounding query reverberated, "How did I get here?" often accompanied by the disheartening encore of "again?"

Yet in the chaos of street insanity, a weary surrender crept in. I retraced my steps back home, fatigued and yearning for a different path. By then, several bridges were smoldering embers in my life's rearview mirror. It was time for a recalibration—I secured a job and tentatively stepped into the realm of responsibility. The journey toward reclaiming myself had begun.

After I returned home, my mom shared some big news—she and my brothers were moving to New Mexico. I chose to stay in Pennsylvania, thinking it would be my forever home. But life had different plans for me. Before turning eighteen, I lived in a holler in West Virginia, chasing a dream of living off the land. Unfortunately, that dream quickly fell apart, and reality hit me.

Over the next ten years, I moved around—New Mexico, Nebraska, and back to New Mexico. While working in jobs that didn't lead anywhere in Nebraska, I realized I wanted more from my life. I loved to travel, so I set that as my goal. I worked several jobs, saved money, and made a plan.

I traveled to visit family and friends on both coasts of the US. Then, I hopped between islands like Maui and the Fijian islands. During a visit to my aunt in Reno, Nevada, two things happened: one about my drinking and one about going back to school. I took the school suggestion seriously but passed on the other.

After finishing school, I moved to Texas to start my career and continue a not-so-great relationship that had been long-distance until then. After just a year of that I realized I wasn't the person I wanted to be—for him, his kids, or myself. I looked around and thought, "This isn't my life." But I had no idea what my life was supposed to look like.

Surprisingly, I ended up in Arizona, the last state I ever thought I'd live in. It's where the most significant changes in my life happened. Shortly after moving there, some really tough things happened, one after the other. Those events made it clear that my life needed a significant change. They pushed me into something I never thought I'd do: become sober.

Good God, those initial years were like stumbling through a painful fog! I had been living on repeat for a couple of decades, a broken record of throwing caution to the wind, indulging in self-destructive behaviors, and spiraling into shame afterward. Not exactly a recipe for success, right?

Suddenly, I slammed the brakes, crashing hard into the proverbial windshield of my life. I found myself lost and alone for what felt like an eternity. I initially reached out to a few people for help, but I resisted their advice, convinced I knew everything even when clueless. It took hitting another emotional rock bottom to swallow my pride and accept the help available.

That was the turning point. I went from a perpetual state of running away to a commitment to learning how to stay. It was time for me to create a life where I could feel safe, sane, and comfortable in my skin.

The journey of personal growth continued, and an epiphany struck soon after I settled into my home. A holiday meal with a couple of women, and it dawned on me—I had a roof over my head, a stable life with enough food, and incredible friends to share it all with. My life finally felt abundant. That day etched in my soul, I realized, "*This* is what my life is supposed to look like!" The revelation echoed through my being, a testament to the transformative power of embracing stability and finding abundance in simplicity.

I've always been passionate about helping people, and this unique life I've crafted made me realize I want to turn that passion into a career. While healthcare involves helping people physically, I felt a calling to assist others in transforming their lives, just as mine has changed. There's immense joy in hearing women say, "Wow. Thank you for sharing that with me. I hadn't thought of it [their issue] like that."

Helping others has become a radiant source of fulfillment in my life. It inspired me to return to school to become an integrative healing arts practitioner. I even got ordained because I sense a profound spiritual connection, especially when engaging with women. To enhance my tool kit, I became certified as a life coach.

A few things guided my journey from the fetal position to being a primarily functional adult: first, I had to lay the SMACK down in my life!

S is for "shit-uations," as I affectionately call them. Take a moment to look around yourself. Toxic people combined with high-intensity circumstances (with or without intoxicants) equal "shit-uations." If your stories often start with, "OMG! I can't believe what happened over the weekend!" or your friends can't believe what you did, it might be time to evaluate your life and distance yourself from toxicity. Seek healthier connections in support groups, with a therapist, or with a life coach. Healthier people won't hinder your positive changes or engage in destructive gossip. Ideally, they'll help you see yourself in a way that fosters growth.

Some of us are delicate and need a gentle, honest approach. Others have walls as thick as concrete, requiring a metaphorical jackhammer to break through. In either case, finding someone nonjudgmental and non-shaming provides a comfortable starting point for vulnerability.

M **is for manageability.** If you're constantly putting out fires due to overextending yourself or feel exhausted from perpetual busyness without progress, setting healthy boundaries with your time is crucial for maintaining sanity.

A **is for action.** Taking action is the key to positive change. Reading self-help books or listening to inspiring podcasts is beneficial, but you won't see much progress without implementing those suggestions. You reap what you sow, after all.

C **is for compassion.** Extend compassion to yourself, and you'll have more to share. Often we're harshest on ourselves, leading to strained relationships.

K **is for kindness.** Even in small gestures, practicing kindness can create far-reaching ripples, and don't forget that the recipient could be you.

On this healing journey another crucial element is **PCP**—not the tranquilizer but *practice, consistency,* and *patience.* Adopting new behaviors is challenging, feeling like an alien among humans. Learning new skills, especially relating to others in healthier ways, requires repetition and patience. It was hard! It often felt like I was an alien life form plopped down among humans, with no communication or coping skills. No one becomes perfect in the first five minutes of learning. Being patient with ourselves allows us to navigate through discomfort and build self-trust and confidence over time.

I am a strong advocate for **THC**—yes, *the healing continues.* Embracing this concept signifies my belief in an ongoing journey of self-improvement, recognizing it as a lifelong adventure. There's profound fulfillment in creating a sanctuary for those on a similar path, sharing the collective journey. Witnessing the transformation of others during their dark night of the soul and responding with love and kindness is incredibly rewarding.

In this shared voyage of pain, challenge, and growth, we discover the power of resilience, the beauty of transformation, and the importance of extending compassion to ourselves and others. As we navigate the twists and turns of our stories, remember that even against all odds, *the healing continues* for us all, weaving a tapestry of strength, empathy, and perpetual growth. Embrace the journey, and may your path be illuminated with self-discovery and profound healing.

About Marie

Marie McDole was born in Würzburg, Germany, into a military family. The family returned to the States when Marie was three. They moved frequently until she was seventeen, and Marie continued to move around for years after. She managed to stay put long enough to graduate with honors from Central New Mexico Community College with a certificate in surgical technology in 2006 and is certified nationally through the NBSTSA. She is a current member of the Association of Surgical Technologists.

She received her Bachelor of Divinity in 2021 through the Southwest Institute of Healing Arts and was ordained through the Universal Brotherhood Movement. She continued her studies to receive her diploma and several certificates of excellence in the integrative healing arts practitioner program. She graduated in 2022.

For a time, Marie volunteered as a teacher's aide with at-risk children ages one through three. She helped them learn basic hygiene skills, assisted during lunchtime, and got to sing along with the cleanup song. She found great delight in seeing the children's eyes light up when they would figure something out on their own, such as how to ride a tricycle.

She has been working with women for the past twelve years, listening as they shared years of pent-up pain and grief, walking beside them through valleys, and celebrating them at their peaks. After a seventeen-plus-year career in healthcare, Marie realized that life coaching is her vehicle to make uplifting other beautiful souls her full-time career. It is her life passion and her calling.

When Marie is not engaged in her life's work, you can find her hiking, backpacking, traveling, or preparing feasts for friends. She gets her own cup filled and replenished in natural surroundings and in her connections with others. Marie lives in Phoenix, Arizona, with her plant, Rooty.

Please reach out to Marie at Marie.Heart2Souls@gmail.com if you are interested in exploring your life's possibilities.

CHAPTER 5

LIVING MY LEGACY

*How My Son's Tragic Death Inspired Me to Live
More Fully and Help Other Women Do the Same*

by Alicia Stingley

fter years of struggle, I was finally starting to dig my way
out of a big hole. I'd overcome crippling physical and financial handicaps and was beginning to see some light at the
end of the tunnel. And then I got a call from the hospital: "Come
quickly; it's your son."

I arrived to find my youngest child, Corey, in a coma. He had
been rushed to the ER after being attacked by three men in an
encounter at a convenience store that had left him breathless, his
brain deprived of oxygen. Four days after Christmas 2012 his
father, siblings, and I made the heartbreaking decision to take our
teenage boy off life support.

When I tell you that shattering experience inspired my passion
to pursue financial freedom and help others build wealth, you
might be surprised. After all, if anyone understands that there is
more to life than money, it should be me, right?

Yes, I know all too well that no amount of material possessions
can ever replace what I have lost. But I also realized through that
awful event that no matter how well we plan and how hard we
work, none of us are promised tomorrow. As Corey used to say,
"Moments only happen once." Life can turn or end in an instant.
We don't know when our time is up, so we can't afford to waste it.

This awareness of the fragility of life hasn't left me desperate,
but it has made me determined. So I am not going to wait until

I retire to enjoy my money because I'm not guaranteed I will get there! Nor will I just leave it as a legacy for my grandchildren. Of course, I will ensure they are provided for after I am gone, but I want to *live* a legacy, not just *leave* one. Legacy is about presence, not just provision. I want to enjoy time with them now, take them on trips, invest in their development—and all that takes money.

Corey's tragic death has inspired me to live fully now and use my financial planning and investment expertise to inspire others, especially women of color, to create wealth.

COMING TO THE END OF MYSELF

I learned to be self-reliant at an early age. Born to a teenage mom in Chicago's notorious Cabrini-Green projects, I grew up in Milwaukee after she moved there in search of a better life. She married and had three more children with my stepdad. As a blue-collar family, we didn't have a lot of money, but we never went without—until my stepdad got addicted to drugs. Then everything changed. He sold our van and household possessions, and became physically abusive.

To escape the chaos, I began to run away, staying with different friends. I decided I couldn't trust anyone else to provide for me and protect me, so I'd have to do that for myself—an attitude that shaped many years of my life.

Thankfully, there were people at Rufus King High School who must have had a sense that all wasn't well in my world and made a point of singling me out for encouragement. In giving me a solo in a production, Miss Jupka, my choir teacher, planted the seed of the idea that I had something unique to offer the world. And by giving me small parts in plays at a time when my spotty school attendance meant I couldn't be relied on for a more significant role, Mr. Mackinson communicated that you still deserve a chance if you are going through something and that not everyone will give up on you.

At Marquette University, Sande Robinson, the director of the

Educational Opportunity Program, and the entire team helped me through the struggles of college and were instrumental in shaping me into the adult that I am today.

I also became a Christian and got married while in college. Because of my experiences growing up, I did not plan on marrying or being a mom. But God had other plans, and my husband and I had four children within five years. We lived a modest but comfortable life, making do on my husband's single salary. When Corey was four, I went back to work part time and then full time when my husband lost his job.

We weren't making it on my lower income, so I got a second, part-time job and went back to school to try to increase my earning power—all while continuing to carry the weight of running the home. Not surprisingly, I could only keep all that up for so long. Diagnosed with a long list of ailments—fibromyalgia, restless legs syndrome, and migraines among them—I was taking fourteen different medications and some days simply was unable to get out of bed. Determined not to be beaten, after a time, I stopped taking all meds and willed myself to rise and keep going.

As our situation continued to spiral—foreclosure, repossession, welfare—I realized that something had to change. My husband and I divorced, and I gradually began to rebuild my life. I did everything legal I could to improve my circumstances, including selling my plasma at one point. But I discovered that even my best efforts could only take me so far one day when I went to the grocery store. Proud to no longer need the food stamp card, I was shocked to have my debit card declined. When I called the bank, I was informed the IRS had cleaned out my checking and savings accounts over a tax lien of my ex-husband's.

I was embarrassed because I was working as a personal banker by now, helping others but seemingly unable to help myself. It felt like I had taken one step forward and two steps back. For the first time in my life, I had to ask for help. My father and my youngest brother gave me some money to help me get by. I vowed to never be in that situation again. So I made a series of decisions that eventually landed me a position as a financial advisor. It was there that I realized that it wasn't enough just to work harder; I had to work smarter. That meant learning how to make my money work for me.

A Quiet Revolution

Coming through bankruptcy, I was starting to make some headway when I got that devastating call from the hospital. Losing Corey galvanized my determination to embrace life as fully as possible by pursuing financial independence and helping other women—particularly Black and Brown women, who historically have been relied upon to be the strong anchors for their families while also being more marginalized economically—do the same.

Creating wealth for women is not just giving individuals a new life but is part of a quiet social revolution because women with wealth have the power to change the world. Why? Because women tend to instinctively be nurturing and generous. They invest in causes that are important to them, their families, and the world at large. Not that men don't have those qualities too, but they seem to be more instinctive in women. Yet women also have some unique hurdles to overcome in achieving financial freedom and security. We spend more time out of the workforce, caring for others. We prioritize the needs of others. We typically make less, save less for retirement, and invest more conservatively. When women attain financial freedom, they are also liberated to make a greater impact by sharing their many other gifts more freely.

That's why it's my God-given mission to help women create wealth even if they've never invested before, feel behind on their financial goals, or fear it's too late to start. Thankfully, as I tell my clients, if you are breathing, it is never too late to make a change. I coach them through a series of action steps: making the required shift in mindset, learning the necessary skills, and developing the proper strategy for implementation.

It all starts with looking at finances differently. I describe it this way: a middle-class lifestyle is like playing checkers, while a wealthy, financially independent lifestyle is like playing chess. It's a different game, and you have to learn the rules. Essentially, building wealth involves making your money work more for you rather than working more for money, by creating multiple streams of passive income. They could be investing in the stock market, real estate, or other businesses that don't require your physical presence.

WIDENING THE CIRCLE

While the details of my three major crises—health, finances, and grief—were different, they produced similar results: stress that wore me down physically, mentally, and emotionally. I've learned that there is no single remedy for this, but a collection of responses has helped me not only survive but thrive.

First and foremost is my faith. Since becoming a Christian, I've always believed that God loves me and has a unique purpose for me. I've tried to follow in his ways, not always successfully, and not always understanding why things have sometimes turned out as they have. But I have held firm to the conviction that he is good, all the time—even when Corey was hospitalized.

During that two-week vigil by his bedside, I fasted and prayed. I told everyone who would listen that God was going to heal my son—I just didn't know whether it would be here on earth or up in heaven. When we came to the decision that Corey's time with us was over, I accepted God's will.

I don't pretend to understand it. And I definitely don't like it. But I choose to believe that "all things work together for the good of those who love God" (Romans 8:28, CSB). One day everything will make sense. Until then I am comforted knowing that Corey is fully healed and I will spend eternity with him in heaven.

Faith doesn't always come easy, though; we must walk it out. I've had to work through feelings of guilt and regret. What if we had never moved to that neighborhood? What if we hadn't divorced?

What if Corey had been living with me rather than his father? Only God knows, and he has helped me find peace in leaving that with him.

Those painful what-ifs were magnified by the public nature of my son's death. Corey had been apprehended and asphyxiated by three men during a petty shoplifting episode. When the news broke, people were quick to rush to judgment about Corey, me, and his father without knowing all the facts. However, ten years after Corey's death, at the time of writing, officials are reexamining what happened to determine whether criminal charges might be due against those who restrained him. We may still get justice for Corey.

As well as relying on God, I have learned to rely on others. As you might imagine, the Christmas season can be distressing. So I have made a point of reaching out to friends and asking them to help me through by checking in with me, praying for me, and keeping me busy so I don't fall into depression. Being vulnerable like that has been a stretch for someone who has always been used to being strong and being there for everyone else. But I have discovered that it truly does take a village—not just to raise a child, but to help their parents come through when they lose one.

HEALTHY TENSION AND HARMONY

In addition to faith and friends, I have leaned on professional help. There's a negative stigma in parts of the Black community about therapy—a sense that it's a sign of weakness or that we shouldn't be involving other people in our business. I have found the opposite to be true—I've been strengthened by being able to talk through issues with a counselor who is independent of my situation and insightful.

That said, it's important to be wise and cautious when inviting others into your pain. Your circle doesn't need to be large, just strong. For friends, shared values are essential. Do they see the world through a similar lens? Are they in low-key competition with you? Can they hold a confidence? Do they pray for you and with you?

If it's professional help you're seeking, then of course you will want to check out their credentials. But there needs to be more than professional qualifications. You want to have a sense of personal connection with someone to whom you are entrusting yourself, whether with your emotional or financial well-being.

Perhaps the hardest part of overcoming my life challenges has been learning to both take control and let go of control simultaneously because both are necessary. We can't control everything that happens, but we can control how we respond.

So I do all that I can. I work hard. I cultivate my relationships. And I accept that even with my best efforts, not everything is going to turn out the way I might like, and that's just the way it is.

Reaching this place of healthy tension requires a shift in mindset for some people. There's a lot of talk these days about work-life balance, as though all of your priorities should be weighted equally all of the time. But that's simply not the way life works. Sometimes responsibilities at work take precedence. Sometimes family demands mean we must pull back from work. Sometimes mama just needs to live her life!

I think harmony is a better word than balance. Harmony recognizes that sometimes the sopranos need to be louder than the tenors, and there are moments when the basses get to be center stage. But when all the different voices blend together in their ebbs and flows, their pauses and parts, you end up with beautiful music.

I know Corey is singing with the angels, and one day I will join him. In the meantime, I find joy in seeing him in the faces of his nephews and niece, and in the lives of the women he has inspired me to help create financial freedom and become the best versions of themselves, secure their financial futures, and impact generations to come.

About Alicia

Alicia Stingley, wealth mentor to mature women, is the founder of Allyn Financial LLC and Finances After 50. She has over twenty years' experience in the financial services industry as a personal banker, mortgage loan closer, retirement plan consultant, financial advisor, and coach.

Having successfully navigated her way through many difficult financial situations, Alicia's superpower is her ability to relate to others in a very powerful and nonjudgmental way. Alicia's God-given mission is to make an impact and income to live unapologetically, give generously, bless her family, leave a legacy, and inspire women to be wealthy. She has a specific passion to empower midlife women who may feel behind on their financial goals, think it's too late to start, or have given up on their dreams, to reach their fullest financial potential.

Alicia has been fortunate to share her experiences in various magazines and newspapers, on CNN, and on local TV and radio programs, as well as on nationally syndicated podcasts. She has spoken on stages across the country and has addressed people from all walks of life at various colleges, organizations, Fortune 500 corporations, and most notably, the White House.

As a worldwide traveler, Alicia has zip-lined in the rainforest of Costa Rica, hiked an active volcano in Bali, parasailed in Aruba, swum with dolphins in Barbados, dove in an underwater cave in Mexico, and climbed to the top of some of the tallest buildings in the world. She loves to dance and eat with the locals, and always meets new friends wherever she goes.

Alicia graduated from Marquette University in Milwaukee, Wisconsin, with a degree in psychology, and earned two master's degrees, in business administration and human resources management, at the Keller Graduate School of Management at DeVry University. Alicia is a mother of four (Cameron, Chloe, Candace, and Corey) and grandmother of four kids (Azra, Auri, Zekiel, and Miel) and a cat (Murphy). She lives in Charlotte, North Carolina.

Learn more at www.aliciastingley.com.

CHAPTER 6

LIVING WITH A MANIFESTED MINDSET

By Dr. Carol DeWalt

The pediatrician at one of the largest nonprofit hospitals in the world balls his fists and shouts, "Do you know who I am?"

I think, "Yes, *and?*"

This is not the first time someone has argued at me, but I am not an arguer by nature. I'm more of a friendly, quiet person.

He throws his arms up and yells across the now crowded nursery, "Well, who do *you* think *you* are? And! Who is your boss?" He pauses. "You don't get to do this to me. You're nobody here," he yells.

I only nod my head in agreement and wait patiently.

We're standing in the middle of the nursery's patient assessment area, discussing the care of a wealthy couple's baby. They had paid for "special" concierge care with this well-known community pediatrician, and he didn't want his patient to go to the NICU. Despite the couple's significant celebrity status, I had to give them the same standard of care required for all patients, which was in the best interest of the baby.

"I'm sorry, Doctor X; he needs to stay on oxygen. Therefore, he absolutely has to be admitted to the NICU."

I watch the doctor turn to speak with the family. He then says, "I'll give the baby oxygen myself in the mom's room."

I calmly reply, "No, that is unsafe, and we don't have a policy for this." At this point the crowd has grown and the people present are of increasing authority.

His eyes bore into me. Seeing that I'm unrelenting, he stomps his foot and spins in a full circle while waving his fists in the air—like a child having a tantrum. Maybe because I was a young African American female, he had no framework in which to deal with my authority as a medical professional. He saw himself as my superior. Despite his behavior, my face continues to remain unbothered and unrelenting; his is beet red. My only responsibility is to the baby.

We're losing time. We can all see the infant's oxygen levels steadily dropping and how he's struggling to breathe. The parents are worried and give me permission to go. I wrap up the baby and announce to the team, "Let's go." I nod to the parents. "You can come with us." As a neonatologist, one of my primary duties is to be the baby's advocate.

———•———

This isn't the only time I've been challenged based on preconceived notions. No matter the situation or people involved, I hold firm to my own moral code and always aim to remain professional.

Conflict is the last thing I'm interested in creating. From an early age I learned to stay quiet and not make waves. I grew up in the South, where for several years I was the only African American student in my elementary school class. Being different had its challenges. For instance, my third-grade teacher, Mrs. Smith, wouldn't let me go to the restroom with the rest of the class; I had to wait in the hallway until they all finished. In response to being marginalized, I focused on my schoolwork. While those around me had a low estimation of what I was capable of, I chose to work hard anyway.

I came into the world with a measure of adversity as well. Born about twelve weeks early, I didn't have any signs of life for the first ten minutes. My father liked to tell the story of how he prayed in that moment and asked God for a miracle—then I cried out for the first time. I was my parents' miracle baby after my mother experienced five miscarriages in the ten years between my brother and me. I consider my being alive a testimony and evidence that I have a purpose on this earth. A caring, loving, and competent soul helped me to survive at birth and even contributed to my having a fruitful life. This is a part of my passion for neonatology, and now I have the honor of being a board-certified neonatologist. One guiding tenet of my life has been the verse "I can do all things through Christ who strengthens me" (Phil 4:13, NKJV). I have so many examples of how God made a way when there wasn't one.

In undergrad at Stanford, and in medical school at UCLA, studying hard no longer set me apart. My classmates and I had chosen similar career paths. Unfortunately, when I entered residency, an old paradigm emerged. Being quiet and the only African American did not serve me well. I still had people telling me what I wouldn't and couldn't do. The first day of residency will be forever seared into my mind, when my attending said, "You probably won't make it here." Most of the world doesn't know what it feels like to be different, subjugated, uninvited, or underestimated. Other people had been putting me in a box my whole life. But I'm proud to say I didn't stay there.

In residency the downside of being quiet was that I had no social life and the rare friend. The upside was no distractions from my studies. My routine consisted of going to work and hanging out with my dog. Later in life I learned that much of my anxiety came from how I saw myself—quiet, insignificant, and unworthy. Studying and passing tests were objective tasks. Putting myself out into the world was scary because I didn't know if I would be accepted. It took me years to figure out who I was, to value who God made me to be, and to be OK being different. God said I am fearfully and wonderfully made. In fact, I daily carried this verse with me in a folder during residency and fellowship to remind myself that even if others devalue me, God has given me value.

When I started valuing myself, my perception of how others saw me changed and likewise my perception of others brightened. The kinder, more mature version of myself blossomed, and I can now report that I am blessed to have wonderful, quality relationships.

My life isn't all trials. I believe God has a plan for me. This deep faith comes from my father. He was one of the most important people in my life. He was a Southern Baptist pastor who truly loved the Lord. He gave me unconditional love and an assurance that no matter what I did, it would work out. I was five when he had me memorize my first Bible verse. "All things work together for good to those who love God, to those who are the called according to His purpose" (Rom 8:28, NKJV). When people ask me how I show such resiliency, I think of this verse. It has become the guiding principle of my life. No matter who or what tries to strike me down, all things work together for good because I am called according to *His* purpose.

Sadly, my father passed away in 2019, but he gave me strength and eternal, unconditional love. Even when things look bad, I know he would never lose faith in me, so I don't lose faith in myself.

Strength comes in many forms. Getting through med school is hard work. My definition of *hard work* is:

- Preparation + Opportunity = Success

PREPARATION

The first part of achieving success involves being prepared. It takes time and effort to meet a goal. Many people say they want to do something, but they're not willing to give the time or effort needed. When we really want something, we have to work for it and not stop until we reach "success." Now, the success we achieve may look different from our original vision, but the satisfaction of that goal will still be fulfilled.

I had to put in the time and the work to become a doctor. I studied four to eight hours a day, most days, and I strictly regimented my time. I even had to schedule fun and rest. The sacrifices and lifestyle choices were necessary preparation to achieve my lifelong dream of becoming a baby doctor.

You must prepare your lifestyle for the goal.

I didn't do it all by myself. I found help when I needed it. For instance, as a senior in college, I took a biochemistry course that normally is taken by first-year medical students. It was over my head. I basically made it through the course with tears and gnashing of teeth. I stood at the crossroads and asked myself: "Do I really want to go to medical school? If this class is the obstacle, how do I climb over it?"

Adjust your plan for who you are and where you're going.

OPPORTUNITY

Opportunity is the second part of finding success.

Not a lot of people take the opportunities given to them. They say they want something, but then an opportunity comes up that requires a sacrifice or astronomical effort, and they decide not to do it. That tells me they didn't honestly want that goal.

You have to commit and not just try. I never said I was going to *try* and be a doctor. *Try* is a dangerous word. When people say to me, "I'm trying to do something," they've already given themselves an out. *Try* is not a commitment to do a thing. You either will do it, or you won't.

Commit.

If you don't want to take the time and effort to make it happen, it's time to reevaluate your goal. We all have a goal that nothing would keep us from reaching.

It was necessary that I passed that biochemistry class to get into medical school. I took the test on a Tuesday and knew immediately I'd failed it. I had never failed anything in my whole life! The next day, the grade was posted. I was devastated.

But later I was up and doing the only thing I knew would help. I prayed to God that this one course wouldn't keep me from my dream.

On Thursday a miracle happened: the professor emailed the students, announcing a makeup test because so many students had failed. This was the first and only time one of my professors re-offered a test during my four years at Stanford. God had answered my prayer, so I made the most of my opportunity and gave it everything I had. I booked a hotel room, where I wouldn't be distracted. I brought my study materials and energy drinks, and locked the door. I studied for seventy-two hours straight—taking an occasional power nap.

I miraculously passed! Medical school was in sight!

The next time you hit an obstacle on the way to your dream, consider a similar approach. Don't let a *no* keep you down. Go to God and watch what happens. Assume you and God can move mountains.

This has been my path to "success."

THE MANIFESTED MINDSET

I've explained how success works for me. Now I want to go a bit deeper into the spiritual side of success. You might consider this the activating agent. Still using the success formula, let's add an even more profound element—God.

Have you ever tried to put the pieces of a puzzle together without knowing what the picture looks like? Most of us live our lives trying to finish our own puzzles by forcing pieces that don't quite fit together, because we don't have the full picture. We may not even have all the pieces.

How often have you asked God to hurry up and finish your puzzle so you can see the outcome? When we allow Him room, He brings the components together, and what appeared as a jumbled mess before is now a masterpiece. He's the Creator, so He alone knows what the components of our lives are, should be, and will be. He's the author and finisher of our puzzles.

We find our truest success when we trust He is bringing us to a good and complete end. Then, when we face a trial or a challenge, we approach Him differently.

Here's a common scenario with my young son. He'll say, "Mommy, can I have a lollipop?"

I'll respond, "Yes, once we get home."

A moment passes; then he'll say, "When can I have my lollipop, Mommy?"

"When did I say you could have the lollipop?"

"When I get home."

"If you know you'll get the lollipop when we get home, why do you keep asking me?"

"Because I want it now."

Prayer can feel like this. We're looking for an answer, a breakthrough, or a "treat." We know God has our solution, but He wants us to trust Him.

What if we asked believing that we'd already received it from Him? Would we keep asking? Of course not. We could then shift our mindset to trusting His timing. This is living in a manifested mindset.

Practice the mindset where our prayers have been answered, we are loved, we are delivered, and we have overcome. Visualize yourself in the manifestation of God's promises.

———•———

When I manifested that mindset, I began living the dream I imagined for myself. I'm a respected neonatologist, a business owner, a wife, and a mother. As part of that dream, I founded Newborn Housecalls, M.D., a practice that provides in-home newborn care and education to parents of newborns. Parenting an infant is stressful, and parents can often use advice and help on the journey as they care for their new little family member. I have a heart to help. I am honored to be a resource and helping hand as parents nurture their infants to their highest potential.

I walked alone a lot during the seven years of medical school and residency. While that's not ideal, it caused me to build an arsenal of mental and spiritual strength. Sometimes the strength we gain by making it through our obstacles develops what eventually becomes one of our superpowers. Obstacles will creep in on the path to our dreams, but we must hold firm to our ultimate destination.

A person doesn't have to be boisterous to change the world. Success looks like preparation, opportunity, and the resiliency of God.

God gives our lives vision beyond anything we could give ourselves. Through discipline and faith we can pursue our dreams. I now know that the only person who can limit me is me. Likewise, you are the only person who can put yourself in a box. And never forget, the only opinion that matters is God's, and He says you're amazing!

About Dr. DeWalt

Dr. Carol DeWalt is a distinguished board-certified neonatologist with a rich academic background spanning across several prestigious institutions. Graduating from Stanford University with a bachelor's degree, she embarked on a journey of medical excellence, earning her medical degree from the joint medical school program between Charles R. Drew University of Medicine and Science and the David Geffen School of Medicine at UCLA. Driven by a passion for community health and pediatric care, she pursued her residency at UCLA within the Community Health and Advocacy Training Program. She then went on to complete her fellowship in neonatal-perinatal medicine at the David Geffen School of Medicine at UCLA.

Following her academic career she joined the faculty as a neonatologist within Harbor-UCLA Medical Center. Her research focused on mitochondrial metabolism and factors that influence cellular damage. Dr. DeWalt incorporates her research background within her practice by educating expectant parents regarding practices to improve maternal health at the cellular level in an effort to improve their infants' outcome.

Throughout her career Dr. DeWalt has been committed to decreasing the incidence of morbidity and mortality among infants by empowering parents through community education. She conducts comprehensive courses year-round, equipping mothers and fathers with the knowledge and skills necessary to ensure the well-being of their infants. With a particular focus on breastfeeding, she champions the importance of breastfeeding and breast milk feeding to optimize infant outcomes. Dr. DeWalt is not only a dedicated healthcare provider but also a compassionate educator, touching the lives of countless families and shaping the future of infant care as the founder and CEO of Newborn Housecalls, M.D. Her unwavering dedication to improving infant health and her pioneering efforts within in-home newborn care and parental education have earned her widespread recognition as a leader in the field.

Dr. DeWalt is also a parent to two lovely children, and an ICU physician. She enjoys biking along the beach and participating in adult classical ballet classes. She takes an active role in engaging her local community regarding the value of diversity, equity, and inclusion. She seeks to take her in-home infant education to the world by reaching seven million expectant parents before 2033. Dr. DeWalt believes that infants deserve the best. Through dedicated encouragement and guidance she endeavors to positively impact the lives of generations of parents and infants to come.

CHAPTER 7

INNER HEALING: MY JOURNEY FROM SHATTERED TO SOARING

What There Is for One, There Is for All!

By Lisa Morgan

Eyes closed, I gripped the marker, allowing my hand to move freely across the paper. Suddenly it came to an abrupt halt and started scribbling furiously in one spot. I thought, "What the heck?" Then it moved again and finally came to a stop. When I opened my eyes, all I could see was a jumbled-up mess of scribbled gobbledygook.

"I don't know," I said to my therapist. "I don't think this worked. I really don't see anything."

"Maybe it's your inner child trying to release the pent-up angst that's been causing your stomachache all week," she replied.

The scribble drawing may have looked meaningless at first, but I knew better. The more I studied it, the more images appeared. First, a side view of a woman's head, reminding me of an old-fashioned silhouette cutout, with a Gibson Girl updo. As soon as I made this connection, I realized it looked like my grandmother's profile. Following the drawing downward, I noticed the outline of two pairs of bosoms, and then the distinct image of an arthritic thumb and finger. It was my grandmother's hand. Suddenly my inner child erupted, going into a full-blown reenactment of an incident of being sexually abused. I was astonished but not afraid. I'd experienced many similar releases but none involving my grandmother. For me it was confirmation—not only had I been abused by her, but so had my father. It's where it all started.

What took root in my father's subconscious was extreme hatred of women. His belligerent, toddler-like outbursts were acting-out behaviors, a release of trapped trauma emotions. My father's abusers were his mother and grandmother (hence the bosoms). Adding insult to injury, his true love connection was his father, who drowned when he was twenty-four.

My father never remembered his mother's abuse. It lay buried in his subconscious yet visible through their contentious relationship. My mother once told me when she was first married their screaming matches terrified her! My father never realized how much he hated women, but I observed it my entire life in the despicable, demeaning way he treated my mother, my stepmother, and women in general.

I've spent over twenty years working with powerful energy-based therapies to get to the root of my shattering. At age seventy-two I finally know my whole truth. I am a survivor of extreme childhood sexual abuse, neglect, abandonment, and soul murder (an attempt to snuff out my light and joy). I lived through years of violence and terror but have no visual memories of these events. It's called amnesia.

A person must be able to "see" a picture in their *mind's eye* to have a conscious memory. I don't see any of the pictures of my abuse, yet I know everything that happened because of soul fracturing. Early in my therapy I started tape-recording my sessions. I wanted to capture the voices coming out and their reenactments. This is how I learned about my past.

Today, I know that amnesia and soul fracturing saved my life! They are God-given survival mechanisms, built into the DNA of every human being, part of the stress response. My version is the six Fs: friend (no stress), fight, flight, freeze (dissociate), fawn/flop, and soul fracturing (amnesia). If anyone ever asked me, "Do you remember your wedding day?" I'd reply, "*Absolutely!*" I can "see" every detail as if it were yesterday. That was forty-eight years ago, so it's not a question of memory problems!

LIVING WITH THE AFTEREFFECTS OF CHILDHOOD ABUSE

First, I want to point out I *always* loved my father. But now I know he didn't want me to be born and tried to force an abortion on my mother. We come into the womb as pure consciousness, knowing everything going on. For my parents it was all about money. My father was earning one hundred dollars a month. Our monthly rental was one hundred dollars. So where did the extra money come from to put food on our table?

I experienced unspeakable acts of violence from birth on, including an attempt to smother me in the crib (my mother rescued me). My body was more of an object than a person, being violated from birth. Thankfully, I do not remember any of this. If I did, it might be like a never-ending video loop, driving me down a rabbit hole. My soul parts came into existence to protect me. I've never had to live with the memories and visuals of these horrifying experiences.

A child is born with a spiritual knowing. We're supposed to be able to trust the people entrusted with our care. Because of my history I developed a subconscious program called "I *do not trust*"—anyone or anything, including my parents, life, and God. This showed up in a lifelong pattern called the Lone Ranger Syndrome. I only had myself to depend upon.

Another devastating aftereffect of sexual abuse was my issue with food. Once upon a time, my mother made an offhand remark, saying she'd put a spoon in my hand (at age three) to feed myself, and "it was like you never stopped eating!" Why would an adorable three-year-old need to stuff her face with food? It doesn't make sense, but *I always knew I used the food to soothe.* When I started gaining weight, my brothers began teasing me. They spoke *pig latin* at the dinner table. I didn't know what it meant, but I knew it was mean. *"Isla itfa atfa igpa!"* (Lisa is a fat pig!) I can still hear that refrain in my brain, an imprint I wish I could erase.

Food was my main focus. When I got home from school, I'd start raiding the kitchen, looking for cookies, cake, chocolate—anything carbs! I even went so far as to sneak into my neighbors' kitchens while my friends were outside playing hide-and-go-seek.

In first grade I weighed 96 pounds. (The other kids were probably 50.) Every year, our teachers weighed us publicly, calling our weight out to the teacher down the hall. I hid in the bathroom for as long as possible. By sixth grade I weighed 196. I know because I lost 70 pounds in seventh grade. What lived inside of me was a belief that the only thing people saw when they looked at me was a fat pig. It was such intense emotional pain, robbing me of my true full joy, for so many years.

The inner wounding spilled into many aspects of my life. Once, my mother tried to convince me to take ballet lessons. I *adamantly* refused. I didn't want anyone to see me in a leotard. Our shopping excursions to the *"chubbette" department* were also excruciating, leaving me scarred. Another incident involved my father trying to give me a pony ride. Again, I refused. I was worried I'd break the pony's back! Then were the daily incidents of my father's looks of scorn and disgust, piercing my heart. I thought he was a monster, a "little Hitler," and shot daggers at him from my eyes. Imagination can be a superpower for a child being squashed and squelched. These examples demonstrate how body distortion and damaged self-esteem take root. There was so much humiliation and shame planting the seeds for extreme self-hatred and self-loathing.

THE JOURNEY OF TRANSFORMATION—OUR TRIGGERS ARE OUR TREASURES!

My inner healing began in 2003, but the groundwork was laid years earlier. In 1996 I left behind a successful career as a board-certified music therapist. For seventeen years I'd created cutting-edge stress-management programs for psychiatry and chemical dependency. It was the toxic effects of corporate downsizing— killing my spirit—that compelled me to quit. I vowed to never be an employee again.

From 1996–1999 I immersed myself in powerful transformational programs, such as Landmark Education's Forum series. My subconscious started inserting itself into my awareness, allowing weird things to surface. In one workshop, called Finding Your Voice, the therapist engaged us in playful interactions, imitating Donald Duck, a Parisian accent, and Valley-girl talk, while talking to each other. Then he instructed us to talk in our own voice. I opened my mouth to speak but couldn't utter a sound. I was shocked! And I vowed to someday find a professional who did this type of body-voice-energy work. My someday arrived seven years later, just weeks before my mother died.

By 1999 I felt an urge to reenter the workforce but knew I wouldn't be an employee. I had to find a new path forward. This is when the *s*#*!* hit the fan! For some reason, volunteering to create an after-school music program for kids triggered a descent into my *year from hell*. With my body/mind hijacked by panic and anxiety, I disintegrated into a state of the *"deadly Ds"*—excruciating disease, despair, despondency, debilitating depression, and crippling dysfunction. I spent this year hiding, trying to shield my husband and kids from my distress. I had no idea what was going on, why it was happening, where I could get help, or even how to explain any of it! At the time, *trauma* was not a well-known commodity.

My breakdown was discombobulating, especially after living forty-eight years with passion, exuberance, vitality, joy, and professional success! Looking back, I see it as a gift of time, being able to build myself up from the inside out. This created an insurance policy of "embodied" experiences, a reservoir, or memory bank, from which to draw *comfort and hope* during my darkest years navigating the dark night of the soul.

When we allow ourselves to get honest and listen to the "call" from within, we open to the magic of inner healing. Even though we suffer, our discomfort serves a purpose. Our higher self is trying to get our attention. Some may call it a midlife crisis. I've always believed it was the voice of my soul guiding me forward, toward growth and transformation.

Oprah was my first therapist, a lifeline to the light while I hung on for dear life. Her "Remembering Your Spirit" episode offered me a daily dose of solace. Her focus on life coaches, such as Cheryl Richardson, Martha Beck, and Dr. Phil, planted the seed. I googled "life coaching" and found International Coach Academy (ICA) on the first page. I knew I was being guided and enrolled immediately.

Life coaching exposed me to the concept of mindset and UACs, the inner gremlins running amok in our subconscious. The more I tuned in to the voice of my "inner critic," the more aware I became of my self-hatred and self-loathing. Can you relate? I was smiling on the outside while dying on the inside!

Our parents are our first mirrors—reflecting upon us their unresolved issues from childhood. We take in whatever is served up. What did you experience as a newborn, infant, or young child? Were your parents calm and loving, or did they vent (dump) their anger, rage, hostility, sadness, or victimhood upon you? It's not just about the words spoken but the energy behind them. Words and actions leave lasting imprints on our psyche, shaping our self-perception and emotional well-being.

During my twenty-year journey, I transitioned back and forth between mini breakdowns and complete shattering. My body felt like a sizzling live wire, with me jumping out of my skin. I lived with stomachaches 24/7. They were not indigestion but rather a soul part wanting to come out. Whatever I'd been thinking or doing in the moment was triggering their terror. The problem was I had no memory of that experience, so I felt blindsided.

When we give voice to the unexpressed words, the trapped anger and rage, and the unshed tears of our inner child parts, our nervous system recalibrates. As adults we get to experience inner peace and calm. This is the process of inner healing. I often used journaling to connect with my parts. The pictures they drew and words they wrote were often disturbing.

In 2008 I started doing EMDR with a trauma-informed thera-pist. I asked, "How long is this going to take?" (I'd already spent eight years in therapy.) Her reply was, "When did it start? How long did it last? How extreme was it? Was your life ever threatened?" It took four more years to get down to the worst of the worst. I became suicidal, yet always knew I was being protected by my body's divine intelligence. Certain incidents were revisited multiple times, slowly dribbling out the details. Too much too soon could have destroyed me. In time I realized even the *food to soothe* had served a purpose and saved my life. It produced serotonin in my brain at a time when I was being flooded by cortisol. My dogs were also no accident (dog = God), sent by the divine to protect the flow of love of my child's heart!

My husband once asked, "Is this all really helping?" My reply was an absolute *yes*! There's no way to heal other than going through it to the other side! I was never afraid of my parts. Somehow I knew they were all just a part of me! I approached every session with an attitude of "*Bring it on*—the sooner the better!"

THIS IS WHAT I KNOW FOR SURE

What if I told you that every belief you've ever held as true was a "limiting belief," the result of taking in flawed messages—*not the truth*! How would it feel if you could rewrite your life story—according to *you*—in your own words, filling your next chapter with your wildest dreams, deepest yearnings, and biggest hopes? Dreams are not merely whims but rather a divine mandate. They exist within each of us because we are the perfect people to bring them to life!

For years I've been searching for the missing X factor to set me free. I finally found it. If you're ready to say *yes* to yourself, then join me on this magical journey of self-discovery and empowerment. My FREEDOM BODY BLUEPRINT© is the culmination of my life's work, a promise for true change and transformation. It's built upon four pillars:

1. **Commitment** to your journey and process, fully engaged in experiential learning

2. **Targeted laser coaching**—Unveiling blind spots, uprooting subconscious barriers, and shattering hidden resistance (avoidance, procrastination, self-sabotage, etc.)

3. **Transformative energy rewiring**—Recalibrating the body/mind/nervous system, reducing chronic stress, taming the inner critic, and restoring inner peace

4. **Unleashing empowerment energy**—Fueled by desire, passion, and creativity; laser-focused; taking risks; and showing up with bold actions!

My mission is to end suffering, provide hope, and be a stand for truth! If I can do it, so can you. Remember, what there is for one, there is for all. I'd be honored to guide you home to your authentic core, where creativity, passion, and joy await. Welcome home!

About Lisa

Lisa Morgan is a board-certified music therapist and certified life coach with an impressive lifetime of experience. She believes her real credentials stem from her "PhD of life," a twenty-plus-year journey navigating the "dark night of the soul." Body-voice-energy therapies enabled the breakthroughs of the subconscious barriers, exposing the hidden truths of her past. Today, she's successfully healed from a history of extreme sexual abuse, terror, and neglect.

Having walked the walk, Lisa now talks the talk. As a survivor, she has an uncanny ability to demystify complex topics, taking them from abstract theories into tangible, real-life experiences. She speaks about a plethora of trauma-related topics, from survival scripts, triggers, and body memories to reenactments, self-loathing, and inner healing. Lisa brings her presentations to life with personal stories, metaphors, and live examples.

Lisa is an expert in amnesia and soul fracturing. Her paradigm for the stress response illuminates six Fs instead of three: friend, fight, flight, freeze, fawn/flop, and fracturing (the most extreme version of dissociation). Lisa knows that amnesia and soul fracturing saved her life. She views both as God-given survival mechanisms, built into the DNA of every human. Her history uniquely positions her to address the ongoing controversy in psychiatry and psychology about *repressed memories versus false memories versus retrieved memories*. With "fractured" soul parts intact, she serves as a living demonstration—i.e., knowing everything about her past despite not having had one conscious memory of any events.

Passionate about challenging DSM-5 concepts—i.e. labeling people as "psychological disorders"—Lisa aims to dispel stigmas attached to mental health. She asserts that symptoms such as panic, anxiety, and depression are not indicators of psychological dysfunction but manifestations of trapped trauma trying to surface to heal.

Lisa's FREEDOM BODY BLUEPRINT© is the culmination of her life's work, a promise for true change and transformation. It's built upon four pillars:

1. Commitment to self and to the process of experiential learning

2. Targeted laser coaching, to reveal blind spots and shatter subconscious barriers

3. Transformative energy recalibration—reducing stress, taming self-criticism, and restoring inner peace

4. Authentic empowerment energy—fueled by desire, creativity, and courage

Lisa's mission is to stop suffering and provide hope for healing. Her coaching methodology creates a road map for lasting breakthroughs and transformation while unleashing our superpower—i.e., living in alignment with one's authentic self and spiritual essence, home to the heart of compassion and self-love.

To learn more, visit lisamcoachingabq.com.

CONNECT WITH LISA:

- Empowered We Rise
- www.facebook.com/groups/385498360900846
- linkedin.com/in/lisa-morgan-018779

CHAPTER 8

THE COURAGE AND POWER TO PERSIST

By Shiressa Johnson

No matter what, I had to get out of that house. My mind briefly flashed back to the murder-suicide that occurred on campus just one year prior, and I had made up my mind. Three, two, one...go! By the time he realized I had slipped out the front door, I was in my car with the gear in reverse. He darted down the hallway and out the door, still gaping from my escape. Shirtless, barefoot, and desperate to detain me, he leaped onto the back of my car, banging vigorously on the rear window.

"Stop the car!" he demanded. But, oh, I wasn't stopping.

I slowed down just enough to say, "Get off now because I'm leaving." I drove faster in disbelief and embarrassment as he began beating forcefully on my rear windshield, yelling for me to stop. I increased my speed, and the message became clear as he tumbled off the trunk and onto the street, but not before shattering my windshield with his powerful fist.

Fueled by jealousy, he had crossed the line from emotional to physical intimidation, which I would never allow to happen again. Nothing would prevent me from leaving him this time. His control over me was over.

Comingled with strong feelings of fear and anger, I also felt compassion. His insecurities led to possessiveness, masquerading as loving protection. The level of toxicity in our relationship grew so high, and I was out of excuses. I now sought protection from the one who was supposed to protect me.

As a recent college graduate, I should have been packing and preparing to move across the country to begin my exciting career in a highly coveted information security role. Instead, I found myself distraught and temporarily displaced without any of my possessions. My survival instincts kicked in.

I drove to an auto shop to purchase a car cover to conceal my car from being discovered by his investigative eyes. I sought refuge at a local hotel for the night to strategize my next steps, including a new rear windshield, a place to stay until I moved, and a way to get my things safely from his house. My sister quickly rallied her friends to secure a safe haven for me, and a college friend arranged to accompany me to transport my things safely with his truck. This was not the first time I had to stay calm under pressure and be resourceful, but it was the first time I embraced my power to persist toward my goals without succumbing to the desires of others. The realization of that power was the confidence I needed to keep pressing forward.

I started a new journey that took me from Texas to a ground-breaking role in information security in upstate New York. From the depths of that tumultuous relationship emerged a stronger, wiser, and more confident version of myself. Evidence of this came a year later when my ex surprisingly contacted me after I had changed my mobile number to tell me he'd found himself in a relationship with someone as possessive as he had been with me in college. He understood how I must have felt and apologized. I forgave him, and we shared a few laughs. Then, I respectfully asked him not to contact me again, and he honored my request. Our season had ended.

Adaptive Leadership

In the coming years, as an information security analyst in 2002, I survived a layoff, which left a void in our team. The gap was in the management of encryption technology and infrastructure, neither of which my senior colleagues volunteered to take on. So, as the youngest professional on the team, I fearlessly volunteered, but little did I know most of the information I would need had already been obliterated. However, I persisted with the support of my peers.

Several months after taking the new assignment, I found myself in an all-male roomful of seasoned infrastructure security architects as I awaited my turn to present on the state of our encryption technology deployment strategy. As my boss presented first, I observed the dynamics in the room and began to question my place among these experts. Recognizing the value of their collective knowledge, in a bold moment of spontaneity, I decided to deviate from my prepared script. I got up. "Hello, gentlemen. Instead of presenting the materials I prepared, today I want to hear from all of you," I confidently stated. As those impromptu words flowed, I noticed the energy shift in the room as the men leaned forward in their chairs and, one after the other, began to share the challenges and issues they were experiencing with the process I had inherited. In that situation, I became keenly aware of my adaptive leadership and courage to admit when I didn't have all the answers. The nod of approval from my boss reassured my confidence.

Feedback from that meeting was overwhelmingly positive, and I gained the respect of my colleagues. Most importantly, I gained my boss's sponsorship, which led to new roles that I expressed interest in.

Healing through Forgiveness

The five years I worked in upstate New York were transformative, particularly when I pivoted from information security to internal audit, which provided opportunities to travel in South America, across Europe, and in Japan performing SOX IT control testing. The enriching professional experiences broadened my horizons, yet the allure of home tugged at my heartstrings. So in 2005 I returned to California as a newlywed, although that would not last long. Pivoting to financial services, nothing prepared me for the 2008 financial crisis or the twists and turns my life would take. The bank I worked for was acquired, and layoffs were imminent, as was the end of my brief marriage. And to top it off, my mother was diagnosed with stage IV pancreatic cancer all within the span of a few months. It was too much for most people to bear, but I had the unexplainable peace that surpasses all understanding. In fact, I had never felt closer to God than I did going through all those trials at once.

I'll explain. The divorce, unlike many, was amicable. Even after a year of separation, I wasn't bitter. In fact, I had occasionally prayed for my ex-husband and the women he entertained during our separation. Once officially divorced, we both acknowledged our flaws in a shared moment of forgiveness and respectfully moved on. The hardest part of forgiveness was being honest with myself long enough to take accountability for my part in what didn't work. Once I forgave myself for my part, I had to forgive him for his, which left no room for resentment.

Shortly after the divorce, I began to date a charming man I met at church, who is my loving husband of the past fourteen years and the father of my two children. Won't God do it?

As for the bank acquisition, I was offered to stay only if I relocated, so instead, I opted for a severance package to spend more time with my ailing mother, and I eventually accepted a managerial role in the biotech industry. Although my mother's cancer was terminal, she survived far longer than the doctors initially estimated. So I never fully embraced the idea that I'd be living without her most of my adult life—that is, until my sister called me that fateful night: "Mom says she's tired and that she's going to wait for you." I vividly remember her words through thick tears over the phone.

My heart sank like a cast iron skillet dropped in my lap. On the flight it became clear the amount of pain my mother had to be in to say she was tired. Those words meant she was tired of tolerating the debilitating pain and constant suffering. I prayed fervently for swift healing and relief of pain, whatever form that might take, aligning my will with hers and God's.

That afternoon, I arrived at the hospital room last, greeted by my mother's smile and relieved she had waited for me. Some of my family who arrived the prior evening agreed to take a break. Alone, my mom shared a few final wishes with me and then decided it was time for the pain medication she had declined all morning. As the nurse delivered the medication, she confirmed my suspicion about my mother's pain.

"We're all surprised how long she went without it. I'm sure she has to be in a lot of pain by now."

A woman of her word, she wasn't going to let anything keep her from saying goodbye to her baby girl. No matter the cost, she waited for me. Realizing the magnitude of her strength and love for me, I encouraged her to close her eyes and rest as I held her soft yet unrecognizably thin hand.

"Go ahead and close your eyes now, Mom. I'll be right here," I said softly. "I love you," I whispered.

"I love you more," she replied, and the medication swept her into a peaceful slumber she never awakened from. Her final words were the expression of the sacrifices she made for me her entire life.

During her battle with cancer my mom found healing from the emotional scars sustained from marriage. She wasn't healed of cancer, but throughout her illness she let go of bitterness and resentment, so in a way, she was healed. My experiences with relationships, layoffs, and my mother's gift of forgiveness taught me that all things can work out for our good if we are willing to see the good amid the turmoil.

A similar shadow loomed over my father after he was diagnosed with lung cancer. Six years later my sister's urgent call would again prompt a change in my travel plans.

She called after work and urged me to visit Dad right away. "He keeps telling me to open the front door for you even after I told him no one is there and you're not coming until next week," she said. Heeding her intuition, my husband and I packed up our children and drove straight to my father's apartment.

Upon our arrival, my dad was in great spirits. He was joking, laughing, and eating unassisted. I began to think my sister had overreacted. However, the next day, things took a drastic turn. My father had a doctor's appointment, and after that he would never be the same. With each word of gloom and doom the doctor spewed, every ounce of hope was drained from my father's face. I wanted to interrupt the doctor and tell him no matter what, my dad was going to live to see my son's next birthday as he told me he would, but it was too late. The damage was already done, and within hours of getting home, my father was experiencing excruciating pain. His pain intensified as swiftly as his mobility deteriorated, and soon, as with Mom, he eventually would fall into a slumber from the pain medication that he'd never awaken from.

When my sister woke me up to say Dad had taken his last breath, I was saddened by the thought of him not being able to watch my sons grow but grateful we got to share his last days with him.

I was there to say my goodbyes to both my parents, a treasure not many people receive. The intricate dance of life, with its joys and sorrows, played out in those sacred moments of intimate farewells.

STANDING UP TO BULLIES

My first encounter with a bully was in kindergarten, resulting in a schoolyard brawl cheered on by classmates who admired my courage. Despite losing recess for a month or two, I felt proud for standing up for what felt like justice. Little did I know that a single childhood victory would shape my confidence and character for years to come. When I regained my playground freedom, I was the most popular kid in the yard, but what struck me most was the newfound respect and kindness from the former bully. That incident taught me valuable lessons that guided my approach to handling workplace bullies.

Workplace bullies are humans with a misguided perception of the personal power they wield to influence others. So when I had to take a stand against a boss who devalued and discriminated against me, I didn't flinch.

After giving birth to my first son, nursing challenges led to relentless pumping every two hours. Despite my working from the lactation room, my manager harassed me for not being at my desk. HR offered no support, only unpaid leave, later threatening a performance improvement plan (PIP). Refusing to sign, I drafted a formal response highlighting discrimination. The manager retracted the PIP, but I was no longer willing to work there. Instead, I took a higher-paying position at a more family-friendly financial institution closer to home, but not before launching a formal complaint.

Facing a tougher challenge later on, I resolved to outlast my toxic boss. Despite being sidelined, I delivered high-quality work and networked with senior leaders. The toxic boss was ultimately fired, and I transferred to a bigger role under a fantastic director. Despite finding a role with career potential, COVID and health challenges prompted me to reevaluate my goals, leading me to make an uncharacteristic decision for someone of my experience: I went back to school.

REINVENTION AND SOCIAL RESPONSIBILITY

Quietly, I applied to USC's full-time MBA program, shielding myself from doubts. With extreme faith and support from my husband, I submitted my application. In December 2022 I received confirmation I was accepted to the Marshall School of Business with a full-tuition scholarship from The Consortium for Graduate Study in Management. Passing the average age and years of experience, I proved to myself pursuing goals regardless of the odds is worthwhile. Returning to USC, where I'd once attended the Multicultural Women Executive Leadership Program, reignited my passion for learning and leadership. As a graduate student, I've held leadership roles and advocated for minority representation, inspired by my late grandmother's service. Serving as a VP of community relations, a coach, an ambassador, and a Consortium liaison allowed me to channel my strengths for the greater good of uplifting others.

My longstanding interest in cybersecurity, passion for music, and yearning for the flexibility and autonomy of entrepreneurship are why I launched Elliott Reese Consulting and Entertainment Group LLC while at USC, hoping to provide women, parents, and professionals facing burnout with flexible ways of contributing to their households. The mission is to provide freedom to balance work and life guilt-free.

I share my story of courage, forgiveness, reinvention, and faith to serve as a reminder to stay positive, find the joy in every challenge, and be for others what you want for your children, recognizing that true fulfillment comes not from personal reward but empowering those around us with the courage to persist.

About Shiressa

A seasoned Certified Information Systems Auditor and cybersecurity professional with over two decades of leadership expertise as a trusted advisory consultant, Reese specializes in guiding organizations through risk management and regulatory compliance implementation. With a distinguished career in financial services, she has served as a vice president of internal audit for several leading global banks and has spearheaded multiple projects helping corporations uphold data privacy, information security, and operations standards.

Reese is a strategic and innovative leader committed to delivering tangible results and value creation. However, beyond her corporate endeavors, her true passion lies in community engagement and advocacy for workforce parity. As an affiliate of the Multicultural Women Executive Leadership Program, Reese supports women of color on their transformative journeys toward becoming better leaders in their professions and communities.

An active nonprofit board member at the Boys & Girls Clubs of Carson, Reese dedicates her time to supporting the educational enrichment of underserved youths. Her contributions extend to organizational governance and development of programs that empower and inspire young individuals to cultivate their limitless potential as future business leaders.

As the founder and CEO of Elliott Reese Consulting and Entertainment Group, Reese embodies a mission-driven approach, aiming to make a lasting impact in her field. Her recent attainment of an MBA from the University of Southern California's Marshall School of Business further solidifies her expertise in strategy and leadership development. As a Marshall Leadership Fellow, an MBA Ambassador, and a VP of community relations for The Black Graduate Business Leaders Association, Reese actively shapes the future of business leadership with a focus on culture and social responsibility.

When not immersed in her professional pursuits, Reese finds solace in creating inspirational music and quality time spent with her husband and two sons, indulging in movie night, puzzles, and board games.

CONNECT WITH REESE:

- **Entertainment (singing and speaking):** https://speaker. innovationwomen.com/users/14662
- **Consulting:** https://www.linkedin.com/in/ Reesejohnsoncisa

CHAPTER 9

WALKING BY FAITH

By Shakera Brinson

After the whirlwind of candles, birthday cake, and three-year-olds running around the house, my husband and I cleaned up the chaos. Parents to a now three-year-old and a two-month-old daughter, we were both exhausted. We got our newborn and toddler to bed, and I immediately fell asleep.

After a few hours I heard a noise. I've always been a light sleeper, but whatever had woken me was so quiet I thought I was dreaming. When I looked at the clock, it was 2:00 a.m.

I jumped out of bed, realizing the noise was my husband calling from the bathroom floor, where he was seated.

"I...can't...breathe," he managed.

Unsure what to do, he instructed me to pour water on him. I grabbed a nearby water bottle and did so. Still by his side, I immediately began praying to God to allow my husband to be OK. To breathe properly. On one phone I called 911. On another I FaceTimed his brother, who was an hour away.

911 asked me several questions and directed me to continue talking to my husband and asking him questions. He responded vaguely, but then his eyes closed. He hit the floor. 911 instructed me to lay him on his back and check if he was breathing. I performed panic-stricken CPR.

By the time they loaded him into the ambulance, he was resuscitated and breathing.

We were still in COVID, so I couldn't even get in the ambulance with him. My mind whirled in frantic circles. As I waited for my brother-in-law to arrive, I was shaken but sure. Whatever had happened was scary, but my husband would be back before the kids woke. He was breathing when he left with the paramedics. Realizing he'd been wearing his pajamas, I packed a bag with his clothes. He'll need these, I figured, as I selected each item.

My brother-in-law and I went to the hospital where the paramedics said they were taking him. When I gave his name, he wasn't there. A twinge of panic ran through my body.

He was breathing when he left, I reminded myself. He'll be home before the kids wake. I clutched the bag with his change of clothes.

Calls were made, but the operators were unsure where he was. I contacted dispatch again to track him down, and we found the hospital where he'd been admitted. We rushed there.

Too late.

At twenty-nine, I found myself an inconceivable combination of things. A mom of two young children. A woman still struggling with postpartum difficulties. A widow.

A heart attack had taken my children's father from them, and I was left to navigate that new reality. My grief. My persistent feelings of guilt. (Could I have done more on that bathroom floor? Was this my fault? He'd been breathing. What went wrong?) My anger. At the paramedics. Life. God.

Overnight I went from security and certainty to the unknown and unexpected.

As I look at my children now, four and two, I know the journey hasn't been easy, but I also know God is good. I wake every day grateful, especially for those five years I shared with my husband.

Even though I was expecting a lifetime of days together, each one we had was a precious gift. Each one gave me the strength and light to carry on, even through those darkest days.

Born into Odds

When my mom became pregnant with me, she was a scared teenager who had no real relationship with my father. Raised by a single mom, I watched as she worked, strove, and persevered to give me a good life. In every example she set and every lesson she taught, she pushed me to be a better woman.

Growing up, I was always a good kid. I made good grades and took all the advanced classes, but as I entered my teenage years, not having a father in my life began affecting my choices.

I never wanted to fall into the trap of teenage pregnancy, but I was looking for love in all the wrong places. At fourteen, I found myself impossibly young, scared, and pregnant. I understood the full force of what my mother must have felt when she first found out.

After much thought and many conversations, my mom and I made the painful decision that having a child this young wasn't my story.

After I ended my pregnancy, I experienced tremendous darkness. I had made this terrible mistake, and I went through a season where I doubted God could still want or love me.

In the second grade a speeding car hit me. The doctors didn't know if I would make it. Once it became clear I'd live, they made their next assessment. I would always have trouble walking. My pelvis was shattered, and it wasn't clear if I'd be able to have children.

When she got the news, my mom, a woman of faith, immediately ran to the scene and began praying. As I lay where I got hit, I could feel her prayers around me and hear her voice telling me to get up and walk.

As I recovered step by step, we prayed together every day. Even from that young age, I knew God would make a way for me. I knew anything was possible if I walked by faith.

After my abortion, I didn't know where to go from there, but slowly those lessons I'd learned lying in the hospital bed returned.

God can do all things. Forgive all sins. With Him all is possible.

It wasn't easy, but I had to set myself free from my guilt and shame. I'd been holding on to this mistake I'd made at fourteen, and if I wanted to do incredible things, I had to forgive myself and I had to accept that God forgave me too.

THRIVING WITH GOD

Once I accepted God's forgiveness and love, I wouldn't allow my past to define my future any longer. He had a plan and a purpose for me, and I was going to fulfill that to its fullest. I had to accept my new identity in Christ and walk boldly in who I am and whose I am.

Always full of drive, ambition, and a desire to be more, I started working at fourteen and graduated high school early. In those teenage years, I wanted to contribute to the family. So I worked, learning a valuable lesson in the process. You can get what you want in life with enough determination and hard work.

I attended Georgia State University and became the first in my family to graduate college. Despite everything it took getting to that point, I made it.

I graduated with a degree in journalism and a concentration in media broadcasting. I'd always had a heart for people and service, and I knew I wanted to use my voice to help people. My grandfather was a Mississippian radio personality, and I dreamed of being on the radio too. Oprah was another role model, and I imagined being on the big screen and sharing my words with the world.

Unsure what route to take, I opened the question to God.

"Lord," I said, "I'll be whatever you want—as long as I can help people."

Teaching presented itself. I'd never thought about that profession, but I followed God's will and became a first-grade educator right out of college. It was amazing, challenging work, and I loved every minute of it. I worked with incredible students, fellow teachers, and administration.

I wouldn't have guessed that was my path, but only God knows the plans for our lives. I didn't yet realize it, but every move was a stepping stone to the next milestone. Those classroom years were teaching me valuable lessons for eventual motherhood.

Even though I loved the work, I knew it wasn't my stopping point. I found myself saying, "OK, God. What's next?"

In 2018, I had a true spiritual awakening. The foundation had always been there, but I realized I must align my life even more with God's will. I needed to change some habits and ways of living to fully walk into the person I was supposed to be.

DIVINE TIMING

I met my husband in February of 2018. Areas of me were still broken, and I wasn't necessarily ready for that relationship. But, as He always does, God presented him to me at just the right time.

By May of 2018, I was joyously pregnant with my son. By August we were engaged. Our path was fast, but this was God's divine timing.

Looking back, it's clear now everything had a purpose. We *had* to move fast because we didn't end up having a lot of time.

In the middle of the pandemic on a beautiful Jamaican beach, we got married.

As we shared those sacred vows, I felt the power of being aligned with God. I had always wanted two children and a destination wedding. I didn't know when or how, but I prayed for those two things.

In 2021, I found out I was pregnant again, and those prayers were answered.

Even though we weren't trying for another child, God's plan was in motion beneath our feet. Our daughter had to come this soon, and I'm so grateful she did.

MOVING IN FAITH

After my husband passed, every day brought unique challenges. The grief journey is never straight or smooth. It's a series of peaks and valleys, but if you keep moving forward, you'll inch toward healing.

I never could have known I'd be a widow at twenty-nine with two small kids. I never could have guessed the difficult questions I'd need to field from a curious, bright four-year-old who remembers Daddy's face and voice.

But every day I continue with my faith in God. I know He's a healer and a provider.

I had bought a house in 2017 and lived there for six years. In August of 2023, I sold it and relocated my family from Georgia to Texas. This was a huge faith move—in more ways than one.

After visiting Texas several years prior, God told me I'd be moving there. I shared what the Holy Spirit had said, but my husband wasn't convinced. He hadn't heard yet. Then, a couple of years later, my husband approached me with house listings for Texas, and we began making plans to relocate.

Immediately after his death, I wanted to scoop my two small children into my arms and fly away to Texas. I wanted to get as far away from our current nightmare as possible. But after a breath, I knew I couldn't run away from life.

I gave myself time to think clearer. To process. To heal.

When we did make the move, I knew that had been the right choice. Once again, God's divine timing shone through.

Life throws so much at you. I know I wouldn't have been able to persevere through all those difficult situations without faith, and I give all honor to God for forgiving me, loving me, and showing me my path. Time and time again.

How to Walk the Path...Even When It's Hard

The one lesson I share repeatedly through my coaching is this: overcoming adversity is within *your* power.

Find your resilience and grit.

Life is challenging. It knocks you down. In those moments, take a beat and breathe. Step back and evaluate your purpose and goals.

When my husband died, I thought life was over. It felt like the end. With him gone, I had to ask God, "Now what?"

Seeking truth and coming up with a meaningful answer required me changing my perspective. Yes, that beautiful chapter had ended, but there was so much more for me and my children. I had to figure out what goals I still needed to accomplish with them.

Keeping my eyes on those goals helped me push through a difficult moment and stop seeing it as an ending.

Embrace the challenging moments.

Thriving isn't about avoiding setbacks. It's about learning how to bounce back. It's about feeling those difficult feelings and allowing yourself to heal from the inside out and build that inner strength.

When my husband died, I wanted to flee to Texas, but it wasn't the right time. I had to embrace this challenging moment. Deal with it. Sit with it. Come to peace with it.

That was the only way I could learn there was light on the other side of darkness and grieving.

Everything prepares you for the next step.

Even when you can't see the plan or path, it's there. Every obstacle and joy is an opportunity for learning and growth. I dealt with challenges I didn't know I had the strength to overcome, and that's because resilience is a muscle. It strengthens with each use, and everything in my life had been preparing me for that next challenge.

Failure isn't failure.

Something's only a failure if you don't learn from it. When you shift your mindset from limiting beliefs to abundance, you start to see change happen.

Failures are opportunities to rebuild something about yourself. When you view life this way, you're always growing and evolving. Mentally. Emotionally. Financially.

The world becomes your classroom, and everything you go through is another subject.

Be clear and firm with your boundaries.

In the aftermath of my husband's passing, I tried to be everything to everyone. Reality still felt like a nightmare I'd wake up from, but I was meeting with his family. Calling his friends. Informing his work. Answering calls back.

It was COVID, so every hospital was at capacity. It took a week just to get the autopsy results and know what had happened. I called every day for updates.

I put myself in an unfair and impossible situation.

I should have looked inside and been more vocal about what I needed to get through this and what help would actually be helpful.

You're more capable than you think.

My mom always says the one thing no one can take away from you is your mind. Once you learn something, that's yours. The more you learn and experience, the more you discover your own capabilities and resourcefulness.

REDISCOVERING MY VOICE

I'd always been a dreamer and a visionary. Even early on, I just wanted to help people.

After my husband died, I went quiet for a period. I lost the voice I'd used my whole life to lift others.

Now, with the gift of time, I'm coming out of that wilderness. I'm doing speaking engagements. I'm talking with people. Coaching them.

I've built an entire community of young women, and I'm helping them navigate life and purpose. I'm showing them God's comfort and love. I'm helping them identify who they are in Christ.

I'm raising my voice again, and it's louder and stronger than I ever could have imagined.

About Shakera

A woman of faith, a widowed mother of two, and a passionate advocate for women empowerment, Shakera Brinson produces content to help women heal to build a legacy of purpose and prosperity through spiritual and practical development.

As a former first-grade teacher, with a heart for service and a deep commitment to her calling, Shakera is dedicated to cultivating transformational experiences that equip women to live purposeful, joyful lives. Shakera has taken her teaching experience beyond the formal classroom to founding Faith Slayer University, a digital learning space for young women all around the world. She is confidently showing women that God can take your broken pieces and make you whole.

As life does, it brought many trials, tribulations, lessons, and testimonies. Her faith continues to outweigh her fear, and she remains obedient to God's call. She's hosted countless women's conferences and retreats; her voice reaches across various platforms and has been recognized in her local community and magazine.

As the founder of I AM SHAKERA TV, Shakera hosts a weekly podcast show, *Identify You*, providing real-life experiences and wisdom to educate, empower, and inspire. You'll find that encouragement you need to be the best you possible.

LEARN MORE AT:

- @IAMSHAKERATV on all social media platforms
- Identify You on Apple, Google, and Spotify
- www.iamshakeratv.com

CHAPTER 10

YOU ARE NOT WHAT YOU DID

By Dr. Carolyn B. Love

A t sixteen, during my junior year in high school, I was a very active, visible, and leading part of my class. I was the fourth of six children living in a loving, close-knit family with my mother and my father. My future was bright and full of possibilities.

This was life right before I learned I was pregnant.

When I found out the news, I lost every ounce of my self-confidence. I had always been a person who was on top of things, but now I was a childhood mother-to-be. In that moment, I didn't just lose hope. I lost me.

Despondent and completely at a loss of what to do, there were weeks of tears. I fixated on how I was going to tell my parents, feeling nauseated even at the thought. I knew I had disappointed my parents, my church, my community, and myself. I knew I had violated the trust of everyone who had supported, trusted, and believed in me.

The father, Leonard, was the man of my dreams, but this was a burden too heavy and too soon. When I suggested we just get rid of the baby, Leonard gently told me that wasn't us. That wasn't what we believed in or how we wanted to live.

"This is not the end of life," he said.

But for me, that's exactly what it felt like.

In the fourth grade I was touched inappropriately by someone I trusted and my family knew well. I never breathed a word of it to anyone. Even at that age, I sensed the outrage and devastation it would bring to everyone involved. In my infinite wisdom I assumed I had to protect everyone and shield them from that hurt. I chose to compartmentalize it and work my way through it alone. I had good days and bad days, but I was able to hide that awful truth.

Now this was something altogether different. Because I would soon start to show signs of pregnancy, this wasn't a situation I could hide from the world.

When Leonard and I met to tell my parents, they were both speechless and brought to tears. My father managed to offer words of support, assuring us we would all get through this.

"Baby girl, it's not the end of the world," he said.

But for me, that's exactly what it felt like. Everything I had known in my life, everything I knew as normal, was gone. The mental anguish of it was too much to bear.

This was the seventies, and at that time you couldn't go back to high school if you were pregnant. This meant my life truly came to a screeching halt.

On September 4, Leonard and our parents gave me a beautiful wedding and reception. We spent our honeymoon in a nice rental, where we lived for four months while our first home was being built. As the excitement of the wedding and building a new house faded and it became time for school to start back up, the facade of happiness drained away. I felt my disappointment keenly, realizing I wouldn't ever have the school year I had dreamed of. I wanted to fulfill the activities and experiences with my senior class at school. Leonard was supportive and tried to make my life comfortable and soothe me as I adjusted to my new normal.

I couldn't imagine how I was meant to go from the comfort of my parents' home and being a spoiled daddy's girl to becoming a wife and mother. I had my own healthy savings account, my own car, and some of the finer things of life. However, I did not have a full understanding of how to make, manage, and multiply house-hold finances.

Leonard was a great husband, friend, partner, and provider.

Every day he would leave for work, and I'd be home alone with lots of time to think. Some days I chose to dwell on the worst of things. Many days I wished there was a way to just drop off into a deep, gaping place. A hole that would consume me and never require me to resurface.

I knew I had so much amazing love and support, and I had a lot to be thankful for, but I had disappointed myself. Most days became a nightmare in my head and heart.

Toward the end of September, I was having breakfast one morning, and my thoughts were as dark as usual on that day. I realized I couldn't go on like that. I had to do *something*. So, I began to pray. I asked God to forgive me and to give me direction because I had no sense of life left.

Later that afternoon, I felt inspired to call the community college. I asked the advisory department what to do when you needed to finish high school but you weren't in high school anymore. The helpful person on the other end of the line told me about their adult education program and GEDs.

Without telling anyone, I signed up for the GED exam the next day. I had to wait for the results by mail. By mid-October I received my results and the certificate of completion.

It was an important accomplishment, but I was still living under that weight of regret and shame like a coat of armor. My GED felt less than, and nothing I did felt good enough to me.

All in a two-week period, our new house was completed, we moved, and our beautiful, healthy baby girl was born. Our daughter became my focal point and a visible reminder I needed to live.

When she was fourteen months old, I entered the world of work. As a struggling young couple, Leonard and I needed the money. As months went by, we learned how to work hard, to save, and to make things happen for our family. We learned what it was like to sacrifice, stretch, and budget with our food, fun, and fuel for our family.

When our daughter turned three, I opened a daycare center

after being gifted a full business, a building, and all the furnishings, students, and staff. It was such a great opportunity for us—with lots of new responsibilities.

When she turned seven, the business was thriving. Everyone was saying how great we were doing—and it certainly appeared that way from the outside. Inside, though, I still didn't feel I deserved it or was good enough. I never mentally or emotionally moved up or on from the shame and pain I chose to hold tightly to.

Once again seeking solace in education, I went back to community college and enrolled in school. I opened and closed the daycare and drove to the community college in the middle of the day or sometimes even at night for my classes. I was determined to finish college, even though I was surrounded by (much) younger students. I finished with my AA and AS degrees in elementary education and early childhood education. Not even taking a break, I enrolled immediately in the University of North Florida and finished my bachelor's degree straight through.

In my final year of that program I found out I was pregnant again.

This news was so different from the first time, and I allowed myself to feel joy and hope and anticipation at the growing soul within me. As a family, we awaited this new addition. At nine months the baby was delivered.

Stillborn.

The devastation of losing a child was unspeakable. In my irrational grief I kept thinking I was responsible for so many children in my daycare but I couldn't even keep my own child safe. I worried no one would ever trust me with their child again now I'd let this happen.

Somehow, as we always did, Leonard and I picked back up the pieces and moved forward.

I graduated from the University of North Florida and wouldn't stop. Couldn't stop. I went straight to Nova University and received my master's degree. The tenacity with which I pursued my education was very much two things at once: me finding a way to deal with my trauma and me reveling in becoming a life-long student.

I kept my daycare center and worked part time for the school system. Three years later I sold the daycare center to expand my reach to others in the education field. I began training beginning teachers and eventually became a vice principal and then a principal.

My journey and every endeavor in the field of education and helping others was forever evolving and advancing. Years later, while still a principal, I started a home Bible study with Leonard that evolved in a few months into a church.

I entered school again and earned my doctorate in theology. We opened a Bible training institute, helping men and women with skills and academia for ministry. This institute grew into an accredited Bible college and now, some thirty years later, a Bible university.

A lifelong learner, I went back to school to become a certified chaplain to help people through grief, loss, and bereavement. I also completed an internship in hospice care and fell in love with end-of-life care.

Through this avalanche of accomplishments and wins, I still had not fully mentally or emotionally dropped my shame and regrets. One day I decided I had been living under this blanket of regret for too long, and it was too heavy to keep carrying. I couldn't keep up the mentally exhausting charade of living as a public success but a private failure.

"Come on, Love," I told myself. "You can do this."

I took a deep breath and began a conversation with myself.

"You know what, Love?"

"What?"

"Guess what."

"What?"

"Love, take a deep breath, and live your life...because you are not what you did."

I stopped short. Then I repeated those words to myself: "You are not what you did."

That day, I unlocked something inside me, and I've been saying those words to myself for the past twenty-five years. They've become my banner, my fuel, and my daily focal point.

I am not what I did. Yes, I made mistakes, but I'm not innocent or guilty.

I began to free myself. I released myself to do more. Become more. Expect more. I was determined to stop hiding behind what was, and even with all the losses and difficulties, I grew more certain.

I am not what I did.

The Hardest Lessons

As an author, speaker, and coach, I'm blessed to help many women, families, and couples. During those interactions a lot of the same advice comes up again and again, and many of those lessons are hard-learned truths I had to discover in my own story.

Fight against the idea that this is the end.

When you're struggling, it's easy to think there's no hope and no way forward. If I had given in when I was young, I wouldn't be here today. I spent hours dwelling on thoughts of suicide. Of driving my car off a bridge. Of ending the shame. In the moment, it was what I desired, but it was never the final answer.

Don't believe *anything* is final. Everything has an opportunity and the option to move forward.

Some things have to happen.

After the loss of our daughter, life once again came to a screeching halt. We'd had the baby showers. We had piles of gifts. We'd done the interior decorating and set up the nursery—only to come home from the hospital with empty arms.

I was on the brink of a nervous breakdown, and the only thing that pulled me out was waking up and deciding to stop wishing to die. I had to decide to get up and stay up.

Even the most painful experiences are part of your journey. For years I walked in shame, disappointment, and discouragement, but those were things I put on myself. I allowed life and circumstances to dictate my journey, and I let my mistakes define me.

I am not my mistakes. I am not the unbearable losses I've suffered. Those are moments in my life that helped bring me to this glorious moment.

What you listen to is what you believe.

When I got the news I was pregnant, it took me years to get the rhythm of life back—not because it wasn't available to me but because I couldn't release myself from the shame. I allowed myself to give my full attention to those dark, self-effacing thoughts, and that became the way I saw the world.

Stay open. Allow your perceptions to change.

It won't happen overnight. It's not easy. There are no shortcuts, and there will probably be more downs than ups. But you can make it.

Don't keep it to yourself.

I kept my struggles largely to myself, and that turned what could have been self-motivation into self-sabotage. I was internally destroying myself. And it didn't matter how much I smiled or how much I presented a sunny front for the public view. My introspective view was a hot mess on steroids.

It's a miracle my marriage survived. It's a miracle our three children are balanced. That's the grace of God at work.

You are not alone.

I'm blessed to have always had people, family and friends, in my corner, cheering me on and supporting me. I worked on and through things with the help of my husband and God. If you're going to win against all odds, you need to respect the process and trust in that relationship with God.

I never had to do anything on my own because I always had Him beside me.

On the Other Side of Things

I have had sixty-nine years of ups and downs. Victories and defeats. Each one is an inextricable part of my story. There were tears and pain and crushing thoughts of ending it all, but on the other side of most things, I can smile, live, and freely love myself now.

I'm a fulfilled wife, mother, grandmother, and great-grandmother. I've had fifty-two years of wonderful marriage to my best friend. Together we've shared every up and down—and too many PB and J sandwiches to count. We've robbed the piggy bank for gas. We've built four homes. We went from a small rental house to beautiful gated community–style living.

I've had an incredibly fulfilling sixty-nine years, and I'm so looking forward to what blessings my seventieth year will bring into my life.

About Dr. Love

Dr. Carolyn Boston Love is a highly respected and sought-after speaker, author, coach, mentor, and entrepreneur. With over five decades of marriage to her lifelong partner, Leonard D. Love, she brings a wealth of experience and wisdom from her everyday life.

In addition to her roles as a devoted wife of fifty-plus years, she is a mother of three, grandmother of nine, and great-grandmother of two. Dr. Love is a CPE-certified chaplain, the founder of Greater Progressive Community Development Inc., the founder of Embodiment Coaching Inc., and the executive director of Operation Love H.P.C. youth program. She has co-pastored alongside her husband for the past thirty-three years at One Church Inc. of Jacksonville.

Dr. Love holds degrees from the University of North Florida, Nova University, and Jacksonville Theological Seminary, showcasing her life-long commitment to education. Her passion for continuous learning led her to University of Phoenix, where she studied in the doctor of management in organizational leadership degree program.

With a rich educational background and an illustrious career, Dr. Love has served as a former classroom teacher, educational professional development specialist, elementary and middle school principal, and adjunct college professor for Nova University and Florida Community College. Currently she serves as the president of Truth Bible University.

Through her diverse experiences, Dr. Love brings a unique perspective and profound insights on how to win in the various cycles of life. Her daily life is a powerful resource for anyone seeking encouragement, empowerment, and strategies to create a lasting legacy of overcoming. With her genuine openness and authentic wisdom, Dr. Love inspires others to discover the secrets of commitment, stability, and thriving in your personal life.

- **Website:** www.drcarolynlove.com
- **Email:** info@drcarolynlove.com
- **Follow on all social media platforms:** @drcarolynlove

CHAPTER 11

IMMORTAL KOMBAT

How You Find the Warrior Within

By Kelli Kombat, PCC

Warriors are not born; they are made. Sometimes we don't know what kind of strength we have until we are tested. My name is Kelli, meaning "warrior maiden," and Kombat—well, that's pretty self-explanatory.

My greatest life lesson came to me at the young age of sixteen years old—I am the eldest of three; brothers Darren and David were twelve and eight years old, respectively—at a time when nothing would ever be the same again.

"I'm going to have a surprise for you when I pick you up," my dad told me before the last day of my junior year of high school. He felt sorry for me, as I grew up timid. I was afraid of my own shadow, had maybe five or six friends, and never wanted to participate in things. My parents strongly encouraged me to be well-rounded. I played the piano for seven years and the flute for eight years. I tried many things, such as ballet and Girl Scouts, for six years. At the same time, all I could think was, "Ah, let me be home with my music and magazines."

On this day, my dad made an announcement. "When I pick you up from work, I want you to change and come outside," he said. I did not know what he had planned and was full of questions. He wanted to teach me to swim. "It's going to change your summer— you will have a better summer for knowing how to swim," I recall him saying.

I agreed and was excited about this activity with my dad. So we went next door to our neighbor's house, as they were friends with my parents and invited us many times to come to their home. After he spoke to them, my dad got in the pool, and there I was, sitting on the edge of the pool, dangling my legs in the water and watching him with my little brother Dave. Then suddenly, Dad stopped swimming. I ran to the patio door to get help from our neighbors. I remember they poked him with the pool pole, *and he just floated.*

Days later he passed away.

Dad was only forty-six years old, worked out every day, lifted weights often, and ran consistently—and his heart just stopped. At that moment, everything in my world did too. *How could this happen?* One moment, my dad was teaching me to swim; the next, he couldn't.

The difficulty of that tragedy was compounded, as I always blamed myself for many years, thinking it wouldn't have happened if he wasn't trying to improve my life. For a long time I carried this weight and questioned everything. This tragedy traumatized me so much that I never wanted to learn to swim to this day.

School also was challenging, partly because of the pressures I put on myself. Sometimes it became so overwhelming in the ninth and tenth grades that I would just leave class and go home. I never felt like I belonged. People would ask me questions such as, "Why is your hair like that? Why do you look like that?" School almost felt like you had to fit in a particular box. And I didn't like that. I didn't like the questions, and I didn't like the spotlight on me. Sometimes I still don't. **Although I was extremely shy, I never ever wanted to be like everyone else.**

Not only was I painfully shy and emotional, but my grades were abominable; I struggled to pass. I just did not understand what I was reading. I remember one high school report card that showed my grades were D, D+, D-, C-, C, and C+. I was relieved that I had not failed any of my classes. Not only did this make me feel like I didn't belong at school, but with my struggles to get good grades,

I actually wondered whether I was adopted because my parents were brilliant.

With a bachelor's degree in physics, my dad received a fellowship for a graduate degree in physics and an electrical engineering degree from the University of Michigan. My dad started his career as an aeronautical engineer at Bendix Aerospace, then worked in automotive engineering as a design analysis engineer and a high-level exec with Ford Motor Co. While there, he owned and managed two apartment buildings with a combined seventy apartments. My dad was way more than just his accomplishments. He was a good father and husband—and a role model for me and my two brothers. My mother is one of the best teachers, literally and figuratively speaking. She is my confidante and one of the only people I trust in the world.

Mom and Dad were always there to ease the pain and emotions of my school years. Dad would say, "I know you're trying; I see you reading"; he would help me study and encourage me.

LESSONS LEARNED

LIFE IS *NOT* A DRESS REHEARSAL!

Despite my struggles in school, **I learned an important life lesson: no day is promised to anyone.** Since then I've always lived my life like every day's my last day, and I try to fit a lot into each day. I want to fit it all in as much as possible before my time is up. Without my dad's support I could have crumbled and fallen apart. Instead, I became motivated. I went to college and turned my grades from Ds to As. Most kids go to college and ask, "What is this?" They're in for a rude awakening. But I started sailing— I couldn't believe it. When I got to college, I thought, "I *got* this."

In fact, I felt like I belonged for the first time in my life. I chose my next journey—over eight hundred miles away at an HBCU (historically Black college and university). I was intentional about attending my parents' alma mater, Norfolk State University in Norfolk, Virginia. I was a mass communications major, played the piccolo in the prestigious Spartan Legion Marching Band, and worked at some of the top radio stations as an on-air personality in several formats. After college I pursued a graduate degree and received my MBA. I even contemplated getting a PhD in industrial psychology a few years ago but decided I didn't want to spend the extra years in school.

During this time, I learned how resilient I am. My grit, perseverance, and tenacity drive me to this day. **I've discovered that success in life is much more than good grades.** There are so many good gifts that each of us brings.

Intelligence is also being able to write a song, compose choreography, and paint a picture in abstract format—there are different kinds of intelligence. I would love for the narrative to shift and to acknowledge common sense, logic, emotional intelligence, reading the room, cultural intelligence, being a great peer, and all the things that make a person successful in life beyond simply grades.

THE ROAD LESS TRAVELED
IN OTHER WORDS, BE *YOU* AND OWN IT!

I'm a testament that the path to success is not a formulaic thing—people saw in me something beyond what most people might think would fit into certain positions.

Success includes grit and talent.

People believed in me, but more importantly, I believed in myself.

I started my career in broadcasting and moved to human resources, first at Ford Motor in Wisconsin. When I took that role, I knew there were a lot of opportunities with Ford, but I knew I could only be in Wisconsin for a year and a half because I had goals that would require me to move. My last job with Ford was at the company's world headquarters, focusing on tasks such as succession planning. I had a lot of exposure to highly strategic responsibilities. It was like a real-life MBA.

After nearly six years with Ford, I was contacted by someone asking if I would be interested in a job at L'Oréal. I went to work for the company as director of HR for a site of around six hundred people, which manufactured all the company's brands of boxed hair color for North America. My next role there was over a whole brand, Multicultural Beauty, where I was on the management committee and gained experience supporting advertising and marketing as head of HR.

After working at L'Oréal for seven years, I became senior director of HR for Volvo, the number two position for North, Central, and South America, an area of about eight hundred employees. Currently, I am a DEI executive at a global media agency.

INSTILLING CONFIDENCE IS MY JAM
BE A *WARRIOR*. REPEAT AFTER ME: WE ARE READY, RESILIENT, INTELLIGENT, OPEN, AND RESOURCEFUL.

Today, I am also a career and life coach, the host of a podcast, and a mentor. The pandemic opened me up to new opportunities. The whole jar cracked open, and in September 2020 I switched my business from HR consultation to coaching. I graduated from the Rutgers Leadership Coaching for Organizational Performance (LCOP) program in January 2021. I got clients, and it went into full gear. I did five hundred hours of coaching in six months. I received my professional certified coach designation with the International Coaching Federation, a prestigious global organization with high standards in ethics, morality, processes, and much more. To this day, I have coached over four thousand hours to hundreds of clients. I wouldn't recommend that pace to everybody, though—it has been a lot—but I am in love with it.

I coach everybody from leaders and managers to retired folx, trying to figure out what's next for them. Beyond business, I do transformational coaching related to inclusive leadership, wellness, and personal self-esteem.

My coaching practice is all about finding your voice (kellicoach.

com). All human beings want to be included, so I've dedicated my life to diversity, equity, and inclusion for all. As a coach, my passion includes helping people of all ages build confidence and communication skills.

As someone who has had a lot of tragedies in my life and recognizes that others have too and feel alone, I want you to have confidence that no matter what you've been through, you can succeed. I. Believe. In. You.

That doesn't mean I don't doubt my abilities—I do; that's being human. What picks me back up is the mindset "I've earned this"— all this hasn't been a fluke. One thing I can say about myself is I'm super resilient.

There's nothing that stops you except you!

To this day, I have to remind myself of that sometimes. I've stopped myself before—I said, "Nah, I don't think I can do that" when asked to facilitate an event, for example. Then I told myself, "Kelli, you coach people about not getting in their way, so why are you getting in your way?" My thoughts shifted to, "Why couldn't I?" So I applied, and I got it. But I had almost stopped myself!

Once you have confidence, you can do anything. I try to teach this to my teenage daughter, Brooklyn, too. I just want her to thrive—I don't want her to feel like she has to conform but to be who she is, which is different. My son, Perry, learned this valuable lesson and lives his best life in Michigan.

When I'm coaching people, and I tell them how I had gotten bad grades and was hoping for Ds, they have this look like, "What? Are you kidding me?" **Remember, you may think the road to success is one way, but it isn't.** And those emotions that discouraged me in high school? They've helped me in my career.

Through my coaching, I have a goal to serve a million people—and I will hit that goal. When I say yes to something, it's got to be with that goal in mind.

Recently, I started my weekly podcast, *Career Kombat*, which has been a longtime goal of mine. It's about getting the career you want and the answers you crave, and you can stream it on

VoiceAmerica or wherever you get your podcasts. I do it live, which honors my days as a radio broadcaster. When I thought of the concept, I asked myself, "Why would I have a script? Why not just have real conversations with people?" This style has resonated with people—they accept my podcast point of view, and I'm happy with how I serve the public.

MY YES YEAR
GREEN MEANS GO!

For me, this year will be all about staying open to opportunities. I don't mean saying yes to so many things that I'm overwhelmed—instead, I'm going to have fun, try new things, and have a "Don't knock it until you've tried it" mentality.

This year maybe I'll get on social media to try to promote my business as well—I've never been into it, but who knows? I'm gonna just say, "Never say never." I may even open myself up to finally learning to swim...finally.

I like motivational speaking and facilitating workshops—I enjoy that live interaction. I can sense the moment when that audience is right there with me and the light bulb moment happens. I love to give back through pro bono coaching as well, through such organizations as The Women's Impact Alliance (WIA) and Dress for Success of Northern New Jersey, helping with how to interview, creating a resume, using LinkedIn, and what to do after getting the job; and coaching on career burnout, getting more autonomy, breaking through to that next level, and other executive coaching. This work is incredibly fulfilling, and it is my purpose while I am here.

Watching people own their confidence—that's my jam. So, I stopped hesitating on my dream to host a podcast, went online, and started looking at mics and baffles. I went ahead and purchased some equipment. **I think that when you actually do what you say you are going to do, it manifests**—whether you write it down, put it on a vision board, even put it on a sticky note, or you buy the equipment, whether that's a yoga mat, a microphone, or whatever will help you work toward your goal. It motivates you to actually do it. You are actually putting it in the universe.

I like the book *Year of Yes* by Shonda Rhimes. In her *New York Times* best seller, Shonda—the creator of *Grey's Anatomy* and *Scandal* and executive producer of *How to Get Away with Murder*—tells how saying yes, forcing herself onto the stage and exploring and loving her true self, changed her life.

I've been closer to my goal of serving at least a million people because I'm confident just being me—the mother, the nerd, the warrior, the crafter, the hip-hop head, the homebody, every single beautiful layer. I'm excited to help people transform their lives; that energy is contagious. The same confidence can be life-changing for you. It will begin a radical renaissance, and you'll never look back.

About Kelli

Kelli Kombat (pronouns: she/her/hers) is a passionate DEI (diversity, equity, and inclusion) executive and coach who believes inclusion is innate and a sense of belonging is infinitely essential.

Her previous experience includes working in human resources at Ford Motor Co., L'Oréal, and Volvo Car USA. Prior to her career in HR, she was an on-air broadcasting personality in Virginia.

Coaching is to Kelli like water is to life!

Kelli was certified in Leadership Coaching for Organizational Performance (LCOP) at Rutgers University through ICF (the International Coaching Federation) and holds a Professional Certified Coach (PCC) credential. She specializes in coaching clients navigating career transition, burnout, and impostor syndrome.

A coach who is eternally curious and kind, Kelli created a coaching business seven years ago called R.I.C.H. (Resources in Coaching Happiness). She is also a certified DEI coach and a host for a variety of workshops to help early- and mid-career professionals find their own voices. Kelli serves as director, DEI on the board for the International Coaching Federation (ICF) New Jersey Charter Chapter.

In her spare time, Kelli moderates a podcast called *Career Kombat* and loves to devour documentaries by the dozens, attend concerts, and edit photos.

Kelli's family grows like branches on a tree. They grow in many directions, yet their roots remain as one.

Kelli can be reached on her website at kellicoach.com. Contact email: yes@kellicoach.com.

CHAPTER 12

SERVING OTHERS: THE SECRET INGREDIENT TO WINNING AN EMMY (AND MANY OTHER THINGS IN LIFE)

By Nick Nanton

From an early age I was addicted to melody, tone, chord progressions, and the poetry of lyrics. Music was my first love. But, as is often the case with young love, it also became the Siren calling to me, pulling me in, and threatening to bash me against the rocks.

Even though I've worked with and managed many successful musicians and am a songwriter in my own right, one professional dream eludes me. I am a goal-oriented person, and when I set a goal, it's usually a big one! This one is no different: I want to win a Grammy—specifically for Song of the Year.

As a Grammy voter for many years, I attended ten Grammy Awards ceremonies in eleven years. It was my great honor to see incredible live performances from some of the most amazing artists working today. (I still haven't seen Eric Clapton or Dolly Parton, but they're next on my list!)

After attending my tenth Grammy Awards, though, I realized I wasn't getting any closer to that goal of winning a Grammy myself. While I didn't tie up any of my self-worth or perceptions about me or my business in winning that trophy, I did recognize and appreciate how powerful awards are when building your brand. I couldn't deny the credibility and positioning they offered. I wanted to open the doors that awards made available, but I began to wonder if a Grammy was the way forward. It certainly didn't feel like it was getting any closer.

While flying home from the awards, the red carpet and paparazzi flashes still fresh in my mind, I opened up my computer and Googled a simple phrase: "How to win an Emmy."

I ended up stumbling on an instructional article that broke the entire process down. The biggest takeaway was that everyone today has access to incredible filmmaking tools. Even the phones in our pockets can take serviceable footage. Technology could create an end product that looked relevant and modern, and those tools were more available, user-friendly, and affordable than ever.

With that technical execution expected, the real differentiator became storytelling. If you wanted to win an Emmy, you needed to find a good story. I stored that simple but powerful piece of advice in the back of my mind.

Not long after, while scrolling through Facebook, I stumbled across the Canon 5D Mark II DSLR camera. I knew a lot of wedding photographers were using it, and more and more filmmakers were starting to gravitate toward it. With interchangeable lenses, it offered incredible depth perception and beautiful focus. It was affordable and ideal for storytelling.

I talked to my business partner and his wife, who often attended events with us and took photos. We ended up buying two of these cameras—one for me and one for her.

Now, I was just on the lookout for the right story...and someone who could really use the camera to its full potential. I was a hack at best!

Stepping back and looking at the facts, I had a lot going against me as an amateur filmmaker. I didn't live in any of the film hubs (Los Angeles or New York). I was embroiled in the music world, meaning I didn't have any contacts or insight into documentary filmmaking. I didn't attend film school or study directing. And, certainly, no one was knocking down my door to say, "You know what? I'd love to give you a lot of money to start making films."

Despite all that, I knew what I did have—a hard-earned toolbox for storytelling. I had gained this over a decade writing more songs than I could count with some of the most talented people in the business. Even though it seemed the odds were against me, I recognized that I didn't have to do what every other filmmaker was doing. I didn't have to have their exact skill sets or talents. I just had to trust what I brought to the table and use my skills to the best of my ability.

My story eventually found me in an unlikely place: Chicago O'Hare International Airport.

While waiting for a flight, I met a man there, and after we got to talking, I learned he and his family had a beautiful, uplifting, universal story to tell.

His son, Jacob, had Down syndrome, and while the family worried about letting him play in their local T-ball club, what unfolded over that season was a story of profound acceptance, love, and friendship.

The parents' concerns of bullying quickly dissipated as the community of Floyds Knobs, Indiana, rallied around that young T-ball club—and four-year-old Jacob. Every time he got a hit and rounded to first, the entire audience would erupt in cheers. On base, Jacob was all smiles, high fives, and thank-yous as he bowed to the crowd.

I knew this was my story.

Shortly after, I hosted a mastermind meeting with a handful of clients. We met periodically to discuss our various business ventures, to talk about what was working or not, and to offer support and insight to one another.

I told them I wanted to read them a story and tell them about something I'd been working on. I read the story Jacob's mom had submitted to her local newspaper, and when I came to the last line, there wasn't a dry eye in the room.

"I want to make this into a short documentary," I told them. "Do you want to help me?"

I raised about $15,000 that day—a meager budget for any film.

But I used what I had, put together a skeleton crew, and flew to Indiana. We shot *Jacob's Turn* in two days.

We ended up submitting the piece to the Emmys and earning two nominations.

As I sat in the audience at the ceremony, I heard our film announced for the first category. I waited with anticipation. Excitement. Extreme pride in what we'd made.

When they read a different title as the winner, I would be lying if I said I wasn't utterly deflated. We'd lost. And while it really *is* an honor just to be nominated, let's be honest, losing still sucks!

Luckily, I'd submitted to other awards in the past, and I knew an important key: if you're going to submit, go all in.

Every award has a committee and a community that run the event. I knew you could actually call them, talk to them, and get advice. So, that's exactly what I had done.

When I called, the voice on the other end of the line at the head office gave me some great advice. One, people often lost awards simply because they didn't enter into the right categories. Two, if you're committing to the process, enter for as many categories as you are eligible for.

Using that advice, I had also submitted *Jacob's Turn* for directing. As a fresh-faced director, I didn't expect to win. But I qualified, so I threw my hat in the ring.

As the category came up and I heard my name listed among the other directors, I was as shocked as anyone to hear Nick Nanton announced as the winner.

I had my first Emmy win. Despite where I lived. Despite my lack of film studies. Despite my inexperience in the medium. I used the film to honor good storytelling, and that was the path that finally opened the door.

I was able to do that only because I was serving someone else. Telling another person's story that deserved the attention. None of it was ever about me.

When I originally brought the idea to my business group, I gave them a reason to want to get involved. I met their important criteria of being a trusted person doing good things and producing good work. I was open to sharing my learning with them along the journey. I invited them to the Emmys with me. I made it interesting and valuable to them, and because we approached the project from a place of collaboration and community, we had strength in numbers.

We were able to overcome what seemed like insurmountable obstacles because we did it together and we worked in service of others.

THE ROAD MAP TO AN EMMY WIN

Breaking into the entertainment industry is considered one of the hardest things to do. And while not everyone has the goal of getting into that field, I think we can all agree that the lessons from such a competitive industry can easily be applied to others. Here are some of the guiding principles that helped me overcome those odds.

Start with how you can serve other people.

Whatever your goal, making it in life often starts with changing your approach. Rather than thinking entirely about how something is going to benefit you, shift that mindset to figure out how you can best serve other people.

Yes, you will likely need to benefit from the venture in some way as well, but when you subjugate what you need and want for the better of others, it's amazing what you can accomplish and how many doors start opening.

Put the needs of others first, and then use your unique gifts and talents to be a conduit and facilitator for what others want. This is how you start to accomplish the previously unimaginable.

Don't think you have to do what everyone else does.

Triumphing against all odds often requires some outside-the-box thinking.

Take Keith Ferrazzi as an example. He's a highly acclaimed,

highly successful entrepreneur and the author of *Never Eat Alone* and *Who's Got Your Back*.

As the urban legend goes, Ferrazzi had heard that Bob Iger and Buzz Aldrin had never met. However, given the *Toy Story* connection with Buzz Lightyear, they were both interested in that opportunity. Ferrazzi called Buzz Aldrin's office and spoke to the secretary.

"I understand Mr. Aldrin would like to meet Bob Iger. Would you like me to help set that meeting up?"

The secretary said Mr. Aldrin was definitely interested and the office would call him back.

Then Ferrazzi called Bob Iger's office and spoke to the secretary there.

"I understand Mr. Iger would like to meet Buzz Aldrin. Would you like me to help set that meeting up?"

Again, the secretary said Mr. Iger would be thrilled and the office would be in touch.

But here's the thing. Ferrazzi didn't know Aldrin or Iger. He'd never even met either of them. When the meeting was successfully set up, Ferrazzi attended as well, earning valuable contacts and an invaluable memory.

You don't have to do what everyone else does. In fact, the most successful people rarely do. Never underestimate the power of creative thinking and resilience, because success often requires them.

Sit in the middle, and figure out all sides.

When you set yourself a lofty goal, it's easy to feel like the odds are against you. When I wanted to make a documentary about Rudy Ruettiger, the inspiration for *Rudy*, the number one sports movie of all time, I knew I needed to raise a lot of funds to make that possible. That's a daunting place to be, but I was able to figure out a system that answered a fundamental question: If I need money to make this project, what can I provide that would be valuable?

As I started the process of making this film, I sat in the middle of all the stakeholders and ensured I would be serving every group.

I was going to make a poignant, respectful film that served Rudy well. I was going to give producer or executive producer credits to those who would contribute funding to the film. I was going to take those contributors to the Emmys, if we were nominated.

With another one of my ventures, Abundance Studios, we work often with celebrity clients, and one of the perks for contributors is getting to meet these celebrities, taking photos with them, and having access to their incredible networks. When dealing with higher-stakes ventures and projects, it's easy for everyone to think exclusively about the money. But what many people end up forgetting is how many other benefits you can offer people.

None of our contributors have any financial stake in the projects. Yes, you read that right. They contribute money to make the film with no expectation of getting any of their money back. In fact, I guarantee that they won't get their money back, but what they will get is an incredible life experience. We've found creative ways to make it about more than just money. We've figured out how to give people great experiences that make them *want* to be part of these purpose-driven projects we create.

We start every project with three crucial questions:

- Whom can we serve?
- What do we want to do?
- Whom is this project valuable to?

From that foundation we can start putting ourselves in the shoes of every stakeholder and figuring out what's enticing, valuable, and beneficial to them.

CREATING MY FUTURE THROUGH SERVICE TO OTHERS

After that first Emmy win, my business partner simply said, "Hey, let's do more of that." And that's exactly what we did.

After more films and more Emmy nominations (and wins…and losses), I had the pleasure of telling many people's stories. Rudy

Ruettiger. Larry King. Dick Vitale. I even earned a star on the Las Vegas Walk of Stars.

As I'd hoped, a major award did open amazing opportunities in my career. With creativity, ingenuity, and purpose, I was able to craft and create the future I wanted.

And while I'm honored with the accolades, I know one thing with certainty. I found my unlikely success in filmmaking and overcame all those odds against me because I always led with how a project would affect others.

In the entertainment industry, it's easy to think it's all about your name in marquee lights, but you get a lot further and create more impactful projects when you stop to think about what's in it for everyone else involved.

Now, about that Grammy...yes, I'm still working on it.

About Nick

From the slums of Port-au-Prince, Haiti, with special forces raiding a sex trafficking ring and freeing children, to the Virgin Galactic Space Port in Mojave with Sir Richard Branson, twenty-two-time Emmy Award–winning Director-Producer Nick Nanton has become known for telling stories that connect. Why? Because he focuses on the most fascinating subject in the world: *people*. As an award-winning songwriter, storyteller, and best-selling author, Nick has shared his message with millions of people through his documentaries, speeches, blogs, lectures, songs, and best-selling books. Nick's book *StorySelling* hit The Wall Street Journal Best-Seller List and is available on Audible as an audiobook. Nick has directed more than sixty documentaries and a sold-out Broadway Show (garnering forty-three Emmy nominations in multiple regions and twenty-two wins), including:

- *DICKIE V* (ESPN/Disney+)
- *Rudy Ruettiger: The Walk On* (Amazon Prime)
- *The Rebound* (Netflix)
- *Operation Toussaint* (Amazon Prime)

Nick has shared the stage with, coauthored books with, and made films featuring:

- Larry King
- Kathie Lee Gifford
- Hoda Kotb
- Dick Vitale
- Kenny Chesney
- Magic Johnson
- Coach Mike Krzyzewski
- Jack Nicklaus
- Tony Robbins
- Lisa Nichols
- Peter Diamandis
- And many more

Nick specializes in bringing the element of human connection to every viewer, no matter the subject. He is currently directing and hosting the series *In Case You Didn't Know* (season 1 executive produced by Larry King), featuring legends in the worlds of business, entrepreneurship, personal development, technology, and sports.

Nick's first love has always been music. He has been writing songs for more than two decades, and his songs have been aired on radio across the United States and in Canada. He is currently ranked in the top 10 percent of songwriters in the world. His songs have been recorded by Lee Brice, Darius Rucker, RaeLynn, Joe Bryson, and many more, and have amassed more than three million streams on Spotify, Apple Music, Pandora, and SoundCloud. He received three Gold records in 2018 for his work with the global touring band A Day to Remember.

Nick has written and/or produced songs that have appeared on the following shows or in promotional commercials for:

- the Fox prime-time series *Glee, New Girl, House,* and *Hell's Kitchen*
- the MLB All-Star Game
- ABC Family's hit series *Falcon Beach*
- the CBS prime-time series *Ghost Whisperer* starring Jennifer Love Hewitt

CHAPTER 13

FROM TRAUMA TO TRIUMPH

By Shonda Smith

My grandmother made me feel at home. Her house, a tiny trailer, was a sanctuary of warmth where her open door welcomed all who sought refuge, regardless of the hour. Whether it was 11:00 at night or the crack of dawn, she was always there to listen and provide comfort.

She was more than just a caretaker; she was a compassionate visionary—a woman of many talents. An amazing cook, hair-stylist, seamstress, and so much more. She poured her heart and soul into everything she did, passing on her wisdom and skills to me along the way.

Despite health struggles and the constraints of living on a meager income, she never hesitated to give of herself. Most mornings before 6:00, like clockwork, she was up, preparing breakfast plates for the workers lined up to buy a meal at her door.

I was almost fifteen when she finally took me in, offering me a haven of stability and love amid the turbulence of my youth. It was a turning point, a beacon of hope in a world that felt uncertain and unforgiving.

NINE YEARS EARLIER, AGE SIX

As a young girl growing up in Myrtle Beach, South Carolina, I was surrounded by the vibrant happenings of this sought-after coastal city. Myrtle Beach was a place of community and connection, where families gathered to share laughter and experiences near the backdrop of the vast Atlantic Ocean. I always loved the beach, but beneath the surface of this idyllic paradise lay the complexities of life and the hidden struggles that shaped my young journey.

At the tender age of six, my world was uprooted from South Carolina, and I found myself thrust into the unfamiliar terrain of North Carolina without my mother! The transition was jarring, like stepping into a new chapter without knowing the plot. Though only one state away, it felt like a continent away from my mom. I learned to adjust to new surroundings and grew up quickly, feeling the pressures of self-preservation as far back as I can remember.

Four Years Later, Age Ten

One hundred thirty-one, one hundred thirty-two... I counted my steps as I eagerly walked to school one morning, carefully avoiding each crack. Something shiny and pink disrupted my counting— a sparkly satin ribbon attached to a metal clip, the type of bow a cheerleader would wear on her flowing ponytail. I stared at it, smiling and knowing exactly what I would do with it.

When I arrived, I hurried down the long, noisy hallway straight to the girls' bathroom. A tightly braided single plait stuck out at a forty-five-degree angle from the back of my head. I boldly decided to undo it, revealing my long, crinkled black hair. I rearranged my flowing ponytail upward, clipped on the sparkling pink bow, and smiled.

"I see you," I told the little girl in the mirror. "You're beautiful."

It was picture day, and I was finally camera ready. I longed to express my true personality, and this pop of color was just what I needed. I rushed to class before the bell rang, hugged my fourth-grade teacher, sat at my desk, and leaned in to her every word.

I was a Junior Beta Club member, was in the National Honor Society, and always excelled with honors. I completed my homework every night with perfect penmanship. I was neatly dressed and always used my manners. I didn't speak unless spoken to, and from my teachers' perspectives, I was an ideal student. School was my safe place.

THE HIDDEN TRUTH

But then came the end of the school day. Every afternoon at 2:45, my teacher would start the dismissal announcements. Tick…tick…TICK went the clock, seemingly louder and louder. My heart pounded to the beat of the second hand, and my head began to hurt. My stomach pains grew more intense. My feet were jittery, and my hands became clammy. I'd shoot a shaky hand into the air. "Mrs. Anderson, may I be excused to the restroom, please?"

I'd rush to the restroom to deal with those uncontrollable behaviors that came near the end of each school day when my body made its own decisions, and I felt utterly sick—all because it was time…to go…home.

My fourth-grade teachers missed something important. Amid the As on my report card, they didn't notice the A that stood for *abuse*.

They missed the B, which stood for *behavioral signs*.

I never made Cs, but if they stood for *confidence*, I surely wouldn't even have earned one!

I had perfect grades, neatly buttoned long-sleeved shirts, and perfectly ironed jeans, yet my teachers missed the black-and-blues. They certainly weren't marker smudges but instead, deep, weeks-old bruises. It's no wonder my attendance was less perfect than my grades. If I could speak as well as I behaved, behind a soft-spoken manner they would have heard the shame and suffering of a sexually abused child.

Every day, I cringed at the thought of returning to that house. But as long as my grades and behavior were good, no one noticed anything.

Much later, I learned to label those uncontrollable behaviors: anxiety, depression, PTSD, and obsessive-compulsive disorder (OCD). I hated that I felt compelled to count my steps, the number of times I chewed before swallowing, or the seconds on that dreaded clock. My obsession with perfection at school and my performance as a student were coping mechanisms that my young mind could not yet process.

By thirteen I was finally removed from that situation in North Carolina and was allowed to return to Myrtle Beach. I transitioned from temporary foster care and then from one house to the other, or "from pillar to post," as my grandmother called it until she finally took me in. Sleeping on the couch or the floor every night in that little trailer was the first place I felt safe, secure, and loved with no strings attached. It was *home*. There's nothing like the nurturing love of a grandmother.

I excelled in school and graduated in eleventh grade with a full-ride four-year scholarship. I eventually became a college scholar, making the dean's or president's list each semester. I was a proud Chanticleer at Coastal Carolina University when I was approved for a paid work-study position as the dean's personal assistant. Life was great!

But beyond the accolades and successes, a shadow lingered. Despite the outward achievements, I grappled with internal turmoil, confronting the lingering scars of my past. It was a journey marked not only by academic triumphs but also by the profound struggle for self-discovery and healing, a journey that would ultimately shape the course of my future.

A HIGHER CALLING

Later, as an adult, when I needed to advance my career and step into my purpose, I couldn't. Struggling with suppressed childhood traumas, I couldn't take the lead in my life. That shy, silenced ten-year-old girl was still inside me, and she couldn't speak up or shine.

Nevertheless, great things happened in my life. After pursuing my passion for becoming an educator, I was nominated for Teacher of the Year. I became a loving wife and a proud mother. I became a business owner and a *homeowner*, creating a safe space for my children to feel loved.

Unfortunately, I put aside what I was most passionate about, what made my heart flutter with excitement yet forced me out of my comfort zone. It required me to take a stand and...speak up. I realized I lacked some inner qualities and that academic success alone wasn't enough to reach my highest potential. A higher calling tugged at my heart, but still I couldn't step into my purpose.

I began to remember valuable lessons that my childhood neighbor, a mother figure, taught me. I began to spend more time praying, meditating, and building a personal relationship with God, and this pivotal point was the start of a personal healing journey.

My soul's heaviness lightened. I began to experience comfort and a reassuring peace. Something inside me shifted, and I sought more opportunities for self-empowerment. I became a crowned pageant queen, holding the title of mompreneur with five children, all of whom are creative, compassionate souls I've been blessed to share with the world!

Given that school was such a safe haven for me, it's no coincidence I became an elementary school teacher or that teaching in my fourth-grade classroom was incredibly therapeutic. During my eighteen years in the classroom I observed countless children's behaviors and emotional needs. Like when I was a child, there was a great need for teaching that focused beyond academics, arts, and athletics.

After doing the hard but necessary work with a qualified PTSD and trauma-trained licensed therapist, I experienced tremendous breakthroughs. I continued serving my community, and seven years ago I took the first significant career step toward living my true purpose. I launched The Queen In Me, a girls' empowerment program with live workshops, online courses, and queen-like events to inspire young girls.

As the mommy of three beautiful girls (twenty-two, thirteen, and eleven), I am confident about my vision and passion for teaching young girls empowering life skills. Indeed, it takes a village. I want to help prepare girls for life in a way that focuses far beyond traditional academics. To do this, I created a virtual classroom. I nurture young girls (little queens) alongside their moms or mother figures, who have a special place in my heart because of my grandmother. Our online "village" includes grandmoms, aunts, stepmoms, foster moms, and adoptive moms. Together we get to impact the lives of girls worldwide.

Our five-session Girls REIGN course focuses on five fun REIGNing Principles. The classes excite and engage girls while they proactively learn self-love, positive body image, body-protection practices, and many more lessons I needed as a young girl. The girls build confidence while learning their true identity in Christ and the importance of sharing their unique gifts and talents with the world. They learn vision planning for their purpose-driven future, and, especially important, they learn the power of their voices.

EMPOWERING AND EDUCATING OTHERS WITH MY VOICE

To every woman or girl who's been silenced, been made to feel worthless, or felt they've had no control over their situation, these are some of the hard-won lessons I wish someone had taught me. Now that I've reclaimed my voice, I want to use it daily to help others heal.

The only true failure is not pursuing what's in your heart. No one else's opinion defines us. Despite my upbringing and uncontrollable past, I could envision a better future for myself, set goals, and accomplish anything I set out to do. I was not broken. We are all valuable, priceless, and more than enough! Just because no one fought for or protected me didn't mean there wasn't a precious little queen inside me!

Your little queen can heal. Your worth and value are not a sum of the mistreatment or neglect you may have suffered. This is not your identity. My broken childhood home and ensuing traumas made me struggle with anxiety, depression, PTSD, and OCD. The depression brought on by sexual, physical, and psychological abuse was a lonely, hopeless place. However, I discovered that days filled with passion and purpose were the cure for depression. And for me, God was the light revealing the way forward. In

Him we're always loved, specifically chosen, and accepted. Having that deep revelation of Him through an intimate relationship was the cure for my anxiety. By fully trusting in God and meditating on His Word, we can cast away all cares, stop the cycle of worrying, and embrace a renewed mind.

Living as your authentic self is living whole and complete. As a young child, I never experienced motherly affection, nurturing, genuine love, or verbal affirmation. That left me with deep-rooted feelings of abandonment and rejection.

I remember like yesterday when I was twelve, and I was adopted into the family of Christ. Once I gave my life to Him and became empowered by His Holy Spirit, I began experiencing the depth of His love—something I'd never experienced before. God is the perfect example of loving and nurturing others. In Him we lack nothing. Even though I didn't receive love as a child, I wasn't incapable of giving love to others. My belief in and practice of godly love made me a loving person.

A Letter to My Inner Little Queen

Dear Sweet Shonda,

From a young age, it was drilled into you that a child was seen, not heard, and whatever happened at home stayed at home. At every turn, your voice was silenced, and you were stripped of power. You couldn't control your environment or what happened to you.

Nor were you supposed to.

You're not alone.

God is with you.

You're not abandoned or rejected.

You're not what you've been through.

You're not broken or forgotten.

Your true identity lies in Him.

You're a beloved daughter of God.

A daughter of the almighty King!

You're a little Queen!

You're more valuable than even His crown's jewels.

He's heard you cry to Him.

He's chosen you, marked you as His own, and saved you.

He's guiding you, teaching you, and molding your heart to be like His. Life hasn't been easy, and you'll encounter more hardships as you grow, but He won't forsake you. He'll carry you through. Just trust Him, and keep your heart secure in His hands. Talk to Him about every concern, thought, and feeling. Most importantly, read His Word in full context. Read chapter by chapter, and He'll turn your sorrows into beauty. He'll transform your thoughts and overall life from traumatic to triumphant!

CULTIVATING, PROTECTING, LOVING, AND BECOMING THE QUEEN WITHIN

Through it all I redefined what *home* meant to me, and I've combined my passion with my profession to bring that definition to those I serve. Every day, I get to help girls and moms by sharing how to raise powerful, self-assured little queens!

As a real estate broker and home designer, I help other moms create places of safety, security, love, and belonging for their children. I help them achieve their homeownership goals and teach them to build generational wealth.

Resilient women don't become that way through easy lives. Resilience is born in the moments when you are truly against all odds. I'm honored to help shape a resilient mindset in today's generation of young girls. I have the privilege of teaching and transforming girls' lives worldwide. The Queen In Me virtual courses empower girls to navigate the challenges they'll face in middle school, in high school, and beyond.

As a voiceless little girl, I needed this program. Now I start each day with purpose and pride because I can help young girls *reign* while *becoming the queen within*!

About Shonda

Shonda Smith is originally from Myrtle Beach, South Carolina, and spent years educating and motivating youth. She has an eighteen-year career as a licensed elementary school teacher in South Carolina and North Carolina. While managing multiple businesses, she pursues her passion to teach girls self-love, self-confidence, body-protection practices, and other empowering life skills so they can overcome challenges and reach their highest potential!

Shonda has three daughters, ages eleven, thirteen, and twenty-two. Her two sons, ages seven and twenty-five, are the perfect "bookends" to help her husband with the responsibility of keeping the girls safe and loved. She cherishes spending quality family time with her children and husband while cooking together, sharing delicious recipes, and communing at the dining room table (which she loves to decorate).

When she's not teaching Little Queens in her online classroom and supporting the women who are raising them, she enjoys guiding families through the home-buying, -selling, and -investing processes and decorating homes with her business HOMEmade By Shonda, based in Raleigh, North Carolina. As a survivor, she believes that home should be a safe haven, and she is fulfilling her true purpose whenever she has the privilege of serving a fellow mom or educator with her talents and professionalism. She teaches girls the power of resiliency, the significance of further developing their gifts and talents, and sharing them with the world, so that they too can live a life of passion and purpose!

"Train her up in the way *she* should go!" As a mompreneur of five beautiful children, a pageant queen, and most importantly, a daughter of the Most High King, she knows firsthand the importance of this mission. She's the founder of The Queen In Me, established in 2016, in which her vision is to transform the lives of girls worldwide by equipping them with the intrinsic tools to "recognize their royalty" and pursue their dreams fearlessly! With her signature online courses, inspirational speaking, and queen-like events, she empowers girls to REIGN while "Becoming the Queen Within"!

Shonda would love to connect with you!

Email:

- Girls Empowerment: Info@TheQueenInMe.com
- Real Estate and Decor: Info@ShondaSmith.com
- Join the email list for free resources and updates: https://bit.ly/QueenInMeEmailList

Social Media:

- Girls Empowerment: @TheQueenInMeGirls
- Real Estate and Decor: @HOMEmadeByShonda
- Join the R.E.I.G.N. Council Facebook group for women raising girls: @TheREIGNCouncil or www.facebook.com/groups/reigncouncil

Web:

- Girls Empowerment: http://TheQueenInMe.com
- Real Estate and Decor: https://shondasmith.com

CHAPTER 14

RESILIENCE THROUGH RACISM

By Ora V. Robinson, PhD

I vividly remember those Sunday visits to my grandparents' house, nestled along a dusty road in Lake City, Florida, where I first drew breath before the dawn of the Civil Rights Movement. It was a quaint little town, but a carload of White youngsters often shattered the tranquility during those Sunday visits. Their shouts would pierce the air as they hurled the vile N-word at us: "N——s! You monkeys, go back to Africa!" Such venomous words spat out with fervor puzzled me as a child. The depth of the hatred behind those words eluded my young understanding.

Our journey northward led us to Milwaukee when I was just a tender soul about six years old. I recall a moment of thirst, seeking solace in a sip of water. I approached the water fountain, eager for relief, but my mother's sudden grip halted me.

"No, this is for Whites only," she whispered with a heavy heart.

Then came a pivotal moment, etched into the annals of my memory. A White lady, her presence a beacon of hope, stepped forward and addressed my mother with a grace that defied the bigotry of the times. "No, ma'am," she asserted firmly, "she can drink from this fountain. This fountain is for everyone."

In that simple act, a glimmer of humanity illuminated the shadows of prejudice. It was a beacon of hope amid the darkness, a testament to the resilience of the human spirit and the power of compassion to transcend the barriers erected by ignorance. Those were the days when Southern fountains bore stark labels: Colored Only and Whites Only.

As a child, I recall posing the innocent question "What color does the water come out of the colored fountain?" Oh, the innocence of youth, unaffected by the evil complexities of racism.

Every time we prepared for a visit back South, my father went to AAA to plan our route, underscoring the sobering reality of our journey. He sought out the "safe" filling stations and sanctuaries where we could pause to rest and sleep. We were acutely aware of the towns requiring daylight passage for our safety; conversations between my parents echoed warnings: "We have to reach this town, pass that one. No stopping, et cetera, understood?"

Before each trip the instructions rang clear: "When we head south, do these kinds of things, but don't do these kinds of things. Do you understand?"

While at my grandmother's down south, she would lead us downtown, a mere few blocks away. There stood a dress store, its threshold a boundary of whispered rules. "You can't touch these clothing items," she'd caution with a blend of pragmatism and resignation. "You can touch the top of the hanger, but you can't try them on."

Being from the North, I questioned, "But why?"

Her response was laden with the weight of history. "That's their rule. They don't want you putting clothing on your back because no White person will want to purchase that clothing."

The only reason we were in this store was because the owner was related to us but would deny our relationship based on the history of slavery. Those haunting echoes of earlier childhood resurfaced as a car prowled the streets. The memories flooded back—vulgarities, the dreaded N-word, and the evil chants urging us to return to Africa. By then I grasped their implications. A chill crept down my spine, a shiver of fear that lingered with me as I grew older, the specter of those moments haunting my subconscious.

In the segregated South, racial divides ran deep. Integration laws in the North, including our hometown of Milwaukee, offered a glimmer of hope. Yet beneath the surface, integration was a facade. We, the pawns in their game, were shuffled to distant schools where acceptance was scarce. Recess and lunch, once communal, became partitions of race.

However, our neighborhood told a different story—a vibrant tapestry where friendships transcended color lines. Despite warnings on the bridge, separating us from friends like J.D., our northside streets buzzed with real integration. But it was a bitter pill, as animosity lurked around every corner.

In the face of adversity, many of us, including me, learned to play the role of the "house slave" in our minds—a survival tactic in a world fraught with prejudice. Yet amid the whispers of caution, my aunt stood as a beacon of resilience, armed with courage, and her "brothers," Smith and Wesson, navigating a world of uncertainty.

As a young girl, I was exposed to heavy stories of racism—a reality that shaped my identity. We, as Black Americans, didn't choose this journey; we simply sought to better our lives amid a world that judged us solely on the color of our skin.

Life in School During the Civil Rights Movement

In my early school days, a teacher labeled my speech unclear, planting seeds of doubt about my future employability.

"You'll never find a job speaking in front of people."

Such remarks, uttered when I was barely eight, weighed heavily on my young mind and decisions made years later as a young adult. High school brought new challenges, with educators deeming my intellect inadequate for advanced studies, steering me away from sciences and toward more basic subjects. The notion of pursuing a healthcare career was summarily dismissed.

At fourteen I grappled with the implications of these decisions, struggling to comprehend their impact on my life's trajectory. It felt like a deliberate attempt to limit my potential, a systematic effort to confine me within narrow boundaries. In those days our public school system offered a structured curriculum to equip students with practical skills by age eighteen. While homemaking, sewing, and cooking were part of the curriculum for everyone, the underlying goal was to help students uncover their true talents and interests. The path led to office education, where I found genuine enthusiasm and aptitude.

Our teacher, Ms. Z, pushed us to excel beyond the established norms. She emphasized the importance of competitiveness, highlighting the disparity between our skills and those of students from more privileged districts. Although the full significance of her efforts didn't register with us at the time, her guidance laid the groundwork for our future endeavors.

LIFE IN THE WORKFORCE, HIGHER EDUCATION, AND INSTITUTIONAL RACISM

At sixteen, thanks to the office education work-study program, I found a job at a bank as a bookkeeper. The women at the bank were in their late twenties and embraced me, a sixteen-year-old, with warmth and wisdom, guiding me into the workforce. They called me Tena, my nickname, which is only for family and friends.

In the bookkeeping department, where I worked alongside another high schooler, a supervisor attempted to undermine me and accused us of ludicrous claims. I excelled in shorthand and typing, but interviews offered only clerk-type positions, highlighting the barriers beyond the office walls. These were harsh examples of my first brush with racism in the workplace.

Upon graduating high school, I faced the daunting question "What next?" I turned to community college, hoping for a fresh start. Although there were some positive moments, ongoing negative experiences served as reminders of the disparities we faced, so I made the rash decision to drop out altogether, forfeiting a two-year scholarship—one of the biggest regrets of my life to this day. I still had a year left on that scholarship, but I felt lost, unsure of my next move.

Intrigued by a free medical transcription course, I embarked on a new journey. Despite being the only Black student, I excelled, only to face disappointment during job interviews. Though I was well qualified, I was only offered clerk typist positions.

Eventually, and for the next fifteen years, I worked as a medical transcriber at Milwaukee County Hospital, nestled in the heart of Wisconsin. Truth be told, it was a pleasant gig. The women and physicians I worked alongside were friendly and supportive. Once again, though, I was the only Black transcriber in the mix.

Eventually, I stumbled upon a scholarship program at the hospital for minority employees like me to pursue nursing. They offered courses at the hospital-based nursing school or options at community college or a baccalaureate degree.

I felt old at twenty-eight. Laugh if you must, but that's how I felt. My coworker strolled over, a cigarette dangling from her mouth, and dropped a bombshell: "Ora, are you gonna seize that opportunity or what?"

"I dunno. I'm too old."

She looked me dead in the eye and said, "Old? I'm fifty-five, miserable over here. You don't wanna end up like me, do you? Get yourself to school."

Just like that her words flipped a switch in my head. I signed up for the baccalaureate program.

My mother and grandmother set benchmarks, steering us away from factory jobs they worked in, where you're bossed around left and right. Meanwhile, I had a friend fresh out of high school at sixteen, working as an associate nurse at eighteen. She'd spill tales about the horrors she faced, how they treated her, and the nasty attitude of nurses and doctors.

"Nope, not for me." Skinny, shy, introverted—that's me. Remember, I can't speak, can't talk properly. It's all subconscious baggage from way back.

So, back to aiming for the medical transcription gig—I applied but was not accepted. I was eighteen, apparently lacking experience. But my crew had my back—they vouched for me, saying they'd train me on the job. Another group of women took me under their wing—White women from all walks of life. It left an impression, a reminder that not all White folks carry racist vibes.

Then came new challenges in nursing school. "You won't be getting a nursing degree from this school," she said, her eyes firm, shattering my hopes as tears welled up.

We were only four Black students among one hundred in nursing school. The experience was a crucible of sorts. A failed evaluation dealt a blow to my self-esteem, prompting me to seek aid from the Black Nursing Association. We probed deeper: Was it truly a knowledge gap? Retaking the class in the summer, I faced the harsh reality—I couldn't leap from a C minus to an A. Yet with perseverance and support, I graduated, the lone Black student among thirty.

After graduating, I returned to Milwaukee County Hospital to work with my seniority intact. But anxiety marred my board exams for two years. Despite a preparatory course, I failed, enduring demotion to a CNA. After taking a refresher course and dealing with anxiety, I eventually passed and transitioned to a registered nurse role.

I enrolled in a master's program and encountered numerous setbacks that could have easily prevented me from graduating. My mentor's counsel guided me: "Do you want to fight or graduate?" I chose the latter, learning to pick my battles wisely. Through it all her wisdom echoed: "You can't fight all these battles that come your way. You have to be selective so you can win the war."

CALL ME DR. ORA

Upon completing my master's, the suggestion to pursue my PhD elsewhere hit me like a ton of bricks. Despite being in my hometown, the University of Milwaukee was deemed off-limits. Capella University in Minnesota became my chosen path, as I asserted my academic aspirations and refused to let others dictate my journey.

Racism lingered, casting shadows even in my role as a charge nurse. My lack of support and cold treatment from colleagues underscored my uphill battle. However, these challenges fueled my determination to excel. Each setback became a catalyst for resilience, propelling me forward on my PhD journey.

I learned an important lesson about forgiveness along the way. Forgiveness is not merely for others but for my healing. How can I expect God's forgiveness if I cannot extend it to others? I've embraced compassion and empathy toward those who sought to hinder me, echoing the words "Lord, forgive them, for they know not what they do."

There I stood in 2006, finally accepting my PhD. I was over the moon.

"Congratulations, Dr. Ora." My mentor handed me a book on African Americans navigating academia, as if to say, "Buckle up. It's going to be a ride." And boy, was it ever.

People have asked me, "Why are you always smiling? How can you? You don't seem to be bothered by stuff." And I quietly say, "Jesus."

As you turn the pages of this chapter, if you face similar challenges—bullies, abuse—know that you can weather any storm with a sturdy support system and a steadfast connection to God. It begins with your mindset and your relationship with God.

Growing up amid the Civil Rights Movement instilled fear within me. Dr. King's death felt personal; stories of lynching trees haunted our countryside. Shyness became my shield as I anticipated the next blow. Recent years brought reflection—I finally rejected the slave mentality, embracing forgiveness and faith.

Education symbolized liberation despite the National Guard's presence and marches. Dogs feared from civil rights images, symbolized danger. Academic pursuits defied societal limits; I pursued nursing despite my fear. In the face of adversity I persisted, finding strength in resilience and determination.

Respect Your Elders, Cherish Diversity, and Never Place People into Narrow Boxes

I'm not just Black but a quilt of cultures stitched together. During my journey to Africa, particularly the Ivory Coast, I was struck by the profound beauty and haunting history. Walking through the remnants of the past, from old cannons to the Door of No Return, I felt a deep resonance with the struggles of my ancestors. It made me realize that blaming everything on the White man oversimplifies the complexity of history.

Traveling can help you expand your horizons and remind us not to be quick to judge. Racism isn't just Black and White; it's a tangled web of ethnicities and experiences. So before pointing fingers, look within yourself and examine your perceptions. And remember, communication is the bridge that connects us all.

Be Remembered for How You Made Others Feel

Even if my kids and students don't remember what I taught them, I want them to remember how I made them feel. I want them to feel valued. I ask God, "Tell me what words I need to say that would edify somebody else. Lift them up versus down," and I pause. I do not tell students they're failing. Instead, I say, "How can we help you be more successful?" Not I, but how can *we*?

Now I stand as an educator at West Coast University, guiding baccalaureate nursing students as I aim to embody the support I once yearned for. I want others to remember I was persistent. I had fortitude. I didn't give up. I want my story to inspire others to push for their dreams. God gave me these gifts, and for me not to use them is dishonoring to Him. These gifts are for more than just me. Life is all about finding ways to give away the gifts we gain to others.

About Ora

Ora V. Robinson, PhD, is a highly accomplished individual in the field of nursing, with a passion for education, wellness, and eradicating racial biases in the nursing profession. As a certified nurse educator through the National League for Nursing, she has demonstrated a commitment to excellence in nursing education.

Ora has received the prestigious Young Publisher's Award through the Association of Black Nursing Faculty, showcasing her dedication to advancing the visibility and recognition of Black voices in nursing. Her National Board Certification as a Health and Wellness Coach (NBC-HWC) and Mayo Clinic certification as a Wellness Coach reflect her commitment to promoting holistic well-being in both her professional and personal life.

She holds a Graduate Certificate in Evidence-Based Coaching, emphasizing her expertise in using evidence-based practices to empower individuals in their wellness journeys. Her research is centered on minority nurse role conflict, with a specific focus on Black registered nurses experiencing racism in the nursing profession. This work highlights her dedication to addressing and mitigating systemic issues within the healthcare field.

Beyond her academic and research pursuits, Ora is a globe-trotter, having traveled to two other continents: Africa and Asia (South Korea, India, and Israel). This international exposure enriches her perspective and contributes to her holistic approach to nursing education and wellness coaching.

Ora's personal mission is to inspire, motivate, and educate one nurse at a time. Her overarching goal is to eradicate racial bullying and other "isms" in the nursing profession. As the author of *The Invisible Black Nurse: Navigating RACE-isms*, she provides a guide on becoming visible in a profession where underrepresentation is a significant challenge. Her book, infused with the principle that "love covers all," serves as a beacon of guidance and empowerment.

A well-sought-out speaker on racism in nursing, Ora actively engages with various professional organizations, sharing her insights and advocating for positive change. Through her multifaceted contributions to nursing education, wellness coaching, research, and advocacy, Ora exemplifies a leader dedicated to creating an inclusive and equitable future for the nursing profession.

CHAPTER 15

THE DANCE OF LIFE

Moving Toward Your Most Authentic Self

By La Toya Davis, PhD

I felt the chill of the bathroom floor up through my body, and I stifled the sobs. My two kids were on the other side of the door, and I didn't want them to hear me. As I sat on that cold floor, I realized something had to change. I could not do what I was doing any longer.

I started dating my husband in 1999, and it was now 2015.

In sixteen years of growing, loving, and living, I had become so intertwined that it was easy to lose my own person in that union. Somewhere along the line, I stopped being La Toya, and I started becoming my husband's wife. We had built a successful business and were leaders in the spiritual community. The community knew us as a collective entity. I still had tremendous love for my husband, but for many years I had been expecting and wanting something from him that he could not give.

I knew deciding to walk away was going to mean a monumental shift in my family's life. I knew it meant disrupting our core of shared friends. I knew it meant the unknown of splitting time with our two children, no longer having the security of his primary income, and not having the safety net of any savings.

Sitting on that bathroom floor, I asked myself the hard, unpleasant questions. Could I get to where I needed to be if I stayed in this relationship? If either of my children were living this unhappy existence of smiling publicly and crying silently, would I think it was OK?

Once I realized the answer to both those questions was no, that was it. If I recognized this situation wouldn't be acceptable for my children, I needed to hold myself to those same standards. I needed to demand of myself the same respect, authenticity, and autonomy in my life.

If I wasn't in a good space, I couldn't be the best parent possible, and that was not an option. Whatever the path forward was, I had a clear idea of what I wanted my children's lives to look like, and I wasn't willing to let that vision suffer because of this necessary change. I would provide my children the type of life they deserved.

My decision to walk away from my marriage was incredibly difficult, but I had to lean in to the idea that the universe always provides. I had to remove my fear and choose to be faithful because I knew one unwavering truth: faith and fear can't exist at the same time.

After the separation I moved to Tallahassee for work. I had no savings to fall back on, and my job was starting two weeks after getting there. That meant at least a month of bills before I'd start seeing a paycheck. I lived on credit cards and trusted the universe would provide.

Those first weeks were anxious and difficult times, but I checked in with myself and realized I was breathing differently. It was like I'd been holding my breath for all those years, and now I could finally take a full, glorious lungful of air. I hadn't even realized I was holding my breath all that time, but in the absence of that effort, my body was suddenly telling me I was on the right path. I'd be OK. All that energy I'd been expending keeping everything together could finally be released, and I felt that relief in a visceral, physical way.

I trusted in the idea it was going to work out, and because I made that difficult, disruptive, transformative decision, my entire family and I found the more fulfilling, more authentic path we're on today.

A Road Map to Demystifying Authenticity

In addition to teaching at Florida State University, I also work as a transformational life coach and a spiritual intuitive. I specifically focus on helping women release fear, shame, and guilt as they embrace an empowered life of freedom. I provide the tools, support, and resources necessary to take back the power they have given away in their lives and help them to move forward in purpose and authenticity.

Backed by neuroscience and experience, the tools and ideas I gift my students are those I used to take my life forward in a positive way.

Lead with acceptance.

Every transformation journey starts with acceptance. It's accepting where you are right now and embracing that however you are is perfect. The work isn't about changing you; it's about getting to the highest version of yourself.

People are always communicating with themselves, but they tend to dismiss that inner voice. They justify and give reasons for why they're feeling certain ways.

I'm there as a reminder that the thing you're feeling is valid, and those internal nudges won't go away until you've investigated the why.

Why am I not willing to accept this impulse? Why am I afraid to move on that idea?

As a coach, I am enthusiastically team "no judgment." I'm there to facilitate the process. I help people identify the gap between where they are now and where they want to be and craft a plan for moving forward.

I'm living proof that you can reclaim your narrative. You can rewrite your story and walk boldly in whatever direction you see fit.

Release societal and ancestral programming.

Conditioning is the totality of what we've learned, taken on in our thinking, and agreed with in the collective consciousness. These are ideas, practices, and ways of thinking that we might not even recognize we're living out.

A significant part of my coaching work is figuring out which conditioning programs are running that are keeping my clients from living their best lives. Then I work with them to pinpoint the origin stories of those blockages and limitations.

Once you've identified where you're operating out of programming, then you must trust and acknowledge what your soul self is telling you. When you do that, you're able to shift the mindset and rewrite your narrative.

You are connected to an infinite source of wisdom at all times. It's available to you. You can recognize why you're making the choices you're making. You just have to trust yourself and lean in to the idea that the universe is wonderful and expansive and always has you.

When you hold on to *that* belief, you're able to release and free yourself from so much else.

For example, being generous, kind, and giving is admirable, but you have to make sure you're making those choices consciously and not out of programming. When it's programming, all you're doing is putting the needs of others above your own. You're pushing yourself to the bottom of the list and shrinking further and further to the back of the classroom.

Make others feel good because it's what you want to do. Make others feel good when it doesn't come at the expense of your own well-being.

One piece of persistent programming I combat with clients is the idea that honoring their needs is somehow selfish. It's not. As you learn to live more boldly, you're simply in a better position to serve others more brilliantly.

Embrace the compounding effect of incremental progress.

One step is better than no step.

In my coaching I'm always wary of trying to do too much too

fast. When you introduce a lot of change at once, a person tends to pull back or the system goes into protection mode and shuts down. So we work on identifying the next best step and going from there.

If you make those small but consistent adjustments, always pursuing progress over perfection, one day you'll wake up and realize you're no longer congruent with the person who allowed you to live in that negative space for so long.

Obviously, each person has to be willing to take action in the first place, but for those who are, small steps over time can add up to a significant journey.

Take up space.

I've always loved dance and began practicing at the age of three. Initially I learned classical dance styles: ballet, tap, and jazz. As early as seven, I was aware my body type was not my ballet teacher's idea of what a ballerina should look like.

For many years after, I struggled to accept my body. I found myself moving to the back of the classroom. Even as the class and the teacher changed, that messaging found space in my body and my mind, and it affected my ability to show up fully.

In so many ways, women are conditioned not to take up space. In our jobs, in ourselves, and in our relationships, we shrink. That's often doubly true for women of color.

In my marriage I never had to be the extroverted, front-and-center one. My husband was always big and commanded the space, and because he took on that role, I allowed myself to stay small. When I removed that crutch from my life, I had to confront the fact it's not about being an extrovert or an introvert.

It's about facing your fear of rejection. It's being afraid of saying or doing something wrong and saying or doing it anyway.

My youngest daughter is also a dancer, but one day at her studio I noticed she was in the back of the class. She loves to dance, and she's not shy.

So I asked her the question. Why was she in the back? I was wondering if this was really an intentional choice, or if she was taking on expectations and programming she didn't even realize. I encouraged her to move around the room, feeling comfortable wherever she needed to be.

Right, wrong, or indifferent, I had to train myself to take up space in a room. Whatever room I'm in now, I give myself permission to be present, to be seen, and to take up space. And that's a lesson I want all my students—and my daughter—to take forward.

Move past fear.

I stayed in my marriage for so many years because of fear. Fear of what everyone would think. Fear of public failure. Fear of judgment in the shadow of my parents' successful thirty-two-year marriage. Fear of the idea that children need two parents to thrive and succeed.

Only after letting go of that irrational fear could I take the next steps in my own journey.

Often we stay in these bad situations out of fear. We think what we're experiencing is the best we can do, but in reality we're often blocking ourselves from the better.

We choose to stay in the comfort of the known, even though everything we want is on the other side of fear. If you just allow yourself to push past it, that's when you get to live life and find true joy.

When it comes to my happiness and going after the things I want now, I'm team "no sacrifice." Yes, it means I have to do things scared. It means I have to push through and trust the universe will provide, but it always does.

Move past guilt.

When your decisions affect others, it's easy to fall into the trap of guilt. In the early days of my separation my husband lived far away, and our young children didn't get to see him as often.

When we all moved closer, my daughter asked me, "Mommy, Daddy's so close now. Why can't we all be back in the same place?"

I told her the truth. I wasn't able to show up as my full self when we were together. Daddy couldn't show up fully either. We were our better selves now, and we could do more for her and her sister apart.

My daughter was six at the time, and she understood and accepted that difficult truth. It was the last time she brought up that kind of question, and on that day, I gave up any remnants of guilt for the divorce.

When you make a decision that puts you on a path to authenticity and fulfillment, never let guilt derail you.

Build your tool kit.

I focus on helping my clients develop a diverse tool kit. This gives them an array of resources to draw on when necessary.

I'm a believer in crafting affirmations, giving the mind a different narrative, and breaking away from entrenched internal stories.

I create playlists for my clients that incorporate specific frequencies and tones to guide and influence their thought patterns.

I provide journal prompts to encourage self-reflection.

I champion visual cues as reminders of the possibilities.

So much of this journey is about learning what you need in different situations and adopting the techniques that work with your life. It's also about giving yourself the grace and forgiveness to be in that moment when none of those tactics are working.

It's knowing and trusting you'll be back at it tomorrow and that it's never too late to make a new choice.

CREATING SAFE SPACES AND COMMUNITY

Dance has always been a source of light for me. Specifically, studying African diasporic dance forms has opened my eyes to the ability of an art form to create meaningful, supportive, collective community.

When I dance these styles, unbound by external influences, I feel free. I'm in a space where I can revel in movement and enjoyment. I know I can bare my soul, and I can receive others in the same way.

The aim of my coaching and all my work is to re-create that profound sense of support and community. No matter what someone has been through and no matter how difficult the choices they've had to make are, I want them to leave our time knowing that the possibility of change is within them and, even more importantly, they are never alone.

Be you unapologetically. Take up space confidently. Trust the process.

About La Toya

Empowering high-achieving women to rewrite the narratives of their lives, La Toya Davis, PhD, stands at the forefront of transformational leadership and personal empowerment. With an illustrious twenty-year journey as a spiritual mentor, teacher, and coach, La Toya's commitment to empowering women is ignited by a pivotal realization: the detrimental impact of external advice, leading women to lose money, time, and trust in themselves. Determined to counteract this, she has dedicated her life to helping women challenge and move beyond the narratives of scarcity, discontent, and compromise that too often dictate their lives. La Toya champions the power of inner guidance, encouraging every individual to reach their highest potential.

Her approach is deeply holistic, blending the spiritual, mental, and emotional aspects of the self into a harmonious state of alignment. Drawing inspiration from luminaries such as Dr. Joe Dispenza, Bob Proctor, and Bruce Lipton, PhD, La Toya has developed a signature four-step process that has successfully enabled nearly a thousand women to overcome societal, ancestral, and personal barriers. This transformative method not only aids in dismantling limiting beliefs but also opens up new possibilities in income, career advancement, and enriching personal relationships. Furthermore, through her My Ancestors Keeper Lineage Healing program, La Toya trains therapists, energy workers, and spiritual healers, amplifying her impact as these professionals continue her work across the globe.

An internationally recognized author, La Toya is also a sought-after speaker and workshop facilitator, celebrated for her dynamic ability to spark transformative shifts. Her work, which has garnered attention in publications such as *Economic Insider*, *CEO Weekly*, and the *Women's Journal*, extends her influence beyond personal coaching. As a recurring guest on WBAI-FM and a featured speaker at events, retreats, and summits, La Toya's sessions are acclaimed for inspiring attendees to embrace their limitless potential and break free from generational chains.

As the founder of the CHI Healing Institute, she has created a sanctuary for high-achieving women worldwide, encouraging them to live with authenticity and unapologetic joy.

Beyond her professional achievements, La Toya is a college professor and mother of two with a profound love for travel and culinary exploration. She teaches African diasporic dance forms, including Afro-Cuban, Afro-Haitian, and Afro-Brazilian. Currently, she is pursuing a PhD in metaphysical parapsychology and is a Reiki Master, further evidence of her commitment to holistic well-being and spiritual growth.

Learn more at www.drlatoyadavis.com and www.chicourses.com.

CHAPTER 16

A DIAMOND UNDER PRESSURE

By Kimberly Bussey Lewis

O n the rainy night of September 2, 1964, in Charleston, South Carolina, my mother went into labor with me. Now ironically, that very summer, the Civil Rights Act of 1964 was passed, which made it illegal to discriminate against people because of their race, color, religion, sex, or national origin. As a Black man with a wife who was about to give birth again, this was great news for my father, who was excited that I would be the first of his four children to be born in a hospital.

My mother went into labor, but quickly felt pain that she hadn't with the other children, so my father rushed her to the best hospital in town: The Medical University of South Carolina in Charleston. He got her there, lifted my mother out of the car, and ran inside the emergency room, carrying her. As he did, my mother began to hemorrhage. I was breech, but of course he didn't know that at the time.

My father ran to the front desk, frantically yelling for help. They ignored him and actually turned their backs to him. My father, now screaming for help, ran to face the doctors and nurses at the desk. "Please," my father pleaded, pointing to the blood running down my mother's legs. "My wife is having a baby, and something is wrong."

But the staff continued to ignore him.

"Please," my father begged.

Finally, a nurse turned to my father and said, "Put her over there; we'll get to her."

My father knew that my mother, and I, may not last long, so he put my mother in a wheelchair and ran as fast as he could out of the building into the pouring rain and down the street to the Black-run hospital, McClennan-Banks. As soon as he got her inside, the doctors and nurses ran to get my mother into the surgery room. A doctor who happened to be visiting from Africa was the person who delivered me by cesarean section and right there named me Kimberly after the Kimberley (different spelling) diamond mine in South Africa, which, as a matter of fact, was discovered earlier that year. It carries the name of the town where it was found. The town, Kimberley, is extremely significant because it is where the first diamond in the country was discovered. That man—and that hospital—are two reasons I am here today. The third reason is through the perseverance of my father.

All my siblings were named after soap opera stars, so when I was old enough to ask where the name Kimberly came from, that's when I first heard the story of my birth. But the most interesting aspect of this story is that it happened fifty-nine years ago. Not a hundred years ago or five hundred. It happened in my lifetime and possibly yours.

My father saw discrimination like this his whole life, and he was always on the alert for it. In the same year that I was born, my older siblings wanted to go to the county fair.

"Daddy," they begged, "please take us."

"I don't know," my dad said, concerned. The hospital incident was still fresh in his mind. Finally, after a great deal of begging, my father agreed to take them under one condition.

"OK," he said, "we'll go, but we'll just watch a bit at first." So he took my three older siblings. They drove to the fair but just parked and watched the front gate from the car. They saw White families get out of their cars and walk to the gate, get their tickets, and walk in. Then they saw a Black family arrive. This family parked their car and walked to the gate to get their tickets. But as soon as this family got close, men came out with fire hoses and dogs. They released the dogs and turned the hoses on the Black family.

My dad and my siblings watched this in horror. Then my dad started the car and drove back home in complete silence.

My father was always cautious after this. When I was five years old, I took an interest in cheerleading and made the youth league cheerleading squad. I was the only Black cheerleader on the entire squad.

I remember when I was in sixth grade, at the age of twelve, I made the all-star cheerleading team, which would follow the all-star football team as they played. And again, I was the only Black child—and it's important to note here that I wasn't just a Black child, but there is a thing in the Black community regarding the shade of your skin. We call this colorism. So I'm not just Black; I'm dark-skinned Black. And there's a whole lot of prejudice that goes along with that as well, from both the Black community and the White community.

So I'm on the all-star cheer squad, and our two coaches decide to have a pool party at one of the girls' houses in one of the nicer neighborhoods. My dad didn't want me to go. At the time, I hadn't really connected the meaning of my birth story yet, so I couldn't understand why my father didn't want me to go. But he was pretty adamant about it.

My mom got involved. "Yes, we're going to let her go," she insisted. So my dad gave in, drove me there, and dropped me off, and I had a great time. But what I didn't know then and wouldn't know for another twenty years was that my dad never went home. He parked the car down the street. He rolled down the windows so he could hear the sound of my screams. And he waited.

He was so worried that something would happen to me that he stayed in that car all night until morning, when it was time to pick me up.

Now when you hear stories of mistreatment and prejudice, the first natural reaction is to get angry, to be outraged. But anger and outrage are not the answer or the reaction we want from stories like mine. The reaction involves the questions that should be asked. And that is, How do we stop racist behavior and biased attitudes?

One of the answers is pretty simple: through engagement. It's difficult to dislike someone, or a group of someones, that you know. Knowing is understanding, and understanding is connecting, and connecting is caring. It's easy to judge or even hate someone from a distance. It's a lot more difficult when they are close or, better yet, connected to us. When you engage with people who are different from you and you share your differences, that's when the change occurs.

My name is Kimberly Bussey Lewis. I am a mother of two amazing daughters, and I have been the CEO of Goodwill Industries of East Texas for eleven years now. Before that I spent ten years as the CEO of Goodwill Industries of KYOWVA Area in West Virginia, and I love my job.

One thing I do in my position is encourage my staff and those we serve to tell their stories. When I have an opportunity to sit and talk with them, I ask them, "Where did you come from? How did you grow up? What did you like to do as a kid? What was it like where you grew up?"

When I was working at the Goodwill in West Virginia, the local library would have this big book sale every year of books that were out of rotation, and whatever they couldn't sell they would donate to us. One of the books that was donated was titled *The African Heritage Cookbook*, by Helen Mendes. The great part is she included the history and origin of many of the recipes. The author traced native cooking from sixteenth- and seventeenth-century West Africa and shows its development in America during the years of slavery.

I love to cook and come from a family of great cooks. I cook a certain way because my family cooked a certain way, but I never stopped to think of the historical reference to West Africa and the Caribbean islands. I just thought that was the way we cook. I didn't even know it was a Southern thing, and I didn't know it was an African thing, as my background is Gullah Geechee, and

Gullah is the combination of the Caribbean and African cultures. When the slaves were brought from the Caribbean islands and Africa, they were brought to Charleston, South Carolina, because it was a major slave trading port. So when these slaves, who spoke different languages, ended up on plantations together, they had to find a way to communicate. That communication became Gullah, which is now a nationally recognized language. Gullah Geechee people are descendants of Africans who were enslaved on the Sea Island plantations of the lower Atlantic Coast.

How we cook our food is a direct relationship to our history, our culture, and our family. And that's just one example of sharing your culture and background with others.

About five or six years ago we had a national Goodwill confer-ence, and I was asked to serve on a panel about "Super Women" in the network. Goodwill's leadership is mostly male dominated, so that theme was unusual; plus, at the time, I was the only African American CEO. I was the chair and founding member of our diversity, equity, and inclusion committee, which developed the Goodwill DEI tool kit that is used around the country. So the plan was for me to talk about my journey as a CEO and my work with the DEI committee. The facilitator began the panel by asking me, "What led you to the space you are in now?"

I had not planned to speak about my birth, but how he phrased the question reminded me that I didn't just start advocating for people, nor did I intend to get into the DEI space—I was born into this work and for this task. So, I told the story of my birth for the very first time in public.

And you could hear a pin drop. And I realized how significant that story was for my colleagues, because many of them were about my age, and this happened in their lifetime. My guess is that some of those doctors and nurses in that story are probably still alive as well. The fact is that they made a life-threatening decision to turn their backs on my parents and put both my mother and me at risk due to their racist behavior, brought on by what was probably a lifetime of biased beliefs.

We all have biases. And our biases shape how we think, how we behave, how we act, how we interact, and what we believe, whether there are factual truths behind them or not.

When I was growing up, my sisters were nine and ten years older than me. I remember they were in high school, and they were beginning to date, and my dad would jokingly make the comment, "Well, if he can't use your comb, you don't bring him home."

And I would laugh with my sisters, not really knowing what it meant. When I got older, and having heard him say it many times, I knew that it meant don't bring a White boy home.

But why? I have White friends, and they're nice. Does that mean that they're not nice? Does it mean that you can't trust them? Does that mean that they're bad? What does that mean? My dad never went into detail, but it did imprint his biases on me of what was taboo at the time.

I now know that my dad's concerns were mostly about safety and protecting his daughters from racist people and possible acts of violence, but they were biases nonetheless.

I share a lot of stories of racism and bias that my family and I have experienced, and it's not always easy. When the George Floyd incident happened in 2020, a lot of my Black friends and Black colleagues couldn't talk about it. And being a speaker, consultant, and executive coach, I started getting calls from other Black and White colleagues, telling me that they wanted to speak about how atrocious it was, but they didn't want to come across as disingenuous.

They said that they felt like they should say something, but what should they say, and how should they say it?

I know this is tough; it took me three weeks to be able to say anything about the murder of George Floyd, as well as the many other acts of violence against Black people, but I finally wrote a blog article titled "Tired of Waiting for Change?" and posted it on LinkedIn. It received a lot of responses.

My advice to anyone who needs to or wants to make a public

statement following any act of hate is to be honest and transparent. I advised them to say, "We know we're not there yet, but here's what we're doing at our company. Here's what I'm doing personally," and bring it back to them, to their vision, to their company, to their community, and to their organization.

Many people reading this might be tired of waiting for change. They may feel like there have not been enough positive moves forward when it comes to bias and racism. But we can take these tragic events—as well as the ones that happen to us individually—and learn from them. Use them. Remember that pain is not in vain; it's a reason to connect, learn, and understand. Don't let the pain take up a valuable space or create poisonous residue in your spirit and heart. You can create a connection with others that pave the way to change. If we all do what we can to build connections and communities, we show that we value all people and that the pressure of the past will not crush us. Instead, we will create diamonds of change.

About Kimberly

Kimberly B. Lewis is the president and CEO of Goodwill Industries of East Texas and the owner of Motivational Muse LLC, a consulting, coaching, and public speaking enterprise. She has more than twenty years' executive-level nonprofit and business experience.

She is an author, a speaker, an executive coach, a consultant, and a frequent contributor to *Forbes* magazine as a member of the Forbes Nonprofit Council and the Forbes DEI group leader. Kimberly is also a member and presenter of the Della Leaders Club, the world's first international lifestyle and business platform. She is a respected professional, and her articles have been published by *Advancing Philanthropy*, Workability International, AFP ICON, *Kahoots!*, Retail Operations Network, The Global Good Fund, and others.

Kimberly is a founding member and past chair of the Goodwill Industries International (GII) Diversity & Inclusion Committee and winner of the GII 2020 Diversity & Inclusion Champion Award, as well as numerous national awards for her leadership and innovation.

She has authored three other books: a historical novel titled *The Fourth Generation*; *A Seat at the Table or Part of the Meal: Creating a Culture of Diversity, Equity and Inclusion*; and the most recent publication, titled *Biases: A Guide for Uncovering Areas of Unconscious Bias*.

She is the mother of two accomplished daughters, and they share a love of traveling, reading, community service, and creative writing.

If you need a speaker, executive coach, or consultant, contact her at motivationalmuse.kim@gmail.com and check out her website at www.motivationalmuse.com.

> "We asked Kim to speak about DEI to a roomful of entrepreneurs. She nailed it. Kim passionately drove home salient points in a way that made a challenging topic accessible to the entire audience."
>
> —Carrie Rich, CEO of The Global Good Fund

> "Kimberly was terrific! Our board retreat began with enthusiasm that only grew throughout her facilitation! The transitions from governance to duties to visioning were outstanding."
>
> —Nick Pesina, Esq., Former Board President, Ninos de Promesa

CHAPTER 17

BORROWING HOPE

By Dr. Crystal Nelson

L ub-dub. Lub-dub. Lub-dub.
I cannot hear anything but the sound of my heart. I am sitting in the car sweating, trembling, and I've never felt this sick in my life, this anxious.

How do I tell her?

What do I even say?

How do I tell my baby girl that her father is going to die—today? I'm scared.

My husband, André, and I were best friends from childhood. We were friends in the seventh grade, dated at the end of high school, and got married right before I finished college. Everyone said that getting married at twenty-one was crazy. They asked, "Why would you want to do that?" But we didn't listen, and we did it anyway.

André just knew we would be together forever, so I borrowed that hope from him. I became a bride at twenty-one, a mother at twenty-six, and a widow at thirty-three. Although I have known since I was five years old that I wanted to be a doctor, I had decided to put off medical school after college graduation. Once we were married, we wanted to see a little of the world. We sold everything we had and moved from Georgia to California. We were in love, and the world was ours. On the West Coast I started as a research intern for a pharmaceutical company—I mean, it wasn't medical school yet, but my biology degree opened the door. We were living in Thousand Oaks, California, and life was great, until it wasn't.

We moved back to Virginia, and I took a higher-level job as a chemist. We decided that I had put medical school off long enough. It was time to prepare and take my Medical College Admission Test, the MCAT. I scheduled the test, and we began preparing for being a young couple with a wife in medical school.

One day my husband was playing basketball with a friend, and he took off his glasses for the game. As he was gathering his things, he stepped on the glasses, shattering the lenses. He made an eye appointment with the optometrist to get a new pair. But the optometrist saw something she did not like during his eye exam, so she sent him to an ophthalmologist, a medical doctor who specializes in the eye, to take a closer look. The ophthalmologist did not like what he saw either.

On my drive home from work, André called me.

"The optic nerves are swollen because there is a mass on the MRI," he said.

"OK," I answered. "What does that mean?" And then he told me.

"There is a brain tumor, and they want to operate in a week."

And this is when things begin to get fuzzy for me. It's amazing how the mind works, because I remember him telling me about the tumor, and the next thing I remember is him coming out of brain surgery. I knew I took the MCAT in between there. In fact, I did well enough to get into multiple medical schools. But I have absolutely no memory of taking the test. None whatsoever. My husband was positive that everything would be all right, so I just used his hope again and did it scared.

My husband had the surgery, and the doctors were very happy with the outcome. They said it was a benign tumor and that they had gotten it all and everything was hopeful. But just to be safe, they wanted to send the mass to Johns Hopkins for a clear identification of the tumor.

A few weeks later Johns Hopkins contacted us and said that it was not a benign tumor after all. It was a malignant tumor, a hemangiopericytoma. This was a rare diagnosis, but the surgeon ensured us that we should still stay positive because the surgery had gone so well. He stated that we should start chemo and radiation to keep the cancer in remission. We borrowed the doctor's hope and marched forward into battle.

This was the beginning of what would be the next eleven years of chemotherapy, radiation, and multiple surgeries. We really didn't have a road map for any of this. Most of the people that I knew our age didn't even have a spouse, much less one with cancer. The challenge was that there was no clear path. No one could tell us what to expect because there were so many variables. It was such a unique journey. Solid advice was hard to come by, besides the general messages to be strong, persevere, and stay the course. So not knowing what else to do, we remained hopeful, and we simply pushed through.

Five years after the original diagnosis and after two years of medical school, we became parents, and our daughter Jordyn was born. Having my daughter gave me a new purpose. She gave us hope and distraction from the looming return of a cancer that we were told was in remission. This blissful ignorance ended when she was only three months old. The cancer had returned, and this time there would be no remission.

This time cancer had spread over his body, and his pain increased drastically. He required more treatments and more surgeries. Our daughter began to grow, medical school ended, and psychiatry residency followed. The years were filled with highlights of our daughter's milestones and me becoming a medical doctor. But the shadow of cancer was always close enough to smother those sparks of joy.

Over time the effects of the chemotherapy, radiation, and all the surgeries started to change my husband physically, emotionally, and the very way he was thinking. He began to deal with serious bouts of depression, and he often wasn't himself. We became great at keeping appearances, but as he declined mentally, so did I.

One day I asked his oncologist, "How long is he going to be like this? What is the prognosis?"

"Well," he answered, "he's already outlived the prognosis of one year. So the prognosis is indefinite."

His words felt as if someone had stabbed me in the heart. I wanted him to tell me that we had a time frame. I wanted to plan out the years we had left, or at least know there was a future ahead that would be better. Indefinite meant to me suffering like this. I was now the medical resident with a sick husband. I felt like I was now being seen as either this superhuman or the fragile person that could crack at any moment. I was finding less and less hope, and André seemed to have less of it for me to borrow.

One night I was out with a couple of fellow resident friends, and we were all drinking at a bar. As the party heightened, I noticed a few other residents started doing lines of cocaine. This was way outside of my comfort zone, but so was my whole life at this point.

And I thought, "Hmm, I've never tried that. I'm a good girl, but who cares? Being good doesn't make a difference.

"Let me try some of that," I said.

My friend turned to me and said, "No, not you."

"What?" I answered, a little angry. "Why not?"

"You're going through too much. You can't manage this. It's time to go home." He drove me home. On that ride he offered me the hope that he had to give. It got me through the night. I don't know where that night would have gone without his hope.

For weeks I was in a low place. One night I contemplated if my own life was worth living. I calculated if all the medications in the house would be enough to end this suffering. But then my daughter called me to her room. As I lay there beside her, she talked about her day, the water day at her school, that she was going to be a mermaid and needed to practice. I listened and laughed. I realized that God had again sent me some hope in that moment that I needed it, hope I could borrow for a while from her.

Knowing that our time was dwindling, André planned a lot with me. We had to have uncomfortable conversations, and nothing was off-limits. We started to plan for the life I would have without him. He knew he wasn't going to be around to watch Jordyn grow up, and we began to discuss that. We made videos she would watch when she got older. He shared about the people he wanted in her life, in my life. We eventually began to have conversations about me dating and possibly remarrying. The conversations were heavy and deep at times. I didn't want to talk about that. I had absolutely no desire to ever marry again. But it was important to him to talk about it, so we did. I went through the paces, I nodded, but getting married was not anything I had seriously considered.

I remember talking to a friend of mine who was a therapist, on how André had brought remarrying up but I had no desire to ever get married again.

"You don't mean that," she said. "You're just saying that because you're scared."

"Oh no," I responded. "I don't want to do that again. Ever."

So she cleverly responded, "OK, then indulge me." And she asked me to do something. "Make a list," she said, "of all the things that the man would have to be so that when God sends him to you, you'll know that it's him."

So I did indulge her, and I made that list. *He has to be over six feet tall. He has to be fun. He has to be able to sing.* I made the list, barely looked at it, and stuck it away.

Weeks later André and I were having another heavy conversation about the future, and he mentioned someone we both knew, a dance instructor.

"What do you think about Kenny?" he asked.

And I thought that was a strange question. "Think about him? Think about him for what?"

"Think about him for a partner?"

It was scary and strange to think about another future with another husband. But over the next year Kenny was weaved into the tapestry of our world. The complexity of this situation had us both scared. Was my first husband, while still alive, actually suggesting and approving of my potential second husband? And as weird as all of this seemed at the time, because he was hopeful that one day things might be different for me, we went with it. This new hope seemed to bring a light back that had disappeared after the years of fighting cancer. This beautifully loving arrangement meant that Kenny was part of our lives during the last months of our cancer journey.

It was a cold Georgian January. The town house was drafty but so quiet. I was home with André, but Jordyn was in school. I walked in to check on André, and his breathing was labored, and he was pale.

"I think you need to go to the hospital," I said.

"I'm not ready yet," he said. "Because I know if I go, I'm not coming back."

The next several days, Jordyn and I went to the hospital every day after school until the evening the oncologist came in to give the prognosis. I went to pick up our seven-year-old daughter from school. She was and still is an incredibly smart and incredibly intuitive child, so I knew I wouldn't be able to lie to her.

Lub-dub. Lub-dub. Lub-dub.

I couldn't hear anything but the sound of my heart racing in my ears. I am sitting in the car, sweating, trembling, and trying to gather my composure. I have never felt this sick, this anxious. "How do I tell her? What do I even say? How do I tell my baby girl that her father is going to die today?"

She got into the car and started her daily chatter.

Lub-dub. Lub-dub. Lub-dub.

I pulled into a McDonald's parking lot. I stopped the car and had her leave the back seat and come up front.

"We're not going to the hospital today," I said. "They're moving Daddy to a different place called a hospice facility, where they're going to keep him comfortable, because he's in a lot of pain. They're going to make him comfortable."

Like I said, my daughter is pretty smart, and she answered right away.

"So that means they've given up on him? He's going to die?"

I told her that the doctors had done all they could do. "But Mom," she whispered. "You're a doctor. Can't you save him?" The tears fell. She knew that I could not. She cried, and I cried, and then we screamed in frustration and heartache.

That was one of the most excruciating moments of my life. It was as if I could actually hear her heart breaking into pieces. I decided in that moment that I don't ever want to break her heart like that again. I decided to use all the borrowed hope from all the people that God had sent me over the years, including her and her father. I promised her that things would be OK, and I meant it. I had no idea how, but I promised.

We went home to get clothes so we could stay at the hospice. My daughter has always enjoyed theater and acting, so I told her to pick out a costume, and she could do a show for Daddy.

She did. My husband watched her show and smiled.

"I'm going to sleep now," he said, and he didn't talk after that.

Lub-dub. Lub...dub. Lub...dub. He passed away at noon the next day.

This was a very difficult time for us, but God and André had plans. I began dating my second husband and realized that he... was the guy on the list. I called my friend.

"Oh my gosh, I think he's the guy on the list."

She had forgotten about the list, and when I reminded her of it, she said, "Well, that's why we made the list. So you'd know if you ever met him."

A little while later I told Kenny about this. We were married a year later.

Our story is not just about survival; it's about hope. And hope always trumps fear.

God could see the end; we couldn't. He knew what was going to be the result, and he had plans. He knows for you as well.

I'm not sure what in your life has you scared or trapped, but I give you permission to borrow hope from me. Take that hope, and let it lead you through the pain, fear, and sadness, knowing there is a new ending planned for you that you can't see yet. And until you get there, take this hope and use it until you can find your own.

About Dr. Crystal

Board-certified and licensed psychiatrist Dr. Crystal Nelson is a distinguished medical authority and entrepreneur in the realm of mental health. Dr. Nelson is the CEO and founder of two Georgia companies, Blueprint Psychiatry, and Blueprint TMS and Wellness Centers of America. In less than five years she has expanded the services to over four thousand clients and has received hundreds of five-star reviews and satisfied clients. She has devoted her career to providing exceptional service and revolutionizing behavioral health treatment with a patient-centered approach. Her approach uniquely combines genetics, cutting-edge technology, and nutritional coaching to produce exceptional outcomes in clients suffering from treatment-resistant depression and other mental illnesses. Her unique ability to translate complex psychological and psychiatric content into accessible language allows her clients to gain deeper insights. Dr. Nelson empowers her clients to reclaim their mental wellness. She has helped to transform countless lives and set a new standard in the field.

Dr. Nelson has appeared nationally on *Headline News* with CNN and Fox. She has been featured in articles for *Working Mother*, *Voyage ATL*, *CanvasRebel*, and *Atlanta* magazine. Recognized as a leading expert, Dr. Nelson earned the title of Top Doc Atlanta 2023 in the field of psychiatry, an honor that recognizes the most exemplary healthcare professionals by unanimous vote from their colleagues. She has treated thousands of patients over her career, including celebrities and public figures. From this vast expertise, she has been a sought-after speaker. She has captivated audiences from coast to coast with topics on entrepreneurship, self-care, pharmacogenomics, depression, anxiety, grief, PTSD, and work-life balance. She recently published her own guidebook titled *A Blueprint to Better Mental Health*. Dr. Nelson is a college graduate of the highly esteemed Spelman College in Atlanta, Georgia. She earned her doctor of medicine degree from Morehouse School of Medicine and went on to complete her psychiatry residency at Virginia Commonwealth University in Richmond, Virginia. She also has some additional training in geriatric psychiatry from the prestigious Emory University in Atlanta, Georgia. Dr. Nelson also serves as an adjunct faculty professor at Morehouse School of

Medicine, where she proudly collaborates to train the next generation of medical doctors.

Dr. Nelson is an avid dancer and traveler. Most of all, however, Dr. Nelson enjoys spending time with her husband, Kenny, and their three children, Kenny Jr., Jordyn, and Kenton.

To learn more about Blueprint Psychiatry or to request Dr. Nelson as a speaker/consultant:

- Visit www.BlueprintPsychiatry.com.
- Follow on Instagram @drcrystalnelson.
- Follow on Facebook at Blueprint Psychiatry LLC.

CHAPTER 18

SIXTEEN

A Symphony of Survival

By Obioma Martin, PhD

When I opened my eyes, all I could see was blood. I knew it was raining and other cars were driving by, but all I heard was my three children calling for me. I couldn't get to them, and I didn't know why.

I later learned the tractor trailer had faulty brakes, causing it to slam into my family as we made our way to church on that rainy Sunday morning. I had to be cut out of the car with the Jaws of Life.

My jaw was wired shut, and I couldn't speak for ten weeks. I couldn't walk and needed physical therapy for a year. My house fell into foreclosure. I was in my bachelor's degree program at the time, and despite barely being able to sit, I didn't drop out.

I had already overcome so much. This was just another hurdle to clear.

THE FIRST HURDLE

As the sun rose on my sixteenth year, the world saw an honor roll student with a creative spark and an entrepreneurial spirit. I was a designer of jewelry, a creator of fashion, a stylist of hair, and a vision of confidence on the runway.

But beneath the surface was a girl who sought solace in places where love's light did not reach. A girl who found false refuge in the depths of alcohol by thirteen yet also found redemption in faith on her thirteenth birthday.

Like a vine yearning for sunlight, my soul thirsted for connection. The absence of family, a gaping childhood wound, sent me searching for solace in borrowed spaces. Stability, a mirage shimmering in the desert of loneliness, fueled my pursuit of belonging. Yet each bond felt fleeting. A temporary shelter against the storm of self-doubt. "Who am I?" "Where do I come from?" Whispered questions echoing in the hollow chambers of my heart.

At the tender yet tumultuous age of sixteen, I was confronted with the reality of impending motherhood.

My unborn child's father was essentially a stranger. When we met, I was waiting at a bus stop. We never had a relationship. At the time, the father, choosing to be absent, left a void filled with rejection, mirroring the absence of my biological father, whom I didn't meet until fourteen. Today, I know that man from the bus stop was just someone I met on the way to where I was going. A bump in the road on my journey.

Becoming pregnant at sixteen disrupted all my dreams, goals, and aspirations. I had been on track to go to Hampton University and receive my MBA. Growing up, my ability to create and make money anchored me. Because I was often alone, I filled my time with things I enjoyed and that put money in my pocket.

At that moment, though, my life became a nomadic quest for stability, moving from one temporary home to another, while the dream of an MBA and a life of modeled success flickered like a distant star in a troubled sky.

More than anything, I had disappointed myself. I had become a statistic. As a sixteen-year-old mother, I couldn't see myself accomplishing any of my dreams. The shame, guilt, and embarrassment were overwhelming.

My mother eventually stepped in, telling me I had to complete school. I was still stumbling through the dark, but it turned out this wasn't the end of my story. It was just the beginning of my journey.

The dichotomy of my existence was stark—a life seemingly rich with potential but steeped in the struggle of a baby having a baby. It was a paradox wrapped in societal judgment and personal trials, yet it became the crucible that defined the relentless spirit within me.

ONE DREAM REALIZED

My unexpected pregnancy brought so much pain, but I delivered a healthy baby girl. My mom and her new husband helped with my child while I set about conquering the first challenge I told myself wouldn't be possible with a baby: graduating from high school.

At eighteen, I not only graduated but did so with honors. I moved out of my mom's house and began renting a room. Wanting to clear the next hurdle, I immediately enrolled in community college, working full time while attending night classes.

I was single, overwhelmed with responsibility, and consumed with trying to provide for my child—while being a child myself. It was too much, and I flunked out my first semester.

With my high school diploma, I landed a job at Keystone Mercy Health Plan. This offered some stability, but after rent, car, utilities, and living expenses, I had almost nothing left over. Public assistance helped with medical care, childcare, and food, but I continued to struggle.

Then, at twenty-one, my life took an exciting turn. I became a spouse and parent of two.

THE ENTREPRENEURIAL SPIRIT AWAKENS

After having my second child, my husband didn't want me to work. He made enough to cover our expenses, so I stayed home for eleven months. Full of unrealized potential, I knew that situation wasn't going to work for me. I wanted my own money and something outside the home to build.

I worked at a credit card company but only for three months.

Believing I had chosen the best, I opted for a premium day care and wholeheartedly entrusted my son's care to their staff. After a few weeks I began to notice he frequently got sick, as did the other children. I decided to keep him home.

That's when I connected with a lady at church. She had five children and couldn't afford to send them to camp. They were around the same age as my children, and I offered to watch them, just asking for some extra money to feed them.

This was July 7, 2002. By the end of August, I had twenty children that didn't belong to me in my house.

My father suggested I start a day care, and by December I was fully licensed as a childcare provider. Using a teaching grant, I went back to school for early childhood education.

With the support of another income and my husband, I could operate my business and go to night school. I graduated from community college in May of 2007 with my AA degree. At this time I also closed my day care, focusing on a consulting business I began in 2005, where I taught others how to open quality early childhood education centers.

Between the sixty-hour day care grind (split between 16th and 21st streets!) and the constant needs of my young son, preteen daughter, and special-needs stepson, I felt stretched thin. A director facing a chaotic, unscripted play.

BECOMING A SINGLE MOM OVERNIGHT

I was married for eighteen years. During sixteen of those we were in business together. Going through frequent separations, I was constantly trying to keep all the balls in the air. Business owner. Mom. Wife.

My priority was taking care of the children, sustaining my clients, and keeping my marriage together. That left no time for me.

Against the odds—young, broke, and steeped in the struggles of the projects—I clung to an unyielding ambition. My children wouldn't be fatherless. Not on my watch. I'd rewrite the script, no matter the sacrifice.

The relentless gnawing of peer pressure, the suffocating grip of societal expectations, the daily grind of stress, the raw pulse of my unhealed trauma, and the all-encompassing fog of depression held me captive in that relationship until the 2018 divorce. Emerging, stripped bare and raw, I clung to the only solace that remained: the children. Testaments to a resilience etched in pain.

After I was loyal and gave him everything of myself, he removed my name from the business we'd built together. This deceitful act meant I must literally start over from scratch.

Like a fledgling breaking free from the nest, I soared past the public-assistance safety net with a silent promise echoing in my heart: no turning back. The system, a web of tangled vines promising false security, wouldn't ensnare me again. I'd pave my own path, brick by brick, fueled by the flames of self-sufficiency.

Though the storefront shuttered, the unwavering entrepreneurial flame persisted. For seven years, lesson plans and textbooks built a bridge, connecting my teenage students' dreams with my own aspirations. Childhood development. Business. Leadership. Each subject was a seed planted for the future. I knew the storefront would reopen one day.

While navigating the challenges of single parenthood, I also prioritized my own well-being. My ex-husband moving meant I could shed the weight of a controlling, domineering relationship, allowing me to reclaim my voice and rediscover my inner strength.

I used to operate within a belief system that limited my agency and well-being. Thankfully, with time and support, I stepped outside that framework and recognized the unhealthy patterns of that relationship. Today, I prioritize my empowerment, building a life grounded in authentic, supportive values.

Abuse manifests in many forms beyond physical attacks. It can be a subtle erosion of identity. The gradual silencing of dreams. The constant whispers leaving you questioning your worth. In a healthy relationship, your spirit soars, not shrinks. Recognizing this truth, even through the fog of commitment, was the first step toward reclaiming my life and rebuilding my self-belief.

Starting to BREATHE

The paint on my self-portrait, painstakingly crafted by others, began to crack and peel. Beneath the layers I glimpsed a canvas waiting for my own colors. My faith, once a borrowed melody, yearned to find its unique harmony. The Bible, no longer a dusty tome, became a vibrant tapestry, its threads woven with stories begging for reinterpretation. Every question was a needle pricking through the veil of assumptions and allowing me to glimpse the divine, not in pronouncements but in everyday life. This wasn't about rewriting scripture but about reclaiming my faith's narrative, a symphony composed by the echoes of the divine within.

God's love pierced the storm clouds of despair, revealing a truth etched in starlight: He desires our flourishing, not our suffering. The suffocating cloak of depression became a tattered garment I could finally shed. I found myself embraced by divine light, not judging my past struggles but guiding me toward a future woven with threads of self-compassion and hope.

Witnessing the crippling power of unhealthy belief systems, I knew I had to offer a lifeline. My goal was simple. Help women fall in love with themselves. BREATHE (believe, release, embrace, accept, take action, heal, elevate) was born from this mission, a methodology crafted to empower women by illuminating their inner strengths and shattering the shackles of self-doubt. BREATHE's transformative power reverberated so deeply. It demanded to be shared on a larger scale, culminating in a book that now serves as a beacon of hope and liberation for women across the globe.

Every transformation journey begins with an introspective glance at your internal compass. It's what steers your decisions, relationships, and, ultimately, happiness. If our beliefs are like worn-out pathways leading us in circles, it's time to explore new terrain. Examining our narratives, gently and openly, allows us to shed limiting thoughts and embrace healthier perspectives. This inner shift ripples outward, impacting not just our mental well-being but our physical and emotional lives. Only when we nurture a positive dialogue within can we flourish on all levels.

Breaking free from the shackles of limiting beliefs required self-discovery. A gentle recognition of my intrinsic worth. Knowing I wasn't a happenstance but a being designed with intent ignited a spark within. This newfound understanding fueled my transformation, empowering me to dismantle outdated narratives and rewrite my story with purpose and strength.

STEPS TO DEFYING THE ODDS

1. Embrace your truth.

Acknowledge your circumstances, but don't let them define you.

2. Anchor in belief.

Faith, spirituality, or personal conviction can be your compass in the darkest times.

3. Cherish education.

Value learning. It's your stepping stone to empowerment and progress.

4. Commit to sobriety.

Like a sunrise casting away shadows, sobriety illuminates the path toward personal empowerment. With each step on this journey, the mind sharpens. The world comes into focus. This newfound clarity grants the power to examine your life holistically, to make informed decisions, and to take ownership of your story.

5. Seek support networks.

Build relationships with those who see your worth and encourage your growth.

6. Define your purpose.

Use your challenges as fuel to drive you toward your true purpose.

7. Demonstrate resilience.

Show the world each setback is a setup for a stronger comeback. Find a way to make your pain work for you instead of allowing your pain to work you.

8. Set healthy boundaries.

Protect your peace by learning to say no to what doesn't serve your well-being.

9. Forgive and forge ahead.

Release the past to move forward with lighter steps.

10. Cultivate creativity.

Let creativity, your soul's language, flow.

11. Strive for independence.

Embrace the strength and courage to stand alone, trusting in yourself and God.

12. Practice gratitude.

Find grace in gratitude. There's power in appreciating the smallest blessing.

13. Prioritize healing.

Dedicate time to heal, acknowledging that journey unfolds in its own time.

14. Lead by example.

Be the leader of your life narrative. Inspire others to do the same.

15. Give back.

Your experiences could be the guiding light for others. Share your journey.

16. Build a legacy.

Today's challenges lay the foundation for tomorrow's legacy.

MY LEGACY

My story isn't just about books and diplomas. It's about defying expectations and juggling aspirations with reality. While others dropped out, I walked into universities, briefcase in hand, a wife, mother, and fighter against unseen foes. Two master's degrees. Two doctorates. Each a monument to the grit it took to build a fortress of knowledge amid life's whirlwind.

My life isn't a single-lane highway but a bustling expressway. While others mourned divorce, I launched five businesses across diverse landscapes. Nonprofit champion, empowering twenty thousand women from GED to PhD. Welfare whisperer, guiding individuals to new business ownership heights. Seven-time best-selling author, wordsmithing triumphant stories. Business strategist extraordinaire, charting courses for countless clients. Founder of a training and development empire, shaping tomorrow's leaders. Each victory, a testament to the boundless potential within us all.

By acknowledging my vulnerabilities and embracing the lessons learned from hardship, I've found my voice in the chorus of those helping others heal and grow. My story isn't a trophy to showcase but an outstretched hand, revealing the power of shared experiences to overcome any obstacle.

The days of sleeping on air mattresses are a distant memory, a relic of a time etched in struggle. Yet that woman, exhausted and driven by necessity, lives within me still. She's the foundation of who I am now, the bedrock of resilience upon which I've built a life overflowing with love, fulfillment, and the hard-won knowledge that even the toughest battles can reveal our most unexpected strengths.

About Obioma

Obioma Martin, PhD, is a luminary in the fields of early childhood education, entrepreneurship, and leadership, with an impressive array of titles that encompass being a business strategist, an accountability coach, a keynote speaker, and a transformational facilitator. As an educator and a philanthropist, she has established herself as a seven-time Amazon best-selling author and an inspiring TEDx speaker, touching lives with her poignant narratives and actionable insights.

At the helm of OMAX Institute, Obioma leads the Center for Early Childhood Education, Entrepreneurship, and Leadership with an unwavering commitment to nurturing growth and fostering transformative learning experiences. Her profound influence extends through her role as the CEO of Omazing You, her publishing arm that empowers individuals to share their stories with the world. Her dedication to societal upliftment is also evident in her founding of OMART Women Supporting Women, a 501(c)(3) nonprofit organization dedicated to supporting battered women with children and teen parents.

Beyond her entrepreneurial endeavors, Obioma is the visionary CEO of Obioma Martin LLC, where her expertise in strategy and leadership catalyzes change and promotes excellence. Her trustworthiness, reliability, and dependability are not just hallmark traits but the very foundation of her successful partnerships and professional relationships.

Obioma, a Lisa Nichols Certified Transformational Trainer, holds a doctor of philosophy, showcasing her profound intellectual depth and commitment to lifelong learning. Her certification in trauma and her role as a certified biblical counselor underscore her empathetic approach to human relationships and her deep-seated desire to bring healing and hope to individuals in distress. As a John Maxwell–certified leadership coach and speaker, she leverages her profound knowledge to mentor emerging leaders, guiding them to their fullest potential.

In academia Obioma's scholarly expertise is backed by a master's degree in early childhood education and a master's degree in leadership, qualifying her as a distinguished expert in her field. Her ordination as an evangelist is a testament to her dedication to spiritual service and her capacity to inspire and guide her community through faith and wisdom.

Obioma's life and work embody the very essence of transformational leadership—she is a beacon of hope, a catalyst for change, and a pillar of strength for those against all odds.

Learn more at Obioma.org.

CHAPTER 19

MIRACLES IN THE VALLEY

Turning Sorrow into Strength, One Step at a Time

By DeLisa Branch-Nealy

I was pumping gas the day my world was rocked, the day I learned my family would never be the same again.

Moments earlier I was holding the nozzle, lost in the rhythmic routine of refueling, watching the digital numbers on the pump ticking steadily as gasoline flowed into my vehicle.

I still remember the weather. It was clear and cool.

I still remember the location. It was a Costco.

I still remember the date. March 5, 2013.

For everyone else it was a normal day in California. Cars streamed by the gas station, their red taillights passing by like a river of rubies, their engines blending with the easygoing vibes of a sun-kissed afternoon. Customers walked in and out of the store, the jingle of the door mixing with conversations about road trips, the weather, and everyday affairs.

They were smiling. They were laughing. They were...happy. At that moment, I was too.

But then my cell phone rang. It was my older sister Denise, calling from her home in New York state.

"Hi, Lisa," she said, not wasting time for small talk. "I have stage IV lung cancer."

I didn't need an expert or the internet to understand the gravity of her diagnosis. I'm a registered nurse. I've assisted lung cancer patients. I've watched them struggle for breath. I've seen them cough up tissue. I've stood by their bedside as they died. Only about half of such patients live past four months. I knew what was coming. I knew the next chapter of her life—and our family's life—would be difficult.

Mind you, Denise wasn't a smoker. Neither were my mother or my grandmother, both of whom died of lung cancer. Denise also wasn't childless. She had three daughters: two were in college, and a third one was on the autism spectrum. Simply put, her prognosis would have a major impact.

She provided a few more details, but they were lost in the fog of emotions. She had a large mass on her right lung, and nodules on both lungs, and a metastasis of some sort. She also told me what precipitated the diagnosis: she had experienced major shoulder pain after shoveling snow and wanted to get it checked.

Those details, though, meant little. After we said our goodbyes, I drove to a safe spot in the parking lot, sat quietly in my car as time stood still, and sobbed. I cried buckets that day.

I didn't give up, though. Perhaps the prognosis wasn't good. Maybe she only had a short time on this earth to live. *We all do.*

Like a coach encouraging her team from the bench, I was determined to help her fight this battle—to do anything that could help extend her days, minimize her pain, and ensure that the last chapter of her life was filled with blessings.

I launched a prayer chain with my friends and family, asking them to pray for the doctors and for Denise. We needed a miracle. I also dug deep into the latest lung cancer research, searching for anything—*anything*—that might provide a spark of hope.

The way I looked at it, I owed Denise.

She was the middle child, the caring sister who helped raise me through thick and thin. Six years my senior, she essentially was my preschool teacher. I, in turn, was her real-life baby doll. She carried me. She protected me. She taught me the alphabet. She taught me how to spell my name. She even taught me the Pledge of Allegiance. She read to me often, including an annual reading of *A Visit from St. Nicholas* (*'Twas the Night Before Christmas*) on Christmas Eve. Those moments were almost magical.

My oldest sister, Deborah—or Debbie, as we called her—was the musical prodigy of the family, a classical pianist who instilled in me a love for music.

I can still remember my father, a World War II veteran named William "Bill" Branch, laughing out loud as he shouted for the "three Ds" to come to the dinner table. To him and to my beautiful mom, Christine (Christie), the three of us were like musical notes harmonizing in the symphony of a loving New York family—first Rochester and then Henrietta. We were a typical middle-class family raised on a typical middle-class street with Jewish, Polish, and Italian ancestry. We were the only Black family in the neighborhood, but no one cared. Everyone looked different. It was like a scene out of a movie.

When I was afraid of the dark at night, Denise would crawl into the bed, sing me a lullaby, and calm my soul. When I wet the bed, Denise would turn the light on and change the sheets—no questions asked. She didn't complain. She didn't yell. She knew I was too young to know better.

She was born with an altruistic spirit. She also was born with intelligence. In high school she won an essay competition for the Alpha Kappa Alpha Sorority and a free trip to DC and Philadelphia. Her name was in the paper. It was a big deal.

Life was like a fairy tale for me. Until it wasn't.

It all started when my mother developed a cough that didn't go away. Gradually, it got worse. In the summer of 1978, she went into the hospital for a lung tap to drain fluid.

I was a teenager back then. I assumed my mom would get better. Up until that moment in my life, I had taken her good health for granted, never truly comprehending the fragility of life. Apparently, though, she didn't want our father to tell us she was terminal with lung cancer.

She was the mom who took me to ballet lessons and to tap lessons. She walked me to elementary school, holding my hand as we crossed busy streets and talked about that day's adventures. When I was in sixth grade, she took a position in the school cafeteria just to be near me, always ready with a warm smile and a friendly wave during lunchtime. She loved to get her hands dirty in the garden, nurturing tasty vegetables that eventually found their way to our dinner table. Her green thumb was a testament to the patience and care she poured into everything she did. She also enjoyed dancing, a hobby that dad too embraced.

Her warm presence was a constant source of comfort. Her unwavering support fueled my dreams.

I was clueless as to what was happening to her health. By Christmas of 1978 she had lost her hair. She had lost a lot of weight too as she grappled with excruciating pain that had her pleading with God to "just take me."

Shortly after New Year's, the ambulance pulled up to our house to transport her to the hospital. As we gathered around her bedside, she told us through a weak but resolute voice to stick together as sisters, to stand united. My sisters were in college by then; I was in high school—but we recognized the weight of her words.

She passed away that night. The next few days and weeks—the grieving, the funeral, the going back to school—were a blur. Each morning was a challenge. Each day was a trial. I did the only thing I knew to do: I took one step forward at a time, hoping and believing life would get better.

I was a cheerleader in high school, walking the hallways zombielike as friends and acquaintances looked away, unsure what to say. I too didn't know how to cope, so I pretended nothing happened. Yet each night, I would lie in bed alone with my dog, crying myself to sleep as I contemplated the void left by her absence. A few months later I purchased Prince's 1979 album, the self-titled one that made him a star. Music and dance helped me rediscover my joy. Music and dance saved me.

My dad found a girlfriend and remarried around the time I turned sixteen. Still grieving about my mom, I submerged myself in schoolwork and extracurricular activities and then graduated from high school in 1981.

Denise was out of the house, but even then, she had a major

influence on my life, encouraging me to apply to Howard University, which accepted me into its nursing school.

Our lives diverged after college: She took a position as an environmental engineer in New York and adopted three girls, while I moved to California and began my own life raising my own children. Still, we stayed in touch, talking regularly on the phone and making occasional visits. We were thousands of miles apart, yet we kept the promise that we had made to my mom. We stuck together. We stayed united.

That's where I was in life in 2013 when she phoned and shared her earth-shattering news. She laughed a few times during our conversation. She remained upbeat. She was a person of deep faith who believed God would heal her—that lung cancer would *not* kill her. In hindsight, God did answer her prayers, just not the way she envisioned.

In the middle of that gas station parking lot, I made a decision to help Denise fight.

I began by doing what was familiar, pulling a few strings through my medical network to help schedule a lung biopsy that paved the way for a tailored treatment—a treatment that likely extended her life for a few months. I also flew to New York for that biopsy and spent quality time with her as we discussed the past, the present, and the future.

Denise lived another eighteen months after that phone call with me, but they were eighteen months filled with miracle after miracle.

She lived long enough to see another birthday.

She lived long enough to watch her daughter graduate in the summer of 2013.

She lived long enough to give her family a few more months of memories.

Her longevity also allowed us to tie up the loose ends in her life.

For example, Denise had signed documents giving me the power of attorney, but she had left the necessary paperwork back in her home, buried randomly among countless piles of coupons, mail, magazines, and other miscellaneous junk. My sweet sister had many gifts, but organization was not one of them. As she lay in a hospital bed in the final months of her life, I drove to her house, filled with angst and uncertainty, not knowing who would be in charge if this problem went unsolved. I got down on my knees and prayed for guidance in finding the proverbial needle in a haystack of clutter. Moments later I stumbled upon a business card with the name of an attorney previously hidden in a pile of receipts. The odds of me finding it were perhaps one in one thousand, and I had found it within a few minutes.

Her longevity gave me the necessary time to find another home—a marvelous group home on Long Island—for her adult daughter, Blessing, who is on the autism spectrum and who had lived with Denise.

Her longevity also gave her time to find another boyfriend! That new relationship had her family members simultaneously laughing and crying as they watched a new relationship blossom.

We gathered around Denise in her final hours, holding hands and singing old hymns as she looked around and smiled.

"I'm so happy," she said in her final twenty-four hours on this earth.

The last night of her life, Long Island experienced a torrential downpour. The next morning the storm had passed. The sun was shining. I woke up crying, instinctively knowing that my sister had passed on from this side of eternity. Within moments someone called from the hospital, confirming it.

I had prayed Denise would not experience so-called "air hunger"—and on her final full day of life her oxygen levels were 98, well within the normal range. She died peacefully, not gasping for air, not unconscious from pain medications. Denise, in turn, had prayed she would not die of lung cancer—and technically she did not. Her cancer had metastasized to her brain, which through a chain of events caused her heart to stop beating. She passed away from a heart attack.

Even after her death Denise kept sending me signals. One of

those signs involved her unique request for a purple casket with a lavender interior. "Promise me you'll do that," she would say. Of course, I agreed—even though I knew it might be tough to find one. Shortly after her death, though, I realized that I had no choice.

Denise died around the same time that a well-known author, Theresa Caputo, released a book I had been awaiting. I drove to the bookstore to purchase a copy and was floored by what I saw: a purple book with a title seemingly penned by my sister: *You Can't Make This Stuff Up: Life-Changing Lessons from Heaven.* Days earlier I had repeatedly used that same phrase—"you can't make this stuff up"—during a phone conversation with a friend in California as I recounted the blessings I had seen.

I chuckled. *I hear you, Denise. You'll get your purple casket.*

We often think of death as a tragedy. But with Denise it was surrounded by unexplainable miracles.

I never would have chosen this chapter of my life. I would have written a chapter void of painful loss and dark trials—a chapter filled with boundless peace and endless joy. That's the type of chapter all of us would write for our lives, if we're honest.

In the end, though, I *did* find joy in the midst of darkness. I *did* discover peace as I navigated my way—often blindly—through the valley. My story is one of persevering, of trusting, of finding faith when all hope seems lost. It's one of taking one step at a time, forward, when you're too sorrowful to even move. Each step forward becomes a quiet triumph, a small victory. Soon you've taken a thousand steps, and soon a thousand more. Eventually, you see the light.

I didn't think I could survive the death of my sister. At times I thought it would end me. It didn't. It made me stronger.

About DeLisa

DeLisa, a registered nurse with an esteemed thirty-seven-year career in surgery, is a proud graduate of Howard University and a veteran of the United States Air Force. Her medical expertise spans breast cancer, ophthalmic, and neurosurgery, with a particular emphasis on plastic microsurgery. Alongside her medical career, DeLisa has been an integral member of The Chinyakare Ensemble, a traditional Zimbabwean music and dance band, for over eighteen years.

This blend of professional and cultural pursuits defines DeLisa's unique journey. Her Howard University education and Air Force experience have instilled in her a profound sense of discipline and commitment, evident in her healthcare work and her passion for African dance. As a performer with The Chinyakare Ensemble, DeLisa celebrates her heritage, expressing the vibrancy of African culture through dance and music.

DeLisa's husband, Mike Nealy, a fellow Howard University alumnus with an MBA from Fordham University, shares her values of education and dedication. Their strong bond, spanning over thirty-one years of marriage, is built on mutual respect and shared aspirations.

As the founder of DeLisa's Life Dance, a health coaching business, DeLisa extends her influence beyond the medical field, promoting wellness, positivity, and holistic health. This venture reflects her belief in the interconnectedness of physical and mental well-being.

Balancing her professional life, DeLisa is a dedicated mother to three adult children, intertwining her roles as a healthcare professional, an entrepreneur, an artist, and a parent. Her diverse interests, ranging from music and fashion to writing and teaching, showcase her dynamic personality and commitment to lifelong learning.

Now transitioning from acute care nursing to focus on her coaching business, speaking engagements, and writing, DeLisa is leveraging her experiences as a Howard University graduate, a USAF veteran, a nurse, and an artist. Her journey is a testament to her ability to touch lives in myriad ways—whether in the operating room, on the dance floor with The Chinyakare Ensemble, or through her inspiring words and actions.

For more information about DeLisa and her journey, visit her website at www.delisaslifedance.com.

CHAPTER 20

FINDING YOUR PURPOSE IN YOUR PAIN

By L.A. Roberts

My Papa. He wasn't just a grandfather; he was my rock, my guiding light, and the wind beneath my wings. Papa believed in me like nobody else ever did. He was the one who taught me that the sky was the limit and that I could conquer any mountain I set my mind to.

In 2016 the world as I knew it shattered when I lost Papa. The pain was unbearable, the loss unimaginable. It felt like the ground had been ripped from beneath my feet. How could someone so full of life, so full of love, be taken from us so suddenly?

He was married to my grandmother for fifty-eight years, until he passed away in 2016. I officiated the service on November 5, 2016, which would have marked their fifty-eighth year together. I stood before the congregation and delivered the sermon, pouring out my heart in tribute to my hero. I sang, filling the sacred space with melodies that echoed the love in the church where my grandparents' beautiful journey began fifty-eight years prior.

The shock, the trauma, the grief—it engulfed me like a tidal wave. I wasn't prepared for a world without Papa. It wasn't supposed to happen like this.

CHICAGO, 1980S

Growing up on the South Side of Chicago, Papa was my constant. He was there when I took my first breath, and held my hand through every triumph and every trial. I spent most of my early years under Papa's loving care. There isn't a memory that didn't involve him. He was my first love, my hero, the heartbeat of our family. Life, to me, was a game best played with Papa by my side.

With Papa, I was invincible.

My Papa owned a home in Hyde Park—a rare feat in the 1960s, especially for a young man who started with nothing, a young wife, and two little ones.

Born in 1928 in Ohio, Papa knew hardship from the start. Orphaned as a child, he and his seven siblings faced the world alone. Life was tough; onion sandwiches were a luxury, and ten-cent hot dogs were out of reach.

But Papa didn't let his humble beginnings define him. He worked tirelessly for the City of Chicago, serving under Mayor Daley Sr. and Mayor Daley Jr. Despite his role as a custodial worker, Papa's spirit was refined. He loved opera, a passion that sparked his courtship with my grandmother at Pilgrim Baptist Church in Chicago.

Smooth as silk, Papa's first question to her was, "Do you like opera?" Now, Grandma was from Montgomery, Alabama. She admitted, "I didn't know what opera was, but I said yes." And yes, they were in church. So, the family joke went, "Grandma, you lied in church." But she'd laugh and say, "We were in the lobby."

Papa always dreamed of more for his family. His journey was one of resilience, hard work, and unwavering love. He held season tickets to the opera without fail, year after year. It was his sanctuary. Grandma grew to love it too, once she understood what it was all about. They'd dress to the nines, sharp as a tack, and make their way to the opera house in Chicago. Together they'd sink into those plush seats, letting the music carry them away.

When I came into this world, Papa had a special trick to quiet me: opera music. Its melodies would soothe me to sleep as he whispered about the beauty of each note. He introduced me to opera, igniting a love that would stay with me forever.

In our living room, with friends around, he'd call me Queen

and beckoned me to sing. I'd belt out tunes, shaking the chandelier with my mezzo-soprano voice, while he beamed with pride.

Ballet was another gift from Papa. With him I learned to carry myself like royalty. He'd take me to class, then watch with unwavering pride as I twirled in tutus and tights. His belief in me knew no bounds; he made me feel like anything was possible.

My Papa would take me to church as a little girl, and we would come home to macaroni and cheese (oh, that smell made me so excited!), sweet potato pie, fried chicken, corn bread, collard greens, and more that my Grandma was cooking. Oh, and salmon croquettes and rice. It was a special Sunday meal each week when we got home from church.

"Go and put on your leisure suit," Grandma said. And we would sit at the table and eat. But I was Papa's baby. You did not see him without me. We were Batman and Robin.

Papa instilled a confidence in me that defied the odds. Despite our challenges, he painted a world where dreams were within reach. "You can do this," he'd say, whether I dreamed of running for president or auditioning for the Augusta Opera Co.

His life was a testament to resilience. Despite battling polio as a child, he thrived, his limp a reminder of his strength. He was a survivor. Even in his seventies, he returned to school, determined to conquer new challenges. Sitting at the table, he'd pore over math problems with me, his determination unwavering. My Papa was part of a program at The University of Chicago. Rain or shine, he'd bundle up all my siblings, take them out in the stroller every weekday, and walk. He'd drop them off at day care and head off to read and write stories, later having them published in magazines. And oh, how proud he was of his work.

A man of prayer, Papa's faith was unwavering. As I grew older, I asked him and my grandmother if they ever worried about me. Without a moment's hesitation, they reassured me, "No." They recounted the story of my mother's pregnancy at seventeen. They took her to church as soon as they knew, where two women who could probably pray the paint off the wall interceded for us. They prayed over my mother and me, declaring I was blessed from the womb. They never doubted or worried because they said I was "touched in the womb" and believed I was destined for greatness.

Papa saw something special in me, something beyond the circumstances of my birth. His belief in me was unshakable, and he instilled in me an unwavering faith—that there was no limit to what I could achieve. With his steadfast support, I dared to dream big.

Launching Papa's Legacy

Papa watched his grandson, who carries his namesake, Leon F. Howard III, become a lawyer and have a law firm with his name on the door.

The *A* in my middle name, L.A., stands for Ann. My grandmother gave me her name, and when I did anything great, she proudly stated, "That's my name." This is the legacy we carry with pride.

I moved to Georgia in my early twenties and got the opportunity to perform. They wanted me to join the cast of *My Fair Lady*. I didn't audition but was invited to watch the rehearsal, and the music director handed me a sheet of music and said, "What's your voice?"

"Soprano," I said reluctantly.

He said, "Do me a favor and have a seat." He'd never heard me sing. I started to follow along and sing with them, and at the end of it, he asked me if I would join the cast. I was the only African American cast member in that production. And whom did I call? My Papa.

Papa wasn't just my grandfather; he was my confidant, my closest companion. Even as I grew older and moved out, we spoke every single day without fail. If I didn't call him by 7:30 a.m., he'd be the one calling me. We shared laughter, tears, and everything in between.

My papa was so proud. After all, he came from nothing and saw this happen. But honestly, he saw it long before it happened, when we were kids. Now, he was experiencing it.

THE DAY EVERYTHING CHANGED

On an ordinary fall day in 2016, my grandma called and said, "Papa fell; you need to come home." She never called to say I needed to come home.

Days later I found myself there, praying his pain and suffering away in his living room. He was in the bedroom under a home nurse's care, and I dropped to my knees and said, "OK, Lord, whatever you gotta do. I don't want him to be in pain." Papa didn't have to hear me to know I released him. He was waiting for me to let him go.

I walked back into the room and watched Papa take his last breath.

When I took my first breath, he was there. And when he took his last, I was there. Mustering every ounce of strength not to lose it, I whispered in his ear that I would continue to make him proud and that everyone in the world would know his name: *Leon F. Howard Sr.*

I kissed him on his cheek. I touched his foot as I turned, and I never turned back. Papa left us on October 27, 2016, at eighty-eight.

BREAKING THROUGH THE PARALYSIS OF PAIN

After he passed, time stood still at 7:30 a.m. every day. The silence echoed louder than any words could. In the first year without him, I went through the motions of life, but I was numb inside. I'd hold on to my phone, playing back saved voicemails to hear his voice again. Where did that leave me if he wasn't on the other end of the line to lend his ear? Where was my drive? My inspiration? Who would reassure me, "You'll be all right. Call me after; I want to hear all about it"? Who else would believe in me the way he did?

The pain was so deep I considered suicide. I didn't want to live. After my grandfather passed away, I told my godmother, standing in my grandparents' kitchen, "You know, if I didn't wake up tomorrow, I would be OK."

For weeks I sat in the middle of my living room floor or in my bed in the dark, crying because I didn't know what to do. I became emotionally and motivationally paralyzed, losing every ounce of willpower to move forward.

But in the most profound moments of pain and depression, I remembered the promise I made to Papa. A friend persisted in inviting me to a conference featuring Lisa Nichols, someone I'd followed for years. Despite my initial reluctance, I eventually relented, sensing a glimmer of determination. I had a promise to keep, after all.

Just two months after Papa's passing, in December, I agreed to attend the conference but was gripped by fear. I booked a VIP ticket, determined to sit up front and absorb every ounce of inspiration possible. Tears streamed down my face as I stood before the mirror in my hotel room, grappling with my apprehension.

I ventured downstairs to the conference room. As Lisa entered, they asked if anyone had any questions. Without hesitation I raised my hand and asked, "How do you keep going when the only person who was your support, motivation, and inspiration is now gone?"

"How long has it been?" asked Lisa.

I replied, "October 27."

"Of this year?!" Her astonishment was palpable. "Six weeks?" she echoed. In that moment, she became my beacon of hope, guiding me through the darkness with her words of wisdom and compassion. Through tears and resolve I began to take small steps forward, driven by the unwavering determination to honor Papa's memory.

From the Person to the Purpose

There came a pivotal moment when I realized that my purpose transcended my connection to Papa. Even when I couldn't see it, Papa always did. He recognized the purpose within me long before I did. Now it was my turn to look beyond the person and embrace the purpose he saw.

When I stood over him and he took his last breath, I inhaled his legacy. God entrusted Leon F. Howard Sr. with me. Now I must grow into what I was meant to be, but only by enduring this journey. So, I had to shift my focus from the *person* to the *purpose*.

Motivating and inspiring people is what I was created to do, from speaking on stages to writing books, talking to people, and encouraging them to move through and beyond painful moments. But I could not step into it without first experiencing this heartbreak.

I had to confront the pain head-on, embracing it rather than skirting around it. There was no avoiding it, no ignoring its presence. It was a journey I had to traverse, ultimately leading me to my purpose.

It's remarkable how many people attempt to evade pain, burying it deep within their souls. It's akin to having a deep gash on your arm and refusing treatment. Soon enough the infection sets in, then festers and spreads until it consumes every part of you.

Your Purpose Is Tied to Others

Loss and grief can be so messy, and that's OK. There's nothing wrong with challenging days and experiencing a range of emotions. What's crucial is *acknowledging* them. I could pretend to be fine on March 30 (my Papa's birthday), or October 27, but that wouldn't be genuine.

If my Papa were still here, undoubtedly, I'd be doing great things, but would I be pursuing the same path? Probably not. I'd likely be gracing stages, singing opera—a noble pursuit, indeed. But would my message be the same? No.

Life makes us discover who we are and who we are meant to be when our backs are against the wall. There is a beautiful story on the other side, if you can see it.

We want the prize, but nobody wants the pain. People see the top of the mountain, but you don't see my valley. You don't know what this cost me. The prize looks good, but you don't want my journey. You want your journey because your reward is yours. And no one can take it from you.

My pain, though immense, transcends my individual experience. Each loss brings a profound shift in perspective, emphasizing the importance of our journey and why we're here. I now understand I was born to touch millions through shared pain. While my pain nearly derailed my purpose, I persevered. Papa would be so proud of me. I know he is.

Reflecting on my battles against all odds, I have a vital message: *Lives depend on your healing.*

Keep pressing forward. There's hope. People need you. If we can shift our focus away from ourselves, we have the power to change the world. Your purpose is intricately tied to others—it may not reach millions, but never underestimate the power of touching a life through your healing story.

About L.A.

L.A. Roberts is a three-time international best-selling author who has more than ten years' experience as a transformational speaker, breakthrough strategist, content creator, and fintech corporate leader. She is also the founder of I Inspire Global, where ordinary people with extraordinary stories change the world.

L.A. has been invited to speak at the UN, Harvard University, Georgia State University, the American Red Cross, the NAACP, TEDx, and many conferences and empowerment events in the US, Canada, and London. In 2021 L.A. was awarded an honorary doctorate degree from Trinity International University of Ambassadors, and the Presidential Lifetime Achievement Award.

L.A. is currently a radio personality on WDRB Media, Apple Radio, Streema, and TuneIn with her show *From My Heart to Yours*. L.A. has received the honor of being named one of the top 50 most influential women in business by *VIP Global Magazine*. She enjoys touring the country hosting Sister Suite Talks and her Relax, Release and Breathe retreats—all while finding time to do radio, TV, and magazine interviews with *Global Woman Magazine*, Shoutout Atlanta, Business Woman Today, *Voyage ATL*, and many more.

CONNECT WITH L.A. ROBERTS:

- **Website**: www.LARobertsSpeaks.com
- **Email**: Breakthrough@LARobertsSpeaks.com

CHAPTER 21

KEEPING MY PROMISES

By Latoya D. Buchanan, MSN, FNP-BC

The hallway from the dean's office to the elevator seemed to stretch out, endless, in front of me.

I could feel the peppermints I had taken from the candy dish on his desk—a force of habit more than need—crinkling in my pocket. I could feel the searing, crushing pain in the back of my head. The pain that had not abated for the last two years, and had sent me into his office that morning, sobbing.

The tears were still dry and salty on my face as I gazed down the quiet expanse.

Since beginning my graduate education in the nursing department, I had worked as the associate dean, Dr. Cecil Holland's assistant. I liked my little station outside his office. The outdated decor and smell of old books made me nostalgic for a home I'd never had, and he was a kind boss. The job had been a godsend, yet another small gift from the universe on my return to school.

Dean Holland knew me as capable, driven, unflappable. He knew that I was a single mom, raising my three kids, and that my schedule was filled from sunup to sundown with classes and practicums and after-school jobs. But he didn't know how much I had been suffering.

He didn't know that two years prior, in my very first month of school, I had been T-boned by a wayward deer. It came out of nowhere—the flash of antlers out my driver's side window, and then the crash as deer met car. It was nighttime, and I was driving the interstate on my way to my job as a registered nurse. I had been working as an RN for quite some time, but upon my acceptance into the graduate family nurse practitioner program at my alma mater, Winston-Salem State University, I had transitioned to part-time work. At the time of the accident I was full of new hope. Back in school, stepping gradually closer to my goals.

I had promised my children a home, and I was going to get it for them.

The impact with the deer left me with injuries to my hip and foot, and after several weeks I began to develop debilitating headaches. Because I had been injured on company time, the accident fell under my employer's workers' compensation plan, and my medical care was in their hands.

But when it came time to pay for treatment, my pain was met with indifference.

They refused to approve any scans to help diagnose the searing ache in my head, even though at times it was so severe I got dizzy to the point of collapse. My vision blurred so much that even driving my kids to the park felt risky. None of which was taken seriously by my employer. The opposition got so intense I had no choice but to take legal action against the company, which also meant that the reputation and friendships I had built there deteriorated along with my health.

The pain in my head started to impact every part of my life. My oldest daughter had begun to ask me why I was "mad all the time." How do you explain to a six-year-old that Mommy is mad because she's in so much pain she can hardly see? Mommy is mad because all she wants is a home for her children, and the path there seems to be littered with obstacles. Mommy is mad because she's not sure how she's going to do this.

My kids and I had only recently found our way free of a difficult relationship with their father, and my sole driving force—the thing that got me out of bed every morning, that kept me up studying for hours on end—was my desire to find a safe, stable home for myself and my children. In order to do that, I needed to control the pain.

So when eventually my doctor—in lieu of other treatment—found a drug to put me on, I was elated. It was a powerful anti-inflammatory, and as soon as I took it, I felt that I'd found a miracle cure. The pain abated. I could live my life!

And for a while I did.

As long as I was taking my medication, I was OK. I managed my punishing schedule, which included waking up at 5 a.m. to get my kids to school by 6:30, then driving the two hours to my morning practicum. All day I would work and study, trying to stay focused so that I could answer any clinical or medical question thrown at me. I would do my work in the dean's office and then drive the two hours back home to pick up my kids, feed them, and put them to bed, then back to studying. It was grueling, but without the vice grip on the back of my head, I was able to manage.

Then, in the middle of our legal battle, my former employer took my miracle drug away. They would no longer approve it. I was, once again, adrift with a mystery pain no one would acknowledge.

I was at a pharmacy, trying to refill my medication, when I found out. I walked out to my car in a daze, then sat in the driver's seat, sobbing. Recently I had been taking my children to church services and had even been singing in the church choir, in an attempt to bring some normalcy to our lives. In the middle of my despair, the choir director called. I don't remember why he was calling, but I remember that he prayed with me as I sat in the pharmacy parking lot.

I'm not a person who quits. I never have been. But in the near dusk, hanging on to the choir director's every word, searching the horizon for some answer, I felt as close to quitting as I've ever come.

Maybe I was asking for too much. Maybe moving my children into yet another temporary situation, working myself to the bone, putting every ounce of life force into my studies and this dream out in front of me—was just one step too far. Was I meant to have what I wanted, or was I going to have to surrender to this pain?

The questions kept me up most of the night, and the next day when I showed up for work in the dean's office—the scent of books and some impossible future in the air—I finally told him about the weight I'd been under. The accident. The lawsuit. This unbearable, unrelenting pain. I told him I was at the end of a rope I'd thought would go forever, and that I needed help.

Dean Holland told me later that he knew it would take a lot to knock me down, so when I came into his office that morning, he felt compelled to act. "There's a physical therapy department on the fourth floor," he told me. "You're going to go there and tell them you're a student and that I sent you. I think they might be able to help."

So that's what landed me at one end of the hallway. At the other, the elevator to the fourth floor, and my possible salvation.

WSSU is a historically black university, so on the walls of the hallway closest to me hung framed photos of the first graduating classes. Rows of black women stared down at me, sturdy and serious. They laid the groundwork for women like me to attend this kind of institution. To study well beyond undergrad. To chase our dreams. I felt them watching me as I started my slow walk, knowing full well the adversaries they had faced to get me there.

Further down the hallway were pictures of the previous years' undergraduates. My own graduating class. I remember being so disappointed in my graduation picture. I thought I looked young and silly, beaming at the camera. I wanted to look serious, in line with the accomplishment I had just achieved. My friends and family all said the smiling photo was a perfect expression of *me*.

I stopped under my photo and saw a younger self, fresh and full of all the fire of plans and potential. I saw in that smile every obstacle she'd already overcome, and all the fuel she would need to overcome those yet to come. I felt her giving me back a strength I thought I'd lost.

I was still that same woman. Full of all the dreams and indomitable spirit. She watched me as I pressed the elevator button for the second floor and ascended.

The dean's name carried some weight, so the graduate students in the physical therapy office were quick to attend to me. The therapist assigned to me sat and listened as I told my story. She didn't jump in or wave off or dismiss anything I had to say. She took me, and my pain, seriously. Sadly, for women—and black women in particular—this is a rare experience in doctors' offices.

Once in the therapy room, she had me sit in a comfortable chair, with her opposite. I was struck immediately by her sense of calm. She talked quietly and without hurry, and I could feel my own system slowing to keep pace with hers.

She took me through several breathing exercises. She asked me where the pain was, and I told her: my hips, my feet, and my head. She asked me to close my eyes and go to the pain in my head, to feel it and breathe into it.

In all the years of doctors' visits and medication, I had never once closed my eyes and actually *felt* the pain in my body. As I focused, I could feel the throbbing in the back of my head, just above my neck. I let my attention stay there, and as I did, it started to soften and dissipate. It was as if the sheer act of acknowledgment had begun to release everything I was holding on to.

For the first time in as long as I could remember, I felt relief. My pain no longer felt like a mystery that only a pill could combat. It was in my control. The sensations that I had been running from, when I faced them, were not nearly as scary as they'd seemed. It was like being let into a cave with a dragon only to discover the dragon was just a fire that had been left burning a bit too long.

From that moment on, things began to get easier. With my new awareness I was able to move fully into and then well beyond my pain. Dean Holland let me work from home and offered me an additional scholarship for disadvantaged nursing students. I excelled in my studies. Near the end of my second year of school, I secured a lease on a house for me and my children.

Up until then, we'd been living in cramped apartments, their three beds lined up orphanage-style, or with friends. This was going to be a real *home*.

Our moving day turned out to be the same day I was set to speak at a prestigious university for a women's nonprofit organization. They had heard me speak at an alumni event, and the opportunity wasn't one I could say no to. That day, my parents picked up my kids and our packed U-Haul so I could attend the event.

I had worked for weeks on my speech. Through my breath work and meditation I had learned that it was only in becoming comfortable with what scared me—facing my own pain, truly asking for help—that I was able to progress. I had a message for women in the same boat: if you have a dream, pursue it with everything in you, and in the pursuit itself you'll find joy.

But if I tell you that God has a sense of humor, would you believe me? Because on my way to give that speech, as I sat at a red light, rehearsing what I was going to say, the keys to our new home jangling in my pocket, I was rear-ended with enough force to land me back in the hospital. Like a bookend to my original accident, but this time it was different. Or *I* was.

This accident wasn't just another obstacle; it was proof of my liberation.

At the hospital I refused any pain medication other than Tylenol and was discharged immediately. Nurses and friends, even the organizer of the conference where I was to speak, all told me it would be OK not to attend. I had just been rear-ended; I could go home and rest.

But I'm no quitter.

As I rode in the passenger seat from the hospital to the conference, I felt the distance between the me of two years ago and the woman I was now. I knew, in my bones, that I was doing exactly what I was supposed to be doing. I knew that I had ownership over my own suffering and could transform my pain into something greater.

As I said in the speech I gave that day, "In your life you *will* encounter opposition. The important question to ask yourself is, "Would I rather have opposition trying to accomplish a *goal* or in my ordinary, humdrum life?"

That night, my kids and I sat on the floor of our new dining room and ate take-out pizza. Even without a table to sit at, it remains to this day the best pizza I've ever eaten.

———•———

I finally graduated in May of 2020. Today, I'm happily engaged. I'm building my dream home with my fiancé on land we purchased for ourselves. I'm practicing as a board-certified family nurse practitioner while pursuing my doctorate. My goal is to one day open my own practice to provide personalized, tailored primary care to my patients.

My children are happy and thriving, and they finally have a safe space to call their own.

The experiences that have shaped me have only increased my desire to do and be more, and they have taught me one crucial lesson: The obstacles that are put in front of us are gifts if we learn to see them that way. All of them urging us forward, reminding us that if we stay the course, there are great rewards on the other side.

About Latoya

Latoya D. Buchanan is a best-selling author transforming lives of thousands of women around the world. Recognized as a motivational speaker, Latoya has inspired families in her role as a board-certified family nurse practitioner having served over fifteen years in the areas of public health, pediatrics, healthcare administration, and marketing.

As the owner of Global Health and Wellness PLLC, Latoya has founded other companies, including A Mother's Milk PLLC and Buchanan Preservation Protection, a property preservation company.

Latoya has been featured in *Vision & Purpose Lifestyle Magazine*, in the *Purpose By Design* podcast, in *A Queen's Roundtable* podcast, and on WUNC-TV.

Latoya delights in being a mother to her three beautiful children, Journey, Jacob, and Calvary, and cat mom to an orange tabby, Tigriss.

LEARN MORE AT:

- **Facebook:** Latoya D. Buchanan
- **Instagram:** Latoya D. Buchanan

CHAPTER 22

FROM NO WILL TO LIVE TO LIVING WELL

My Journey to Complete Wellness

By Annmarie Waite, ARNP, CHC, PhD

The day had come. I would go from Ms. to Mrs. and start a new life out on my own. A dream come true, right?

Not for me. Not then.

After my father died suddenly at the young age of forty-three of a massive heart attack and a stroke, my mother was left with three girls and a boy. I was twelve at the time. The product of a broken home, I felt like I did not fit in, that I was not loved or worthy because of the rejection I felt as a child.

After my father passed away, Mom and Grandma decided they needed to arrange marriages for us girls so we would be taken care of. The idea was not unusual considering my mother's background. She is half Indian and half Spanish, and arranged marriages are common in Indian culture.

I was sixteen. He was twice my age. While many girls that age were going to movies and having sleepovers and pizza with their girlfriends, I was saying, "I do."

But I didn't want to.

At seventeen I had my son. I had to grow up with him. I don't remember being a teenager. Every choice I made had to be in the best interest of both him and me.

Early on in our marriage I felt mentally disrespected and unhappy. When I started to rebel, the relationship got worse. As a result, I had low self-esteem. When I think back on my first days of marriage, at the time, I thought, "I might as well die." I contemplated suicide because I felt that was the only way out. But something inside me thought, "This can't be it."

That's when I went into therapy—that was my way of thinking about how to get out of this relationship and unbearable situation.

In therapy I met my guardian angel, who helped me plan to leave. I left Jamaica alone and went to live with my family in Connecticut. My husband later sent my daughter to live with me, and when my son got depressed and his grades suffered without me and his sister, my husband bought a house where our two kids could live with me, closer to him, in Miami. He planned to come visit the kids there.

It sounded like a good plan—until about five months later when he moved into the house and the bad relationship started all over again.

Whatever I was going through was not how I saw my life unfolding. I had very strong faith. I believed that God would take care of me. I had to keep the faith and keep believing there was better to come. I had to accept full responsibility for who I was and what I wanted to do. I had to believe in me.

Having gotten married at such a young age, I never had the opportunity to go to college. But now, since my mother instilled in me that to get anywhere in life, you had to get an education, I decided that's part of who I wanted to be. So I entered nursing school and began a new path for my life. When the relationship deteriorated even further, I felt I had to move out, and, after a long process, I got divorced. The day I walked out of the court no longer attached to him was the happiest day of my life.

I became a nurse, and my kids came to live with me again. Because my goal was to climb to the top of my professional ladder, later on I became a women's health nurse practitioner. Once my kids graduated high school, I obtained my PhD in nursing. I want other women to know that regardless of where they started, regardless of what has happened to them, they too can thrive!

Through my years of experience, I've seen a lot of women stay in toxic situations because they don't know any better. When you lose sight of yourself, you end up suffering.

My daughter's relationship with her father was not a good one, and as an adolescent, she didn't want to be with him. I wanted her to have a relationship with her dad, so I arranged for him to pick her up for dinner—he did, but eventually, she didn't want to do that anymore. Being an adolescent, coupled with the effects of the divorce, things also got difficult for her at school.

NEW BEGINNINGS

A year after I graduated from nursing school, I remarried. A few years later, when my husband had an opportunity to work in Singapore, we decided to take advantage of that, and it was the best thing that happened to our family. My son graduated high school at age sixteen and was now in college. So it was just the three of us in an environment where we had only ourselves to rely on, and it worked out well for everybody. While we were there, my daughter decided to forgive her dad. Now she's on good terms with him. We have since moved back to the States.

Looking back, I know my father's death instilled in me the desire to dream big—and to know that I have a choice in everything I do. I was determined not to follow in his footsteps in terms of health, but that decision also taught me I could dream outside the box.

I decided then to be as active as I could be. I joined a gym and developed a healthy addiction to exercise. And I became a vegetarian in my late teens. I know for sure that the modification of my lifestyle changed my genetic health trajectory. My siblings did not take the same path, and I watched sadly as my older sister went down the same path as my father. I tried to help, but she was not willing to change her lifestyle. She died at fifty-five years old.

I am now sixty-two. People ask me why I'm still working—it's because I believe there's so much more in store for me. I believe there is more to me than I could ever imagine, but most importantly, more than I have been told. I want to continue living my soul purpose: being in service to others.

GIRLFRIENDS HEALTH

Because my father died so young of heart disease, I have had a passion for wellness from a young age—twelve, to be exact. My father's health journey became my personal growth journey. Of course, my sister's death also affected my wellness path. Losing a sibling was traumatic, and it shaped my decision to look at health coaching during COVID because the medical system could not save my sister. I knew in my heart of hearts she did not have to die. Nursing has taught me that humans all experience a version of the same challenge, just at different levels. I decided to become a health coach and share my journey. It's a story people don't typically share with others, but I know that when we reveal our truth, we create space for others to heal theirs. Sharing our vulnerabilities is one of the best ways we can support others. I created Girlfriends Health to empower women to take control of their physical and emotional health and healing. Our bodies never lie; we just need to learn to listen to them more keenly. To become healthy, we must have enough courage to be in touch with the wisdom of our female bodies and to follow the desires of our hearts. The painful lesson is that while I learned to take care of my own health because my father died, I couldn't save my sister, because you can only help someone if they are willing to receive help.

While my past pains led me to become a certified health and wellness coach, I also took that path because I know how to heal naturally, and helping others is fulfilling. I want to help others get back into the driver's seat of their health and live their best life—not one shortened by disease.

Through Girlfriends Health, the focus is on prevention, helping women who may have a negative health history and want to prevent diseases. My areas of expertise include conscious goal setting, transforming your mindset, and holistic engineering of wellness. I focus on the inside and the outside. When you can find happiness on the inside and couple it with lifestyle changes, you have a pretty good guarantee of living a happy, vibrant, and healthy life, regardless of your genetic makeup. I am living proof, and I hope my story empowers others to move to deeper levels in all areas of their lives.

The name Girlfriends Health was inspired by the bond that developed between my daughter and me when working through her adolescent complexities to find her voice. To help her establish her place in the world, mother and daughter became "girlfriends." To this day, my daughter still calls me "girlfriend." In addition to that special meaning, "girlfriends" also describes the power of women supporting one another.

SMALL CHANGES, BIG RESULTS

I have learned from the hundreds of patients I have nursed back to health that you can turn things around with small changes. It doesn't matter how many years have passed. Taking the first step can open years of possibility for you.

It did for me. Research shows when you change your lifestyle, you can divert even genetic disorders. You can lower your risk of cardiovascular disease, hypertension, and diabetes, among other things—real threats as we get older. Whatever issues you are having, we want to find a way to help you.

One issue is preeclampsia in pregnant women. Having preeclampsia raises a woman's risk of having heart disease to 60 percent. I want women to know that they can do something about this through a program I offer. I help women work on their diet, exercise, and mindset—which determines what they eat and how they exercise—as well as how they manage stress. It gives them a game plan for working to prevent heart disease.

Another issue Girlfriends Health addresses is problems losing weight. Most times, the focus is on losing weight, but oftentimes, there's something more deeply rooted that's causing the extra pounds to stay on. When a client comes to me, I might know the root cause right away, but my purpose is to facilitate their health journey, so as much as I would like to tell them my assessment, they should glean it through introspection. Having accountability is a big part of health coaching. Diet, mindset, and movement are all part of the process. Growth and healing occur through taking action, so each session ends with homework. Often, I use journaling because you have to track your progress. In all my health coaching, there's no judgment—I'm not judging you; you're not judging yourself. You have to love yourself in order to get better.

I recently got certified as a Happy for No Reason trainer, so I offer a happiness workshop. Happiness is the one thing we all need and can never get too much of, yet so many of us do not make happiness a priority. That was me years ago—the happiness of others came first, over mine. I thought happiness was an impossible goal with everything going on. The root of that was I did not believe I deserved to be happy. The fact is, everyone deserves happiness, and it was only by pursuing joy that I was able to create the life I love. I want to inspire others to do the same.

This four-week workshop teaches different strategies for being happy—and how to pursue joy. It is about knowing how to heal yourself by accessing your deepest master systems, and to live by the truths rising through your body, guiding what is true for you. We work on changing habits to start your day with a grateful mindset—having an attitude of gratitude will change the way you see things, and you'll embody the things you want. It's important to remember that whatever you're putting out into the world is what's coming back to you. Are you what you want? When you do this, your energy flows, and when energy is flowing, happiness and healing happen on every level of your life. You learn the tools to help you break free from blame, fear, shame, and guilt. And finally, it is about embodying and harvesting a greater love, so it becomes the fabric of who you are rather than what you seek.

Part of my dreaming outside the box and growth is giving back because I'm so grateful. Nursing taught me to care even more deeply and have so much compassion. I'm very grateful for the ability to love people unconditionally. When I decided to leave nursing, I unconsciously fell into a state of depression, and through self-diagnosis I realized I was mourning the loss of my identity of thirty years. I wanted to give back to my profession for all it gave to me, so I created a free Happiness workshop for nursing students and healthcare providers. My vision and mission are to help decrease the nursing shortage and burnout rate by helping nurses to be happy for no reason.

TIPS FOR LIVING YOUR BEST LIFE

Other tips for living a happy, vibrant, healthy life include the following:

- Don't allow toxic people to hold space in your life. When you do, you are often bound to create more damage than not having them there at all.

- Heal the parts of you that past generations could not heal for themselves. By speaking your truth and living in self-awareness, you can grow and build confidence as you expand into the next best version of yourself.

- Exercise and get moving. What you put in your body needs to be supported by what you're doing.

- Couple that with your mental health—if you're healthy on the outside but you're stressed out, it's not going to help. You have to be happy.

- Eat a healthy diet.

- Think healthy thoughts. When someone gets a diagnosis, I teach them to realize the diagnosis is just a name—you can work your way out of that diagnosis.

But if you believe it, you're going to have more of it because that's what you believe.

- Believe in yourself. Whenever I lead a course, I instill self-resilience.

I have come a long way since heart disease took my father's life—in fact, it is the very thing that saved mine. And I desire to help you become healthier as well. I want you to embark on a profound journey of well-being and self-discovery to live your best life—I really do.

About Annmarie

Annmarie Waite, ARNP, CHC, PhD, is a distinguished figure in the realm of nursing, with a rich tapestry of experiences spanning over three decades. Armed with a doctor of philosophy in nursing, her multifaceted role as a healthcare provider, researcher, and educator encompasses a wide array of critical health-related domains, particularly focusing on women, children, and families.

Throughout her career, Annmarie has been a beacon of advocacy and care, addressing issues ranging from health promotion to cardiovascular disease and mental health. Her groundbreaking research on nurse practitioners in independent practice not only propels the nursing profession forward but also significantly contributes to enhancing healthcare outcomes for individuals across the spectrum. She ardently believes that nurse practitioners are pivotal in alleviating primary care shortages, emphasizing the urgent need to modernize outdated laws to ensure timely access to care for all Americans.

As the president and CEO of Girlfriends Health PLC and the nonprofit foundation Girlfriends Guild Inc., Annmarie channels her passion into tangible initiatives. For three decades she has dedicated herself to improving the health and social standing of women, children, and families through a combination of hospital nursing, community outreach, and health awareness programs.

In the face of adversity, Annmarie remains steadfast in her commitment to providing care, whether it entails supporting children born with AIDS or conducting examinations for sexually assaulted women. Her expertise in women's health, child abuse, and pre- and postnatal care underscores her invaluable contributions to these critical areas.

Driven by a vision of empowerment and holistic well-being, Annmarie established Girlfriends Health PLC to offer vital resources, educational materials, and counseling support to women seeking to enhance their physical, emotional, and mental health.

Annmarie's journey began as a registered nurse in pediatrics, and she evolved into an advanced registered nurse practitioner (ARNP). She obtained her undergraduate degree from the University of Miami before delving into medical training at Jackson Memorial Hospital. Further academic pursuits led her to earn a master's degree from the University of Miami and ultimately a PhD from Barry University.

Over the years, Annmarie has worn many hats, including roles as a professor, nursing administrator, child protection team medical examiner, and sexual assault examiner. These diverse experiences, coupled with her extensive expertise, continue to leave an indelible mark on the nursing profession and the broader landscape of healthcare.

To learn more about Annmarie Waite, visit:

- **Website**: girlfriendshealth.com
- **Facebook**: Dr. Annmarie Waite
- **Instagram**: girlfriends_health

CHAPTER 23

THE EVOLUTION OF INNER-STANDING

By Janell Westley-Edwards

I t was my cousin's fault, this late-night terror.

We had been together earlier that day, goofing around as we always did. She had fourteen years on my twelve. She was visiting my home in Savannah, Georgia, from hers in Maryland—the two of us traveled together a lot, visiting family during the summer months. Those summers were filled with laughter and fun visiting uncles, aunties, and cousins. On this particular day, out together in the sticky heat of Savannah, she started a conversation about religion. (My religious coding was Catholic, and hers was Jehovah's Witness.)

"Whatcha gonna do when you die?" she asked me, her head cocked to one side. *As if I knew!*

"What do you mean?" I pressed.

"If you're not saved—," by which she meant in *her* way, in *her* faith, "then you're gonna go to hell."

It was far from the first time I'd heard such talk. I knew all about hell and salvation, but something about the way she asked—implying that if you weren't a Jehovah's Witness, you weren't going to heaven—shook me. Only a certain number of people would be allowed through the pearly gates, she told me. Would I be one of them? The thought left me dumbfounded and anxious.

What was *I going to do when I died?*

Why was I even here in the first place?

Why had God brought me here, if at the end there was a chance I'd end up in hell?

An inner turmoil bubbled up, such as I'd never experienced before. I tried to sleep that night but instead found myself pacing, wearing divots in the beige carpet of my childhood room, silently shouting my questions up to God. "Why? Why?" I asked. "What is this life for? Why am I here? Why didn't you just leave me where I was? Why did you bring me here to die?"

It felt like I'd suddenly discovered the punch line of some cruel joke. Did I have any control? Any say-so? And if I did, what was I supposed to do to make my life have any real meaning? My pleas were punctuated with surges of anger. I would rage and question and then collapse onto my bed. I muffled my cries with my pillow so that my parents—right across the hall—wouldn't hear my distress and come knocking. Mama would have said something like: "Janell, why are you so upset?"

"I don't know why a loving God would have us to come here to die!" It didn't seem like a convincing reason to be up so far past my bedtime.

That night in my childhood bedroom would prove to be the catalyst for every step I've taken since. But I didn't know it then. All I knew was that I needed some answers, and would you believe it? Eventually...they arrived.

Toward the end of the night, as the sun started to glint beyond my windows, a peace descended upon me. I felt a kind of calm I'd never felt before. I didn't hear actual words, but a response emanated up through my spirit, and somehow I knew it was the Spirit of God:

"OK, God, I want to understand you. I want to know what this existence is for. What's the end game?" It soothed my pounding heart. I could sleep.

God hadn't given me the answer, but maybe Spirit had dropped in the fortitude to start to live my questions.

———

I spent most of my life living up to being a good little girl. I was raised by two amazing parents, and I did all the things I was "supposed" to do. We had a middle-class life, and my parents were both pillars of our community. I went to private school until I graduated high school. I was a debutante and a Red Cross volunteer. I played basketball, volleyball, and softball, and was on the cheerleading squad. I performed and volunteered and smiled when I was supposed to smile. From the outside I lived up to every standard set out for me on the road to success.

In all those years I spent most of my time listening—to what my parents thought I should do, what my friends thought I should do, what my college advisors thought I should do. But always somewhere inside me lived the questions:

What am I here for? What is this human existence for? Why do we come here to die?

It wasn't until I met my first husband and married him for the first time (we'll get into it) that I started to stray from my prescribed coded path. My parents felt that I could do better, for reasons that might prove to be prophetic. He was the first man who challenged me, different from all the other suitors I'd been dating up until then. We dated exclusively for about six months, and shortly after, he asked me to marry.

We soon had our first child, a beautiful baby boy. It was then that problems started to arise. He lost his job, and his temper exploded. I suffered through it while straining to make our family healthy and cohesive. We went to counseling, separated, and then reconciled before we had our second child, our sweet baby girl. All the while our finances dwindled. We moved from a luxury apartment I had shared with my girlfriend in my single life to a small duplex home in the lower-income area of Savannah.

It was a tumultuous time, and it wasn't long before we finally divorced. I moved back into my parents' home with my two children, where I tried to start over again. After a year or so, tension died down between my ex and me as we co-parented our children. Then, because life is full of surprises, and because he presented a transformed version of himself—we found our way back to each other. I truly believed he'd changed and that things would be different this time.

We remarried, and soon our last baby boy, child number three, was born. Once again, from the outside my life looked just as it was supposed to: perfect.

My husband had come into some money from a large settlement, and we were living high in our beautiful home on Wilmington Island and driving the big whip—our Lincoln Navigator. Life was good, until soon what had seemed different slowly became the same. Again, I strained and suffered to make it work. Throughout this time, I was learning the scriptures, studying Greek and Hebrew. I became a ministry leader at our church. I attended church conferences, thirsty for the knowledge and inner-standing that my spirit craved.

What am I here for? What is this human existence for? Why do we come here to die?

I started a home-based business; I completed cosmetology school and received my master cosmetologist license. I was teaching, working at a salon, and building my home-based business—busy and productive, but still the questions that clung to me, like a cloak I couldn't shed, continued to get louder and louder:

WHAT AM I HERE FOR? WHAT IS THIS HUMAN EXISTENCE FOR? WHY DO WE COME HERE TO DIE?

I'd like to tell you that an answer dawned on me, enlightenment fell, and I knew my place in the universe in an instant. But that's not how it works. Growth is a gradual process of getting to *know* yourself, like becoming reacquainted with an old friend you never knew you lost.

I believe my first original thought was when I decided to move to Mississippi. All I knew was that I had to set myself free, free my mind from the embedded codes—put there by well-meaning others—that did not serve me any longer. My home-based business was doing exceptionally well, and I had created networks all over the country. I formed great relationships with a team out of Mississippi, and there was a profound need to establish economic sustainability in the small rural community there. So, to the dismay of my friends and family, I sold all my furniture, packed up my three young children and a U-Haul, and moved to Mississippi to continue to build my business. And my life.

It's funny how at the moments we are our freest, the world around us can be the most judgmental. It's why so many of us live in prisons of our own making. We live our lives to make the people external to us happy when our own inner beings are in turmoil. That's what I'd been doing, and what I refused to do any longer. The people around me thought I was nuts, leaving a good home, a good life, a good man. But I felt the happiest and most purposeful I'd ever felt.

I remember coming home to visit not long after I'd moved and running into an acquaintance in the local grocery store. He smiled when he saw me. "Heeeey!" He said in greeting, "You still crazy?"

I laughed. "Is that the word?"

"Yep."

"Well, I guess I'm still crazy then!" I told him. It holds true today. If crazy means following your joy. If crazy means breaking out of the chains that bind you and starting to really and truly live for yourself; if crazy means sending a self-created virus to disrupt the codes embedded in your subconscious mind by others—codes that do not serve your soul's purpose for being on this planet...then call me crazy.

For years, since that long, traumatic night in my bedroom, I had been growing slowly in this inner-standing: that in life we must write our own story. Our own coding. I told Spirit that I would do what it took to know the God Source mind inside of me, and stepping away from my life and into my inner being was the very first move toward that knowing.

Through all my life experiences, studying spirituality, watching countless podcasts, listening to a plethora of speakers, and reading numerous books, I have found that knowing *your* soul's purpose begins with answering two very important yet simple questions.

1. Does it feel good to me?

2. Is it working out for me?

The answers to both questions must be yes, simultaneously. It cannot be yes to one and no to the other. *Does it feel good to me?* meaning, Does it bring me joy and happiness in my body? My mind? My soul? And, *Is it working out for me?* meaning, Am I experiencing inner peace? Am I witnessing the positive impact on others? Is this making the world and humanity better?

When I left my life in Georgia and moved to Mississippi, I was the only one who could know the answers to these questions. *Did it feel good?* Only the best and most on-purpose it's ever felt! *Was it working out?* Sure, it was challenging. Moving, especially with three little children, isn't easy. But "working out" isn't about being easy and comfortable all the time. Working out means you're growing and evolving and moving closer and closer to your soul's purpose for being on this planet.

My failed marriages to the same man were an awakening. I learned over the span of those thirteen years that I was worthy of more; I was worthy of being my authentic self, I was worthy of being heard, and I didn't need anyone else to complete me. I am complete and whole within myself!

By leaving, I found my way to a true understanding of what my boundaries are. I stopped writing energy checks for things that wouldn't give me a return on my investment. I learned what it means to love someone in a relationship without needing them to complete me. My new husband is complete, and I am complete—we are two *whole* people who decide every day to be each other's help meet! His family has a large plot of land in Mississippi where we built an award-winning nonprofit organization, Fayette Community Service Organization (FCSO). It has helped us serve our rural community several times over through gardening, establishing a farmer's market, and working to build infrastructure for economic sustainability.

Where others saw poverty in our community, I saw potential. Under my direction FCSO has implemented the Seed to Need Gardening Project to help bring produce to what has long been considered a "food desert." My husband and I created the annual FAT to Fit Olympic Games (FTFOG), an evidence-based community health engagement program to eradicate childhood obesity. We've created youth intervention programs of all sorts and served on task forces and action committees to uplift this region. Most recently, *Our Mississippi Magazine* named me one of the Top 25 Most Influential African Americans in the State of Mississippi, and I was recognized as Nexstar Media Group's Remarkable Woman for the State of Mississippi 2022–23.

So, is it working out for me? Yes indeed, it is!

When I stood in that bedroom at twelve years young, I wanted to know everything. I wanted to understand why we are and how we are, and what we're here for. God is still in the process of answering that question, and might take my whole life to do it. But in the meantime, I've stepped closer and closer to knowing.

What am I here for? To graduate from Earth School as a spiritual being having human experiences, to deliver the gifts hidden deep inside from the Creator, to serve humanity by showing up in the highest frequency of love in every situation.

What is this human existence for? This human experience is for data collection for the God Source based on the five senses. We are small parts of a whole, here to represent the infinite perspectives of mankind, sharing our understanding through thoughts and emotions stored in the shared subconscious.

Why do we come here to die? We don' t come here to die, because energy does not die; it only transmutes into other forms. Once we leave the form of the human body, we transmute back to the spiritual essence of Source endowed with all the emotional knowledge of a human existence.

Your inner being is like your piece of God on the inside, helping you see what the future holds and what the right steps are. If you listen, you can create the life you want. All you have to do is stop entrusting your joy, peace, and happiness to the codes of others. Listen to your inner being, the God Source who has all the answers for your soul's purpose, and begin the journey of inner-standing *yourself.*

About Janell

Janell Westley-Edwards is a born leader, a humanitarian, and an inspiration specialist. She is driven by compassion and love, as she takes supreme confidence in providing the best thought-provoking knowledge possible.

As a mathematics teacher, master cosmetologist, live radio/social media talk show host, public speaker, entrepreneur, published author, and executive director of an award-winning nonprofit organization, her goals are to share her experiences with other young men and women (including youths) to impart knowledge that will help elevate them to the *next level of greatness* in their personal life's journey.

Edwards has received numerous awards and recognitions that span twenty-plus years, including, but not limited to, being crowned Miss Savannah State College 1989–90 (now Savannah State University), receiving a Bachelor of Science Degree from Savannah State College, becoming a member of Delta Sigma Theta Sorority Inc., being appointed by Sen. Sally Doty as Sub-Committee Chair under the State and Local Action Committee of Governor Phil Bryant's Healthy Teens for a Better Mississippi Taskforce, being honored as *Our Mississippi Magazine*'s number 12 of the 25 Most Influential African Americans in the State of Mississippi, and being cofounder of the annual FAT to Fit Olympic Games, created to eradicate the epidemic of childhood obesity.

For her dedicated work as executive director of the award-winning nonprofit, she has been recognized by notable academia; local, state, and federal government officials; and radio and television entities, with her most recent accolade being Nexstar Media Group's Remarkable Woman recognition for the State of Mississippi 2022–23 and this particular accolade being recorded in the September 14, 2022, 117th edition of the United States Congressional Record by the Honorable Bennie G. Thompson of the State of Mississippi and a congratulatory video made from the governor of Mississippi, Tate Reeves.

Edwards has an impassioned and extraordinary commitment to fostering health and wealth among young men and women through service and guidance. She has planned, implemented, and created fun interactive programs, events, and workshops throughout her tenure. She has been invited to speak on stages since 2004. She has dedicated thousands of hours to studying personal power and reaching one's greatest life potential. She has taken this knowledge and developed a fun, interesting, interactive, and *highly* impactful Life Is a Puzzle, Life Is a Game workshop.

CHAPTER 24

THE CRY OF THE VOICELESS

Finding Light in the Darkest Corners of the World

By Keiko Izushi

As I reflect on my career with the UN World Food Programme (WFP), first at headquarters in Rome, Italy, and then spanning diverse corners of the globe, including Cambodia, Bangladesh, Indonesia, Afghanistan, Kyrgyzstan, and many more—I am humbled by the vast experiences woven into the fabric of my journey. Serving as a leader among a global team dedicated to ending world hunger, I have lived in and/or visited some seventy countries. Each encounter marked my understanding of humanity's shared struggles and the wonder of triumph.

Decades ago this was a dream I dared to nurture without fully comprehending the challenges that lay ahead. Yet with each step of the journey, the depth of experience and breadth of insight grew exponentially, shaping me into the leader, advocate, and humanitarian I would become.

CAMBODIA

The bustling streets were a symphony of chaos and determination, pulsating with the rhythm of existence. Tuk-Tuks zipped through narrow alleyways, horns beeping while leaving a petro odor in their wake. Their engines echoed against weathered walls adorned with colorful murals depicting stories of victory and tragedy.

Amid the hustle and bustle, the air was thick with the scent of spices mingling with perfumes and the sweet aroma of tropical fruits or street foods. Market vendors called out in a melodic chorus, their voices blending with the chatter of locals haggling over the day's catch or the freshest produce.

But an undeniable heaviness lingered—individuals robbed of limbs languished on pavements, their eyes imploring for mercy. Haunted by ubiquitous land mines, Cambodia bore witness to innocent lives altered by hidden terrors. Unaware of the danger, curious children approached these malevolent relics, mistaking them for toys until tragedy struck—a cruel irony echoing in distant corners.

My sojourn in 2000, through the heart of Phnom Penh, Cambodia, revealed a portrayal of despair and resilience. Walking alongside a Japanese donor to the WFP project sites, little did I anticipate the vivid scenes we encountered—a haunting display of land mine–inflicted suffering, a cruel legacy of a bygone war. The journey unveiled scars on bodies and the collective psyche of a people crippled by history.

In my tenure of nearly three decades working for the United Nations System, I've traversed the agonizing landscapes of war and disaster, bearing witness to the haunting echoes of starving children and vulnerable populations. Yet against this somber backdrop, I've glimpsed the undeniable spirit of humanity.

Tales of tragic family histories, brutal regimes, and a repeating darkness unfolded. Covered with a putrid odor from acrid, gray air and smokey fumes, "Smokey Mountain," Stueng Mean Chey, is Phnom Penh's municipal rubbish dump. Thousands work there, including hundreds of children, recycling the city's rubbish dumped there by trucks every day. I encountered orphaned children sifting through refuse, their tiny hands injured from the needles, glass, and metal among whatever recyclable material and food they found.

As we strolled toward a village on the edge of this wasteland, a baby girl in a surprisingly decent dress caught my eye. The mother thrust the child toward me, her cries echoing anguish. It was explained to me that through tearful pleas, the mother implored,

"Take this girl with you!" believing her child would have a brighter future under my care. Overwhelmed, tears streaming down my face, I pondered the unthinkable choices borne of dire circumstances.

Fortunately, beacons of light emerged amid the shadows. An NGO provided shelter, housing, and essential skills and tools needed to forge a new path of hope for a brighter future. The UN World Food Programme, a lifeline against hunger, provided food assistance and nourishment to empty bellies.

Soon after, a restaurant was built by the children of carpenters in training and painted by an art learning group. They served foods cooked by a culinary team trained by a former celebrity chef, who volunteered his time to the project. Meals were served by boys who were learning about tourism and hospitality. I remember the meals were the best I have had in any restaurant in the world, in a sunny atmosphere painted with bright colors. The children's big, proud smiles showed their joy in serving and making their guests happy. Classes for aspiring restaurateurs, beauty professionals, and more blossomed, creating a symphony from the hands of eager learners.

In the face of adversity, the resilient spirit of Cambodia shone through, encapsulated in the smiles of children determined to forge a brighter tomorrow from the ashes of their past.

BANGLADESH

Moving to Cox's Bazar, Bangladesh, a makeshift haven emerged—a testament to ethnic cleansing and the displacement of the Rohingya people. A lifeline was woven through joint efforts with the Bangladesh government amid this somber landscape. Vegetable gardens sprouted amid rudimentary conditions, offering fragile sanctuary.

Life persisted in camps threatened by floods—families formed, and children found solace in play, oblivious to the complexities of the daily affairs of humankind.

During a visit to a stopgap structure to meet with the beneficiaries, it was revealed that one woman was pregnant, her large belly indicating she was soon to be a first-time mother. She sat silently, looking down, in the dimly lit and stiflingly humid space, her expression a mixture of confusion and sadness, haunted by desperation. Yet within the darkness her commitment and determination shone through—a belief in new beginnings, a testament to the indomitable spirit that refuses to be extinguished.

INDONESIA

During my tenure in Indonesia from 2002–2007, a chapter of profound significance unfolded, marking a pivotal moment in my journey with the World Food Programme. It was a time when the resilience of the human spirit clashed with the ferocity of nature's wrath—a time when the Aceh Tsunami left devastation in its wake, shattering lives and communities with merciless force.

As I stepped onto the shores of Aceh, the magnitude of the devastation struck me with an intensity that words fail to capture. The once vibrant coastline lay in ruins. Nothing was left except some coconut trees and a huge steel ship in the middle of nowhere, and I wondered, "What force could bring this gigantic lump of iron to the middle of the land?" Yet amid the muddy soils and despair, there burned a flame of hope—the people in the community started to pick themselves up, helping the old and vulnerable, a flicker of resilience that refused to be ignored.

Assigned to the WFP's emergency food-assistance operation, I witnessed firsthand the profound impact of our efforts in alleviating the suffering inflicted by the tsunami. Biscuits fortified with vitamins and minerals were provided at schools so children could return to study. Our global teams worked tirelessly to ensure that no one was left behind in their hour of need—things only humans can do for other human beings out of compassion from the very heart.

Beyond the logistics and numbers it was the human stories that etched themselves into my soul—the tear-stained faces of mothers grateful for a meal to feed their children, the weary smiles of survivors finding solace in the midst of desperation, the resilient spirit of a community refusing to be defined by tragedy.

AFGHANISTAN

I was stationed with the WFP in Kabul, Afghanistan, from 2013–2015, shouldering the head of donor relations, reports, and communication responsibilities. Despite the precarious security conditions, I ventured beyond the safety of my office. I wanted to understand the true impact of our efforts by meeting the beneficiaries face-to-face.

Draped in a burka to navigate the cultural expectations of Afghan society, even under the scorching summer sun, I traveled in an armored vehicle—to connect with those whose lives were touched by the WFP's food assistance. Our Food for Education and Training initiative aimed at empowering girls by providing a monthly family ration of nutrition-enriched wheat flour and oil upon completing literacy and skills training. These skills included tailoring, poultry production, carpet weaving, and tree nursery establishment.

Young women seized the opportunity to read and write within the confines of a cramped training center and against societal norms. I witnessed a poignant moment as sixteen-year-old Fatma confidently approached the whiteboard, inscribing her name. In her wake a chorus of names followed—a tangible declaration of identity, proof that they existed in a world that often overlooked their presence. Never was I more proud of the role of our food provision in empowering these girls to become proud individuals.

The overwhelming gratitude of these young women resonated deeply within me. In a curious moment of self-reflection I posed a difficult question that would inadvertently expose my ignorance. "If you like the training so much, would you be willing to attend the course for three hours a day for three months, even without food?" The immediate response was etched with the word *impossible* on their faces. Without family support their fathers, husbands, or brothers would never permit her to attend and learn. The incentive was not for the girls but rather for the men around them. The privilege to learn was a transaction, an exchange for food and sustenance for those they represented at home.

I felt shame for my lack of understanding, underestimating the girls' determination and the intricate complexities of their lives. These young girls, reminiscent of teenagers worldwide, reveled in the joy of learning, relishing the camaraderie forged in that small space. They clung to optimism, aspiring for a future even in the face of daunting circumstances—resilience deepening following the Taliban's assumption of power. I hoped the girls we touched would eventually become mothers, fostering the next generation with the same patience, resilience, and determination.

As I departed from that small haven of hope, my prayers lingered with those resilient young women. Their courage, often concealed and voiceless, was the silent keystone of our shared history. Thanks to the unwavering courage of these women and others in history, humanity has not only survived but triumphed against all odds, paving the way for a future anchored in hope and resilience.

KYRGYZSTAN

I concluded my incredible journey and my final post as the deputy representative (2016–2020) and bore witness to the WFP's steadfast efforts in spearheading poverty-reduction programs to combat climate change and ensure food security. The country gained its independence from the USSR in 1991 but had an adverse effect after independence, with the harsh reality of poverty and endless efforts to build a new nation. Despite enduring tumultuous power shifts and political changes, I witnessed the resilience of ordinary people shining through. They carried the torch of their beautiful culture and traditions within the country's breathtaking landscapes, offering a glimpse of hope for future generations.

Amid the chaos of the 2020 global pandemic, overseeing operations while safeguarding the well-being of staff and their families was a monumental challenge. Yet our operations persisted without pause, driven by the unwavering strength of humanity to assist the most vulnerable–a humbling experience, to say the least. When I close my eyes, I can still see their faces and tears, behind which lies an unshakable commitment to carry on in the face of adversity, refusing to let go of the torch. It's a vision and a memory I will never forget.

These diverse country experiences have profoundly impacted me and created unforgettable memories that have shaped me into the person I am today.

A Girl's Dream

Among three daughters, I was in the middle—skinny and shy. At age ten, I agreed to embark on a journey to Europe with a student group during the summer holidays. Scared but curious, what unfolded was an experience that left an indelible mark on my young soul.

In Sheffield, England, I encountered the wonders of studying English for the first time, relishing English breakfasts in the university cafeteria, surrounded by green fields and the soulful tunes of a guitar playing the Beatles song "Yesterday." The majestic churches of Paris invoked awe, and tears flowed naturally as I gazed upon the Pieta in Vatican City. Italy brought the joy of discovering the pasta, a previously unknown taste. This adventure was a gateway that opened my eyes to the world and shaped the course of my life. I owe immense gratitude to my parents for providing this opportunity and early experience, which stirred within me a profound awakening. The kaleidoscope of cultures, the taste of unfamiliar delicacies, and the awe-inspiring landmarks ignited a passion to dream big and bold. At that tender age a seed was planted—an ambitious dream to "save the world" to alleviate the pervasive hunger that haunted so many lives.

THE HOPE OF RESILIENCE

As I sit down to inscribe my experiences, extending across nearly three decades, I find myself entwined in a delicate tension—woven with threads of tragedy and the unbeatable beauty of the human spirit. The vivid memories of the dire cry of the voiceless, the haunting scenes of anguish and hunger, cast a weight upon my heart. Yet a glimmer of hope emerges—a resilience inherent in the human condition, a light that persists even in the darkest corners of despair.

It is a privilege to carry these poignant stories to a world often devoid of the context of such struggles. Amid these reflections, I uncover a profound sense of purpose—an imperative to persist as a voice for those whose stories go unheard, to illuminate the unseen resilience flourishing amid adversity, and to aspire toward a world where these narratives aren't just tales of hardship but tributes of hope to those who struggled and overcame against all odds.

As you read through these reflections, consider the intricate weaving of *your* resilience—the strength that resides within you, capable of facing life's complexities and uncertainties. The human spirit's resilience is not just a collective lesson but an invitation to explore the boundless potential within.

These narratives of tribulation and triumph are not meant to simply inform or entertain. No, they are meant to invite you to consider how your own resilience can be harnessed for good, how your actions can ripple outward, shaping a world brimming with compassion and hope. Let these stories not merely wash over you but stir within you a fervent call to action—a challenge to step forward, to be an active participant in crafting a brighter tomorrow.

For it is in the active pursuit of positive change where the true essence of resilience is realized, not just in weathering the storms of life but in bravely charting a course toward a future steeped in kindness and possibility.

May these stories ignite a spark within you and serve as a catalyst for your journey toward making a meaningful difference around you and in the world.

About Keiko

Renowned as a two-time TEDx speaker, international best-selling author, and Effective Results Coach, Keiko Izushi is a beacon of inspiration and resilience. She spent more than twenty-five years with the United Nations World Food Programme, where she played a pivotal role in advocating for global peace and eradicating hunger.

A distinguished figure in the realm of global leadership, Keiko's dream to heal the world traces back to her childhood, where at age ten, a summer in Europe opened her eyes to the world and ignited a passion to help others. Armed with a master's in agricultural economics, poverty, and development, as well as an MBA, she embarked on a career with the United Nations, serving in diverse locations such as WFP headquarters in Rome, Italy; Indonesia; Afghanistan; Japan; and Kyrgyzstan. Fluent in five languages, including Japanese, English, Spanish, French, and Italian, Keiko traversed more than seventy countries, leaving an indelible mark on communities worldwide.

In 2018, Keiko's encounter with world-renowned motivational speaker Lisa Nichols in San Diego became a turning point. Contemplating the impact of her voice on changing the world, Keiko transformed her UN experiences into two TEDx talks, international best-selling books, and the establishment of the Harum Sari Retreat in Ubud, Indonesia. This sanctuary, born from Keiko's realization of the need for personal peace, has become a haven for healing.

In *Against All Odds*, Keiko shares the poignant stories she witnessed during her tenure with the WFP—tales of starvation, famine, and the resilience of those facing adversity in places like the smokey mountains of Cambodia and war-torn Afghanistan. Her message resonates deeply: within us lies the strength to thrive against all odds.

Recognized with an honorary doctorate from University Azteca Mexico, Keiko authored *What Grandma Taught Me: World Tribute to Grandmothers and Their Legacies*. A sought-after speaker, she addresses schools and business communities in Japan. Married with a son, Keiko now calls Bali, Indonesia, home. Her life story is a testament to the power of resilience, compassion, and the unwavering commitment to making the world a better place. Explore more about her impactful work at izushikeiko.com and harumsariretreat.com.

CHAPTER 25

UNCHECKING BOXES

By Dr. Fred Harvey

*"Your life does not get better by chance;
it gets better by change."*
—JIM ROHN

You could say that I've been in medicine since I was four years old, because that's when I would follow my father around when he would make his rounds. My dad was a doctor, and so was my brother, my uncle, and my great-uncle. My grandmother was a nurse, my mother was a nurse, my cousin was a med tech, and my other cousin was a nurse. So I guess medicine was the family business, and it was assumed that I would go that way as well. But I really did love it; I had the desire and the interest, so it made sense for me to become a doctor too.

I was a Doogie Howser kind of doctor, which is one of those young kids who got fast-tracked through the entire educational process. I interviewed for medical school when I was a senior in high school and got into a five-year premedical program with Penn State and Jefferson University. When I started this program, I knew this would be a challenge, but I thought, "Hey, I can do this; it will be fun." Well, it was not fun. Not in the least. But I did like the people that I took care of, my classmates, and a few of my teachers. I completed the program and was a doctor at twenty-three.

Looking back, the emotional trauma for a concentrated medical school program like that is way too much for a teenager. I mean the psychological manipulation that happens in medical school and residency, it really is abuse; it takes so much out of the most well-adjusted young adult, but it can absolutely wreck a teenager. It changes you, alters your personality, and it trains a person to put up with a grueling workload, extreme stress, and long hours. It can really affect faith and self-esteem.

As I said, I started my career as a doctor at twenty-three, and I quickly realized that medicine was about the relationship with the patient and the doctor. Which was a great realization, except that the challenge was when you're working in a practice where you see thirty-five patients in the office each day and then another fifteen at the hospital. By doing this, there is little time for a patient-doctor relationship, and that's what happened when I joined a medical group after residency. It looked like a premier internal-medicine practice from the outside but really was more of a patient factory and worse.

Work was busy and kept getting busier until there was a point where I was actually working harder as a practicing doctor than I did during my residency. I remember one holiday weekend I had three hours of sleep that entire three-day weekend. I was exhausted. My marriage was suffering from the long hours and stress. I suggested to the group that we reduce the on-calls we did for the local hospital, but because this was about a third of our practice, that didn't happen. Days seemed endless, and nights too short. I was practically living at the hospital on a diet of donuts, coffee, sausage bagel sandwiches, and whatever else the hospital cafeteria had to throw at me. Each missed dinner took me further from my family. Sometimes when we get so focused on what we think is the right thing to do, we lose sight of what is truly important. Have you ever felt like you lost sight of what makes you joyful?

Finally I officially asked to have my workload lightened to give me time to work on my relationship with my wife, which was suffering at the time, but that request was not approved or even really considered. Which, looking back should not have surprised me, because almost everyone I worked with was impaired in some way. In our practice one person was hooked on benzodiazepines and alcohol, another one was an opiate addict, another was embezzling, one partner was doing Medicare fraud, and one of the partners was having an affair in the office only days after the birth of his new child. It was a nightmare practice. But I just kept working harder and harder because that's what spiritually and emotionally unhealthy people do. Then they get physically unhealthy.

During this time I was trapped by contracts and obligations that seemed impossible to fulfill. The tension seethed in my muscles, and I was so tightly wound that I started to get horrible back pain, but like most men, I just took ibuprofen, got in the hot tub, and pushed myself through the day. That seemed to work for a while, until one day I got out of bed and fell flat on my face. Literally.

I hit the floor and stopped in shock. I tried to move. NO! It felt as if someone had put a hot poker in the middle of my lower back, and that's when I realized that my right leg was completely paralyzed. I was only thirty-three years old; I thought this shouldn't be happening. There was no physical injury or trauma to the leg, which meant that it was completely anger and toxicity had crushed the disc, which had popped out and pressed against the nerve, which paralyzed my right leg. And as I lay there, I thought, "How did I get here?" I realized over the next weeks that I was responsible for what had happened. I had stopped caring for the important relationships in my life. I had stopped loving myself and caring for my temple. I had lost faith. I was joyless.

I crawled across the floor and made it back to bed and started to put a plan together. I had to fix this. My spiritual, psychological, and physical health were what was important, not this toxic practice. Fortunately I could take time off to get well. My best friend was a neurologist, and his wife was an amazing physical therapist, so they were some of my first phone calls, and we started working together. Then I went to a neurosurgeon who was a very conservative guy, who looked at the MRI of my back, and I saw his eyes get really big when he did.

"Mike," I asked, "how can we fix this nonsurgically?"

So we all came up with a plan. I took steroids, muscle relaxants, narcotics, everything. I went to a local holistic nurse for energy medicine, and I slowly began to get some energy back. I found two types of chiropractors, one that does just the upper neck and one that does the whole back. I received acupuncture; I got herbal remedies. I didn't want to be addicted to the narcotics, but I was also afraid of the pain, so I just kept doing little things that made the pain better. I took healthy steps each day, and it got me stronger. I meditated and prayed. Yoga was really important, and then I slowly got back into walking and weight lifting. I changed my diet and my relationships.

I was dedicated and went to physical therapy every day and received Reiki therapy, polarity therapy, and homeopathy. I did every possible non-Western medical approach there was, and within three months the paralysis was gone, and I stopped steroids and muscle relaxants. Within six months the pain was gone. And I weaned myself off the opiates. I maintained with nutrition, yoga, walking, herbal remedies, and homeopathy as well as regular chiropractic, massage, prayer, and meditation.

I did it. Through a nonsurgical, holistic method, I had gone from paralyzed and broken to strong and healthy. I was functional again! Physically, mentally, and spiritually I was all there! Because of all this I began to review these personal experiences to see how I could change my approach as a physician. How could I use this incredible example to help more people? I began to focus on the important details of what I learned and jettison all the distractions that I had been taught during my time in that medical office.

Up until that point, if I had a patient who came in with a runny nose, the normal process would be to give the patient a pill for the runny nose. This is called reactionary medicine or illness care. But what if I transitioned from this standard Western approach to actual healthcare? More questions need to be answered. Why do they have a runny nose? What's causing it?

Hippocrates would have evaluated his patients' *dieta*. This Greek word, which means "mode of life," has become the modern word for *diet* (habitually taken food or drink), but it goes way beyond that. *Dieta* covers everything about you: what you eat, when you eat it, whom you eat it with, whom you sleep with, whom you work with, what kind of work you do, where you work. It includes the time spent indoors, time spent outdoors, how much water and alcohol you drink, how much sleep you get. Because all these things matter.

Over a year a typical patient will most likely have an annual physical with cholesterol and sugar tests and possibly a prostate exam or Pap smear. But there is no information from these tests that will empower the patient's health in any way. None. It may help give guidance on illness risks and an opportunity for a shiny new prescription, but that does not improve health.

So I began to wonder what the flip side of this was. Well, that would be a deep dive into a patient's full history and finding out how they live, what they eat, why they eat, what they do for stress, what causes stress. But no one in a traditional illness practice has time to ask all these questions. Plus, there are several things a doctor needs to ask a patient in the current system that if they don't, the insurance company won't pay them.

Think about this concept: a doctor has to mark 95 percent of the checkboxes to get Medicare or insurance to pay them. But what if you've known somebody for twenty years—you're going to ask them if they've ever smoked every time they visit? It's a waste of time, but the current system is requiring us to waste time because some bureaucrat decided that these boxes need to be checked to prove that the doctor is doing the job. In my career I've never checked one of those boxes, because I don't care if I get bad grades on busywork. It has nothing to do with healthcare! It has to do with insurance companies monitoring doctors to improve profit for shareholders and bureaucrats justifying jobs.

By eliminating meaningless routines like this, we can spend time on actually talking with the patient and developing a solid physician-patient relationship. One based on trust and understanding where the physician, who understands the patient's background and life, can make solid recommendations to improve their health, not just one ailment, but in every aspect. Then the patient can choose because the patient has control over their life and their health.

In Western medicine we give the patient very few choices. "Do what we say, or you'll die" is usually how it goes. And the truth is, there is usually no actual evidence that the patient will die from that issue.

Let's say the doctor recommends a cardiac stent. Should the patient have the stent? Specialist answer: yes. Why? Because they may get better, and many people have survived having a stent. So the process is to default to the next expensive procedure because our current medical delivery system doesn't allow us to do the right thing, which is care for the patient in all areas of their health. In reality, medical management, controlling symptoms, is less costly and has fewer adverse consequences than stents.

In my career I have seen many women and men have their gall-bladders removed for no real valid clinical reason. And after they did, they still have the right upper quadrant pain. Why? Because they still have the wheat and dairy allergy or bacterial overgrowth that was causing the abdominal pain to begin with.

The same is true with a patient who has mood changes. Depression and anxiety are not diseases but descriptions. Bad mood can be caused by many things, such as food sensitivity, mercury and lead toxicity, infections, and mold exposures. Stopping gluten intake or removing mercury from the body will change mood and in many cases eliminate the issue entirely! Too often we see that mood symptoms are treated with mood-altering drugs, rather than looking for the *why* of the problem and getting rid of it. Permanently. Primary care is focused on managing chronic disease, but let's eliminate disease instead!

I realized that I wanted my medical practice to focus on transformation because that's what's important. I want to help people transform their lives. I want to help my patients get relief from chronic pain, brain fog, and fatigue to get their mojo back. I want them thriving by creating a partnership between the doctor and the patient.

I can work with the patient and show them all kinds of techniques. I can provide for their access to all kinds of tools and provide all kinds of information. But unless the patient trusts me, unless the patient believes that I genuinely want what's best for them, it doesn't matter. It's only through the cooperation and the relationship—that's how transformation happens.

This past year I met Lisa Nichols at the When My Soul Speaks workshop, which was truly amazing and transformative. In her community you work with the other people going through the program, and you help one another and hold one another accountable. And that's exactly how our world needs to work, as a team, as a family of choice that helps people lift up. I was called to a new level of commitment to my career through Lisa's work. And that's what I want to create in my healthcare community, both virtual and live, a transformative environment designed to help and support one another in living healthy and important lives.

As I end this chapter, I'll leave you with one wish. And that's to take the time—to really take the time. Give yourself the moments you need to be with yourself, to get calm, to get ready, to be resilient, to plan, to be you, and to *love yourself* as you would your creator, because you are your life's cocreator. And if you feel yourself reaching for that medication at the first symptom that comes along, stop, breathe, and listen to your body and feel it. Spend a few moments trying to determine where that symptom came from.

And down that path is where the new you awaits. Are you ready to start your journey to abundant health?

About Dr. Harvey

With an illustrious career spanning over three decades, Dr. Harvey stands as the longest-standing functional medicine physician in the Sarasota community, earning recognition for his expertise in addressing a wide array of health concerns.

Dr. Fred Harvey obtained his medical doctorate at Thomas Jefferson University in Philadelphia and completed his residency at Mercy Catholic Medical Center. His commitment to advancing medical knowledge and improving patient outcomes has propelled him to the forefront of functional medicine.

As the host of *The Healthy Steps Radio Show*, Dr. Harvey utilizes his platform to educate the public on a variety of health topics. His passion is in helping people recover from chronic illness, including addressing fatigue, symptomatic aging, insomnia, chronic Lyme disease, fibromyalgia, allergies, Alzheimer's, dementia, heart disease, pain, sleep issues, hormonal imbalances, weight problems, COVID long haul, and mold toxicity.

With a quadruple board certification in internal medicine, geriatric medicine, functional medicine, and holistic/integrative medicine, Dr. Harvey's expertise is both comprehensive and highly regarded.

Dr. Harvey's philosophy centers on preventing disease rather than merely treating symptoms. His approach to healthcare emphasizes personalized, one-on-one care, empowering patients to be proactive in understanding and meeting their bodies' unique needs.

Affiliated with esteemed organizations such as the American Academy of Environmental Medicine, the American College for the Advancement of Medicine, and the Institute of Functional Medicine, Dr. Harvey remains at the forefront of medical advancements and holistic approaches to wellness. He was a founding member of the scientific board of Xymogen, the premier nutraceutical company.

With over thirty years' experience, Dr. Harvey has become a trusted figure in the Sarasota medical community. His commitment to preventative medicine aligns with the evolving landscape of healthcare, emphasizing the importance of lifestyle, nutrition, and holistic practices in achieving optimal well-being.

Dr. Harvey is also an author of *Against All Odds*, coauthored with

Lisa Nichols, which is coming out August 2024 and will be available on Amazon.

Dr. Fred Harvey is highly recognized for his exceptional contributions to the field of medicine. His dedication to preventative healthcare and patient well-being has left an indelible mark on the Sarasota community and beyond!

CHAPTER 26

SICK, FAT, AND SLOW? NO, NO!

*How to Heal Your Gut and Feel
Phenomenal at Any Age*

By Jackie Bowker

W hen I was a teenager, I fell in love. And boy, I fell hard. I was infatuated with, enamored by, and obsessed with…sweets. Anything sugary. Throughout my teens and twenties I indulged in this love affair, carrying evidence of my dirty little secret everywhere. I was a successful corporate executive, and while my colleagues carried notebooks and laptops in their handbags, I had candy.

After a long workday, I would walk home in anticipation of a supermarket stop, filling my basket with snake gummies, Chicos, Jelly Babies, Milk Bottles, Strawberries and Cream, those little candy Coke bottles, and Minties. (Ahhh, the Minties.)

I'd make awkward conversation with the cashier about having a party. Then, on the way home, I'd rip into everything straight away. Stuffing my face and reveling in the familiar sugar rush. It was *so* good.

One day while living in New York, my husband and I were going to brunch with Uncle Dave and Auntie Marilyn. I was so excited—to see them, obviously, but mostly because they were taking us to a fancy Upper East Side restaurant. It was winter, and I was wearing my puffy jacket. I could see my breath as I dreamed of what I was going to order. Three fluffy pancakes drenched in maple syrup, cream, and ice cream. When they arrived, I tucked in, eating every last morsel.

I sopped up the last of the syrup, hearing my mom's voice in my head. "You can't watch television until you've finished everything on your plate." As we walked out of the restaurant, a now familiar feeling overcame me. My body started shaking. Despite the cold, sweat dripped down my face and soaked my clothes. My heart raced. Everything went blurry.

I made it to the park bench just in time. Feeling like I was going to pass out, I opened my bag, fumbling for my self-discovered remedy: a banana and a diet Sprite. A few minutes after consuming both, I could see clearly again, but this episode scared me enough to see a doctor.

After a finger prick and some lab results, the doctor told me I wasn't diabetic. "Everything's normal, Jacqueline."

I was confused. I didn't feel *normal*.

At the time, I didn't think to question what the good doctors told me about my own body. I assumed they knew best. I continued the banana-and-diet-Sprite technique to manage my episodes.

Banana. Diet Sprite. Another banana. Another Sprite. Another and another—for nearly five years.

I didn't look sick from the outside, but my health continued to decline. My body was riddled with viruses. I couldn't function like I wanted, and doctors told me I must cut back on my working hours. I had two small children, my husband frequently traveled for work, and most days I'd get the kids home from childcare, throw together something (anything) for dinner, and end up asleep on my children's bedroom floor before they were asleep themselves.

Finally, after yet another doctor visit, I got my answer. Hypoglycemia.

"Thank goodness," I thought. "A diagnosis!"

That euphoria lasted about five minutes. Then I realized the diagnosis was only that. There was no plan to get me better. Again, I was left confused and frustrated.

I was sick and tired of being sick and tired. I was done with being exhausted, and I learned something. The medical industry does a lot of good saving lives, but it's failing us. It's not designed to help us feel phenomenal in our bodies. Today's biggest issue is that we're getting sick, fat, and slow. More depressed. More infertile. Yet when we listen to debates or news reports about what's wrong with our world, this is absent from the conversation.

I realized I had a choice. I could stay suffering or take my power back and create possibility. Learn how to advocate for myself. I left my corporate job to learn everything I could about why illness starts, where symptoms come from, and how to use food as medicine to restore function to my body. I gained two master's degrees, in science and nutrition, and a diploma in functional nutrition. I specialized in the areas of gluten and energy psychology so I could understand the mind's power. I launched a podcast with top health subject matter experts from around the world. I established a global gut and nutrition private practice, which I ran for seven years, helping thousands of people in Australia and around the globe recover from seemingly impossible health issues.

What I discovered shocked me to my core. Our food system is utterly broken. We spend over $4.3 trillion on healthcare—mostly on preventable chronic disease. Our academic performance is declining because our kids are cognitively impaired due to the food they're eating. There's increasing violence, aggression, and divisiveness, which are tied to the mental health crisis, which is also linked to food.

I'm here to explode some myths. And I want to explode them because I bought them. I lived them. My father lived them. My mother. My husband. Maybe you've bought them too.

The biggest myth of all is that it's natural between your forties and sixties to get fat, sick, and slow. To lose focus and to gain weight. That your body must change. That's all wrong.

What if we rejected this myth being handed to us? I don't know about you, but I came here to be healthy, lean, and trailblazing. I'm done with the conversation that as we age, we get worse…like a beat-up car ready for the junkyard. I'm exhausted with our society allowing illnesses to keep going. If you agree, you're in the right place!

Our bodies don't age and naturally decline. We age and decline by what we feed, think about, and do to our bodies. I started aging my body by eating candy. Then drinking. Then partying. Pizzas. Sleepless nights. Overexercising. Late nights working.

By the same token, though, you can begin to *unage* your body whenever you choose.

You might be suffering right now in some place in your life. You shouldn't have to! Maybe you're not getting enough sleep, or you need sleeping medication, or your stomach talks back at you after you eat. If that's you, know you don't have to stay in suffering any longer. As long as we stay inside suffering, bloating, lack of sleep, fatigue, and brain fog, we're choosing to *age* our bodies instead of being the authors of our health stories.

Not to mention there's big money in keeping you ignorant about how to restore your body. Our ignorance is someone else's income, and it's profitable. Antidiabetic medication alone is a fifty-billion-dollar industry. Here's the truth: the pharmaceutical and healthcare industries are the largest funders of government, news, medical groups, and most institutes.

I hope you can tell by now I'm committed to the whole truth. Even if it's not popular.

Did you know diabetes is expected to grow annually by 3.2 percent, with more than 38.4 million adults in the United States currently diagnosed with diabetes? That's 11 percent of the population. More concerning is the 8.7 million currently undiagnosed. (These statistics are publicly available from the CDC). Roughly 25 percent of young adults have prediabetes, 20 percent of teens have fatty liver disease, and 50 percent of teens are now overweight or obese. That number's 80 percent for adults. This is a *man-made* disease. Which means it's preventable.

This truly is the biggest issue we face. There has been a 500 percent increase since 1980 in diet and lifestyle diseases, and they alone cause 6.7 million deaths annually. With three-quarters of men, two-thirds of women, and one-quarter of children overweight or obese, surely there's a better way.

So I invite you, against the odds, to become a health resetter.

Resetting is the ability to make a clean slate. Rebuilding is the ability to create a new body. Remember, the biggest myth of all is that you can't reset your body.

I got back my leanness, health, vitality, and speed. I have energy to run with my son. I can cartwheel with my daughter, who's a dancer. I have the legs to ride for thirty kilometers before 6:00 a.m. It's possible.

To me, the moment there's one exception to the rule, it's no longer a rule. It's just people's experience. Every day, I'm grateful for the ability to restart my health and be in control of my health destiny.

How to Reset, Rebuild, and Revitalize *Your* Health

I want to share three things that really helped me and will put you on a path to being a health resetter too!

1. JERF. (Just eat real food.)

When Jackie today looks back at young Jackie, I understand why she loved sugar. Sugar is addictive. When this Jackie looks back at that Jackie, I have compassion. I love her. I care for her. She didn't know she was slowly shortening her life. I never forget young Jackie. Jackie today isn't perfect, but she is wiser.

In retrospect, the most alarming thing I've seen is that our food is making people sicker and sicker. The ultra-processed food industry has designed addictive food. Fast-food and processed-food companies are about a sixteen-trillion-dollar industry globally. We, including our children, are being poisoned by toxic food, and every chronic disease is skyrocketing as a result.

257

I support nutrients. Whether you choose to eat omnivore, carnivore, vegan, vegetarian, or pescatarian, the quality of the food you choose to put in your body is one of the easiest ways to be well. To feel energy. To eliminate pain. To be metabolically healthy. To improve the quality of your life. Calories are not all created equal. One hundred cookie calories are not the same as one hundred blueberry calories. Despite what some industries might try to push, what's on the end of your fork does matter. The evidence shows ultra-processed food dysregulates your appetite and causes obesity, depression, and many chronic diseases. For every 10 percent of your diet that's ultra-processed food, your risk of death increases by 14 percent, making it the number one killer globally.

I challenge you to start the process of quieting your gut, getting better sleep, and having more focus by eliminating three of the top inflammatory, disease-creating foods: wheat, dairy, and sugar. Cut them for three weeks, and see how you feel.

2. Your poo is talking to you.

Your body talks to you. Even your poop talks to you, giving you indicators. You might not know those indicators. But guess what? You deserve all the answers to your questions.

Over two thousand years ago, Hippocrates said, "All disease begins in the gut." My one piece of advice to help you feel better is, hands down, to heal your gut. Develop a healthy microbiome. Heal the intestinal permeability. Nothing is more important.

The gut and the brain were born from the same embryonic tissue. One grew up. One grew down. Sixty to 70 percent of our immunity sits in our gut, and 95 percent of our serotonin (happy neurotransmitters) is made in the gut.

One easy, fast, free way to check your gut health is to examine your poo! Your poop reveals a super important piece of your health. Check the consistency of your poop to determine your stool type using a chart called the Bristol Stool Chart. (Google it.) Types 1 and 2 indicate constipation, where the poop is hard and becomes difficult to pass. Types 3 and 4 are "normal." Types 5 and 6 indicate the poop is too loose. You are looking for a smooth "log" or "sausage" that sinks to the bottom. Did you know your poop isn't supposed to float? If you're not digesting your fats properly, your poop can carry that fat, making it buoyant.

It's OK to need answers. It's OK to have a problem that needs solving. But it's imperative to review where you're at so you have your own data. Don't stop until you get your answers. Solutions, brighter days, a better life, and a happier body exist.

3. Learn to advocate for yourself.

The system for managing and preventing chronic conditions has completely let us down, and I invite you to take much more responsibility for your own health and that of your children and loved ones. I invite you to become the expert on your own health. A health resetter.

Studies on ultra-processed foods are often based on low-quality evidence, and the public should be aware of these limitations. Major funders can include Coca-Cola, General Mills, Hershey, Kellogg, Kraft, McDonald's, Monsanto, Nestlé, PepsiCo, and Procter & Gamble.

I believe the biggest issue in the world is the food industry, where roughly 85 percent of deaths are tied to preventable food-related metabolic conditions. As a functional medicine nutritionist, I'm passionate about the root cause…and then the cause of the cause. People are missing the warning signs and the interconnectedness of those signs. There's a link between what we eat and the conditions we suffer (depression, anxiety, infertility, insomnia, heart disease, diabetes, Alzheimer's). Once we understand we have control over that, we can transform our health.

We're in a national emergency and public health crisis. Narcotics, such as OxyContin, kill around seventy thousand people a year. More than ten times that die from ultra-processed food. These are millions of unnecessary, early deaths for our children.

I now look forward to undertaking the next step in my journey. I was recently awarded a scholarship to complete my PhD in the first-ever global holistic health intervention for childhood obesity. We should be protecting our children. Instead, we're literally killing off our human capital. The next generation of adults is going to be sicker and die younger than their parents and cost society more. They're going to suffer more from chronic illness, including mental health issues. The brain and body are connected.

We've been caught sleeping at the wheel. Our bodies breaking down. Becoming fat, sick, slow, sad, and infertile. My hope is that people wake up. That experts stop recommending processed food. That our nutrition guidelines discourage sugar. Trillions of dollars would be saved, and it would have a profound impact on the population's health. This is such an incredibly big problem that's not talked about enough.

But what happens if we create hope instead of fear? I challenge you to be greater. I challenge you to find ways to never settle for the person you were last year. Are you willing to be part of the solution? Will you give yourself permission to live a healthier life? Are you ready to eat and to fuel your body so you can live a long, vital, energetic life? You have great things to do. Each one of us has a calling. Between your birthday and transition, you have one job. Make that dash dance!

About Jackie

An award-winning gut health functional nutritionist and the creator of the Gut, Brain, Body Reset, Jackie Bowker helps health enthusiasts heal their gut, lose weight, and sleep through the night around the world.

Recognized as a leading expert on the gut and nutrition, Jackie has two master's degrees in health, is undertaking her PhD in holistic health and nutrition in the prevention of childhood obesity, and hosted the *Feel Better Now with Jackie Bowker* podcast. Jackie speaks to audiences internationally at conferences and events on the topics of gut health, using food and our minds as medicine, and how to eat to turn our bodies into fat-burning, high-performing machines. People leave with the motivation and tools to feel phenomenal and confident in their bodies, be the very best version of themselves, and have the energy and focus for work and for play.

As the CEO of the Global Feel Better Institute, Jackie founded the institute to transform the gut and metabolic health of one billion people, reverse the epidemic of preventable chronic disease, and elevate the standard of healthcare globally.

Jackie is a member of the Complementary Medicine Association, and has studied under functional medicine pioneers including Dr. Tom O'Bryan, Dr. Natasha Campbell-McBride, Bruce Lipton, Rob Williams, speaker-coach Lisa Nichols, the Nutritional Therapy Association, and many more. She was the recipient of the Melrose Health Eat Your Way to Health Award in 2019.

Jackie enjoys making easy, healthy recipe creations that use real food, sunrise beach walks and body surfing, immersing herself in nature, and going on adventures with her husband, Mark; their two children, Huddy and Coco; and their dog, Cookie.

Jackie Bowker
Gut Health Functional Nutritionist
Creator of the Gut, Brain, Body Reset
CEO of the Global Feel Better Institute, Speaker
BSc (BioMed), Grad. Dip. & Master Human Nutrition, GAPS & Gluten Practitioner, PSYCH-K Facilitator

Learn more at:

- **Web:** feelbetterinstitute.com
- **Instagram:** https://instagram.com/jackiebowker
- **Facebook:** https://www.facebook.com/jackiebowkernutrition
- **LinkedIn:** https://www.linkedin.com/in/jackiebowker

CHAPTER 27

MY RISE FOR SERVICE

The Wisdom of the Elders

By Deborah McClendon, PhD, RN

When you spend your childhood constantly learning at your elders' knees, you don't realize how much your subconscious mind is recording programs that will influence your life behaviors. The lessons you see and hear are already influencing your thoughts and shaping your future without you even knowing it. Looking back on my long career serving as a registered nurse and nurse practitioner, I understand I was learning how to become a servant healer when I was still just a child.

How did I do this? By listening to the women sitting around in the quilting circles, cooking in the kitchen, or out on fishing trips. Most often, however, it was visiting the sick in the community.

Whenever someone in our community would turn up ill, I remember my grandmother and other ladies in the community would step up. They would organize and take turns, rallying to help provide whatever was needed to keep the family in homeostasis.

My grandmother would drag me with her whenever it was her turn to answer that call. On one occasion I can still remember complaining to her about taking me. I was so young. She explained that I needed to go so I could learn how to help serve in case there would come a day she was not able to. Right away I understood, and it was from that point that I began to look forward to these visits. I remember receiving and feeling so much love just for being present. The needy families were so grateful to see the expressions of love and receive our care.

The visits usually consisted of taking food. We used a variety of herbal remedies, anointing the sick person with oil, and said lots of prayers. There were also times when we would just sit and chat. Sometimes when I came home from nursing school, I would just visit people and chat. Everyone was always so happy to see me.

There was not a name for this kind of care back then; it was just what people did to help out. But now, looking back on those long-ago days, I understand that I was learning the roots of what now has been branded as "holistic care." When I think about the kind of care we administered, it's hard to separate from my early community experiences.

I learned that serving my community of family, friends, and neighbors was just one of many ways of expressing unconditional love. Those childhood experiences taught me the art of valuing community health, providing wellness, and doing so with a whole heart filled with love. I learned how to sit down and listen because one day, as my grandmother said, if I was fortunate, I would have the privilege of serving someone in need.

If only it were that easy, though. The challenge in serving people is often far more complicated than merely providing food and herbal medicines and talking about life.

TREATING THOSE IN NEED

That glimpse into ancient wisdom was a wonderful gift. In hindsight I wouldn't trade those experiences at Grandma's knee for anything. I ended up working my way up professionally to where I achieved a master's in nursing, another master's in public health, and ultimately a PhD in nursing.

While working to establish myself in the system, I discovered that just because you bring wisdom to the table, it does not mean the world will listen to you. Our system of Western medicine tends to be rigid. Healing your ailing neighbor with a dose of roots and a bowl of hearty soup is one thing. Serving professionally in the role of an acute care nurse in a hospital is another altogether.

Before I became a family nurse practitioner (NP), I first considered becoming an herbalist and opening my own store. While in NP school, I met a colleague at a conference who had written a book about the use of home remedies and herbs. She advised me that when writing papers and presentations, I should include alternative remedies. I took her advice to heart and felt I had the best of both worlds. My peers even began to confer with me when they had clients who were already incorporating or asked questions about herbal remedies.

Over time I learned another lesson: Just because people seek help and advice to improve their health, it doesn't necessarily mean they'll follow the advice given to them. Sometimes it takes more than just suffering and pain to influence people to adopt consistent self-care behaviors.

I know a person who developed type 2 diabetes as a complication of obesity. Over time his diabetes and the complications continued to get worse. He developed neuropathy (nerve damage), nephropathy (kidney damage), and retinopathy (eye damage). The damage to the blood vessels in his eyes progressed to blindness. By a miracle of God he regained his eyesight and was healed to the point of full recovery. However, less than six months after his recovery, his healthy behaviors, food choices, and physical activity reverted back to unhealthy levels. Every day, in fact, he insisted on stopping in at the local store for an ice cream cone, which was not in alignment with his treatment plan.

I was able to see that having knowledge and education was not enough for people to consistently choose health and the behaviors to match. I came to understand that lasting change comes from internal rather than from external motivators.

I have also come to understand that sometimes people are unaware of what drives their choices, and they need help getting to the root cause. Sometimes they need someone willing to walk alongside them during their healing process. Their healing process may include their physical, mental, emotional, social, and spiritual health.

Designs on Real Change

The facts about our collective health are complicated. More and more often healthcare providers are seeing patients with chronic conditions such as type 2 diabetes and high blood pressure that have reached advanced stages. In many cases these are preventable diseases.

Despite our discoveries about prevention and innovations in healthcare technology and treatments, an increasing number of patients are finding themselves forced into more-invasive care because of disease progression. There is strong evidence to support that diet and physical activity are effective for helping prevent, manage, bring into remission, and even reverse the complications of many chronic diseases and some cancers. Yet there is a lot more work we need to do around how to close the gap between knowing what we need to do and doing what we know needs to be done.

I remember one of the first patients I encountered in the clinic as an NP student. He was diabetic. He had been told on numerous visits by his providers how to take care of his feet and what to look for to make sure they were healthy. One day he came into the clinic saying he knew he had waited too long. He tried to heal a sore on his foot himself. He saw the sore was getting worse, but he continued to self-treat and waited to come in. When he took off his shoe and sock, we were able to see that not only was he going to lose a toe, but part of his foot needed amputation as well. The mood around him sunk. He came in prepared for the loss of the toe but not for part of his foot.

In spite of all of the teaching, education, and knowledge this patient had received, here we were, arriving at the scenario we all wanted to avoid. I wondered what more we could have done to serve him that would have helped prevent this ending.

While working in the city hospital, my heart was burdened.

I was able to clearly see groups of people who represented the health statistics I read about in my books and research journals. They were walking around in living color. I felt that our health-care system was failing them in some way, but I was not sure how.

There came a time when I became compelled to learn what else I could do to close the gap between knowing and doing to help avert chronic conditions reaching life-ending progression. I knew I needed to strengthen my expertise with some way to help before the end stage was reached. I felt the need to touch people when there was the most hope for recovery, resulting in their best possible health. That meant trying to touch their lives before they got sick in the first place and helping them start their healing process from within.

Helping people achieve their highest form of health and wellness from the inside out is my life's passion. This has been my passion for as long as I can remember. Charting a new course for myself into this latest chapter in my professional journey, I have embraced a new path to becoming most effective at promoting real change in a person's life. This is using the tool of coaching.

Using the coaching model, I help the person I am coaching (the coachee) discover what they want for themselves, identify what things are keeping them from having what they want, and help them get to where they want to be. I recognize the person's faith as a core tenet of their living and being. Principles from their belief systems are included to guide them along in their healing journey to maximize effectiveness from the process.

In addition to medications that may be needed, identifying their limiting beliefs, what caused them, and adjusting the mindset helps get to the root of behaviors that delay forward movement toward becoming the ideal self.

MIND, BODY, AND SPIRIT

Subsequently, I began to learn how to incorporate intrinsic coaching and health and wellness coaching techniques, adding them to my toolbox for counseling and treatment. As I have continued to learn and grow as a coaching practitioner, I have begun to draw on transformational coaching techniques in my practice. With my whole heart I believe this is an essential piece underused and sometimes missing from the healthcare puzzle.

I understand the role as guide, facilitator, supporter, and collaborator. The success of transformational coaching is due to the relationship of the coach and coachee. The coach works with the coachee while the symbolic layers of the onion are peeled back one at a time. They do the work together one step at a time, nurturing new beginnings one thought at a time.

Transformational coaching is a walk-alongside process that helps the coachee examine the beliefs, values, and perceptions that guide their thoughts and behaviors. The overarching intent is to get to the root reason behind behaviors and subsequent habits. A tenet of transformational coaching is that learning why, with professional guidance, should yield healthier choices, positive impacts, and desired outcomes for developing even better lives and valued relationships.

As a transformational coach, I am able to build on traditional coaching methods and dig even deeper into the complex layers of the coachee's beliefs, values, and mindset. This powerful and holistic coaching approach exposes critical spaces for self-discovery, desired personal growth, and ultimately intentional transformation. I am able to work closely with the coachee to penetrate and disable the limiting beliefs, fears, and self-imposed barriers that keep them from receiving the healings they are in need of physically, mentally, emotionally, spiritually, and socially.

Developing new thought patterns leads to sustained transformation. This empowers the coachee to become the best, and progressively an even better, version of themselves. As the coachee develops, so does the family, healthcare team, and community.

What a wonderful world.

My personal and professional rise for service is as transformative as it is endless. As I continue to rise, I am being served with greater love, joy, peace, and hope. I am being served with greater grace and wisdom to deliver greater love and care.

I am so happy and grateful and blessed to have been given a heart to help people to heal and live. Raised to serve, I am able to help others heal and rise to serve.

About Deborah

Deborah McClendon, PhD, RN, is a board-certified family nurse practitioner, Certified Health Education Specialist, Certified Paracletos Counselor, National Board for Health and Wellness Coach, and Lisa Nichols Certified Transformational Trainer and Coach. Deborah has spent over fifteen years in postgraduate formal healthcare education and over forty-five years in nursing practice. Deborah is known as a gifted teacher, an international speaker, a mentor, and a clinical practitioner who helps people to heal. Additionally, Deborah has earned a certificate of advanced education for nurse practitioners in obesity medicine and has completed a diabetes certificate course. Deborah is recognized as a clinical innovator and a cutting-edge research-guided practitioner.

Deborah has developed a strong and concentrated set of clinical skills that have proved to be a track record for success. As a result of working with Deborah, each client is guided through to achieve their desired transformations. Clients enjoy weight reduction, blood pressure reduction, and normal hemoglobin A1c levels achievement. They also experience type 2 diabetes remission and reversal. Deborah has dedicated her life to helping people find the lifestyle behaviors specific to them that will last.

As a coach, Deborah believes every person is complete, creative, and capable. Her clients experience a safe and supportive environment where open communication and freedom of expression are encouraged. Her practice is inclusive, is culturally sensitive, and recognizes and respects diversity. She helps clients set clear and achievable goals and build resilience through the use of their own unique experiences and strengths. Additionally, Deborah takes care of herself by regularly practicing self-reflection and obtaining personal coaching.

Deborah also enjoys spending time with family, friends, neighbors, and her pets. Her hobbies include gardening and photography.

Learn more at https://ibwell.org.

CHAPTER 28

MAGIC WITHIN

Stories of Subconscious Healing

By Dr. Shilpa Wadhwa

I n bustling New York City, I met a client with dreams as vast as the skyline. Despite success, the dream of writing a book left her entangled in hesitation and self-doubt. Our journey began with a transformative subconscious therapy session, delving into her past to unravel the beliefs holding her captive.

Uncovering layers from her past revealed a powerful forgotten memory: at four she fell into a lake, unnoticed by her parents, saved by her uncle. This incident became a cornerstone belief, leaving her questioning her worth.

Deeper exploration unveiled many more neglected instances, reinforcing her belief of insignificance. Discovering these false beliefs marked the crucial start of her breakthrough.

It was evident her subconscious mind shackled her aspirations in chains of unworthiness, falsely whispering the lie she couldn't write. Our subconscious, aiming to shield us, sometimes misinterprets our desires. Here, it sought to shield her from potential heartbreak, suggesting she might feel irrelevant if her book didn't succeed or be received well by the world. Together we dismantled these false beliefs, crafting a new narrative where her voice resonated with importance. By the session's end she embraced the belief that she mattered, her purpose was significant, and she could impact others through her words in her book.

With newfound strength and a shifted identity, she defied past echoes, writing not one but several books, leaving a lasting literary impact.

On the other side of the coast, in the greater Los Angeles area, Emily, a tall, attractive, and remarkably intelligent woman, had navigated through most of her life without a partner, despite her external charm. At the outset of our conversation it was evident that she harbored a belief in the scarcity of good men in the world. Her narratives about men painted a portrait of despair, echoing the tales of heartbreak that seemingly justified her conviction.

As we delved deeper, an unexpected revelation emerged—a memory of Emily as a baby crying in profound sadness due to her father's departure. This early experience left her with a profound abandonment wound, instilling a fear of solitude that hindered her from forming meaningful connections, causing her to unwittingly undermine relationships with decent men and endure unhealthy ones.

Childhood experiences of witnessing parental flaws often make us feel insecure, as our parents are our pillars of security. Desperately seeking understanding, our childlike minds construct narratives, unfairly assigning blame to ourselves. We internalize our parents' shortcomings, cultivating a haunting sense of guilt and inadequacy, convincing us that we are undeserving of the love and attention we desire.

In Emily's case her young mind wove a tale of unlovability, linking her father's abandonment to her perceived inadequacy. Subconsciously believing, "If I was lovable, he wouldn't have left," became a formidable barrier to love, compelling her to unconsciously sabotage connections with decent men, driven by the fear of abandonment.

Through our session Emily glimpsed the truth—she was inherently worthy of love, a lovable baby born into the world. Her parents, like everyone, were flawed and capable of mistakes. Her dad's departure had nothing to do with her worthiness. Witnessing this transformation was nothing short of miraculous.

Reframing and crafting a new narrative unveiled the

reality—Emily was deserving of love. Her evolution marked the end of a heartbreak cycle, allowing her to love and be loved by good-hearted men. It was a beautiful testament to the power of rewriting one's story and embracing the happiness that had long eluded her.

Meet Aisha, a courageous woman living in the vibrant city of London, deeply rooted in her South Asian cultural background. Aisha sought my guidance for her struggles with binge eating and weight issues, carrying the heavy burden of a long-standing history of bulimia that had haunted her since the age of seventeen.

As we took a deep dive into our sessions, a poignant narrative unfolded. Aisha's past was overshadowed by a narcissistic mother who wielded control with an iron grip—dictating her clothes, restricting her relationships, and even controlling her daily meals. Frustrated and feeling trapped, Aisha turned to bulimia as a desperate attempt to regain a semblance of control over her own life. The act of purging became a twisted solace, a way to dictate what would stay within her body when the rest of her world felt beyond her influence.

Interestingly, her bulimic episodes intensified whenever she struggled with a lack of control in her external surroundings. Aisha's difficulty with confrontation, a product of her controlling mother, translated into enduring a toxic work environment and staying in a marriage that she longed to escape.

It was a revelation for Aisha when she recognized that she, now an adult, held the reins of her life. The realization dawned that rebellion was no longer necessary; she had the power to make decisions independently. As this newfound understanding settled in, the frequency of her bulimic episodes gradually waned.

Empowered by this self-discovery, Aisha summoned the strength to break free from her unhealthy relationship, pursue a new job, and reclaim control over her narrative. In the transformative journey of our three-month subconscious therapy program, the chains of twenty-six years of bulimia were finally shattered, and she finally developed a healthy relationship with food. Aisha's story is a testament to resilience, self-realization, and the incredible capacity for healing that resides within all of us when we find the strength to rewrite our narratives.

Another client, Sarah, was drowning in the suffocating sea of inadequacy and unworthiness, held back by the haunting notion that she was never doing enough in her work. As we went into the depths of our sessions, a series of childhood events emerged, where she constantly measured herself against peers, always feeling average, never quite good enough, and inherently different from the rest.

This deep-seated belief in her mediocrity held her captive, preventing her from stepping into the spotlight and demanding the value she truly deserved. Unearthing the painful memories of her early years, we confronted the harsh judgments she had cast upon herself.

The breakthrough moment arrived when the revelation struck—childhood comparisons were an unfair yardstick. As an entrepreneur, embracing uniqueness was not a flaw but a strength. The peers she had measured herself against had not soared higher in life; they were not the epitome of success she once perceived. Sarah, in essence, was as worthy as any of them.

With the wounds of inadequacy healed, a deep feeling of enoughness unfolded. Sarah emerged from the cocoon of self-doubt with newfound confidence, bravely showcasing her worth in meetings and boldly charging what she deserved. In a remarkable turn of events, her income skyrocketed in a mere span of time, and her name earned a prestigious place on the Forbes list.

Sarah's transformation stands as a testament to the profound impact of healing the wounds that echo from the past. In reclaiming her worth, and healing her not-enoughness wound, she not only transformed her professional trajectory but also embraced the unique brilliance that had always set her apart; her relationship with her partner also changed for the better. The financial results and thriving relationships came as side effects to the deep inner work and transformation. Her journey is a symphony of resilience, self-discovery, and the triumphant ascent from unworthiness to undeniable success.

An enoughness wound stems from a deep-rooted belief that one is not unconditionally enough, hindering the ability to attract desired experiences in life. We all have this wound to varying degrees. This often originates in early childhood as a protective mechanism, formed when we lack control over external experiences and develop beliefs to shield ourselves from overwhelming emotions.

Our beliefs shape our reality and become self-fulfilling prophecies. When we are unaware of the subconscious enoughness wound and its influence, it can limit us, preventing us from receiving our deepest desires in love, wealth, success, health, and abundance. We have to feel worthy of receiving our deepest desires.

Through these client transformations you can see that your subconscious mind holds the answers to all your current problems, blocks, unhelpful beliefs, and self-sabotaging behaviors.

Through subconscious therapy you gain an adult understanding of how the experiences in your childhood created the stored subconscious limiting beliefs, and how your body and nervous system adapted in order to survive. It quite literally is soul surgery, as it goes beyond talk therapy, addressing the root cause overlooked by most. To create lasting change, we embark on the journey of unearthing subconscious limiting beliefs and identifying the lingering childhood wounds that continue to shape our present. Like upgrading devices, our subconscious mind, functioning on outdated programming, requires reprogramming for lasting results. Neuroplasticity empowers us to rewire our minds, accessing immense potential. By imprinting empowering beliefs, we forge new neural pathways, fostering positive change. Deprogramming precedes reprogramming, ensuring lasting transformation in both thought and behavior.

Most of these wounds emerge from unmet emotional needs, carving deep imprints in our psyche.

Examples of these profound childhood wounds, like banners of struggle, include abandonment, betrayal, rejection, shame, inadequacy, imperfection, loneliness, feeling unlovable, helplessness, failure, and worthlessness.

Each represents a fracture in the foundation of our emotional well-being, a scar from times when fundamental needs for safety, predictability, love, affection, playfulness, acceptance, praise, belonging, healthy risk-taking, and freedom were left unfulfilled.

Interestingly, a lot of these wounds can be passed down generationally.

Just a few years ago I was in a very different place in my life. I was stressed out, overwhelmed, and anxious, and was living a life that was nowhere close to the deeply fulfilling and wildly expansive life I desired.

No matter how much "inner work" I did, I always felt like I was still the same person, living the same life and creating the same experiences on repeat.

Not only was this wildly frustrating, but it was also incredibly painful because I knew all these things were possible for me, and yet I didn't know how to show up in the world and what gifts I had to offer.

As I became a mother, I changed in ways I never could have imagined. I noticed my daughter began to learn so much by just watching me every single day. I decided I needed to be deliberate about the behaviors I was modeling. I started to notice that the one thing that all my limiting cyclical, dysfunctional, unwanted experiences had in common was me.

I was tired of living on autopilot, constantly trying to fill the void inside with food, shopping, Netflix, vacations, and parties. I needed to discover who I was beyond the labels of mother, daughter, and wife. Despite seeking validation externally, through achievements, money, and possessions, I still felt an unfulfilled emptiness. No matter what I accomplished, I was stuck on a treadmill going nowhere.

I finally decided I was tired of constantly chasing things and being in this endless loop of feeling like I was not good enough, like life wasn't good enough. So I went on this journey to find out who I was, and to expand beyond this part of me that needed to have things a certain way. I felt like the physical world had me on a little string. I felt good when things went my way, but the second they got taken away or, god forbid, the opposite of that happened, I felt terrible again. And I wanted to just get off that ride entirely.

Through my journey I found that most people, no matter how beautiful, smart, accomplished, and successful, all suffer from not feeling good enough in some way to varying degrees. And this is what keeps us stuck and playing small. And because it's our early experiences that shape us, fancy degrees, multiple revenue streams, a number on the weighing scale or even in your bank account, or even the status of your relationship doesn't make you immune to this feeling of not being good enough. I dove deep into all things neuroscience and the study of human psychology and discovered subconscious therapy.

Once I started to become aware of the fact that there was this voice in my head, this conditioned sense of self that wanted and feared and liked and disliked and had all these preferences and desires and aversions and attachments, I felt peace for the first time in my life. I finally realized that I'm not anxious, I'm not depressed. That's just my mind. I don't need these things to feel a certain way. It felt like this was what I was looking for my whole life. I was just looking for it in all the wrong places while it was always here within me.

And to my surprise, as I stopped getting in my own way, I started to become an entirely elevated and upgraded version of myself.

Everything in my reality began to reflect this change back to me as I discovered how to show up as this free, nothing-out-there-can-make-me-shake-me-or-break-me person. And from this place I can play in the physical world. As the fullness of who I really am. Without doubts, fear, lack, resistance, without needing, wanting, obsessing, controlling, attaching, hoping to achieve, become, or arrive. I know who I am on the deepest level, and I play at the highest level and cocreate my reality because of it.

I now have a soul-based, heart-centered business that I love, lights up my soul, elevates my purpose, and is the reason that I came to this planet, that changes lives every day at the deepest level from doing it my own aligned, intuitive way.

What I love most about my work is healing intergenerational trauma through subconscious therapy.

As we heal our old trauma, our inherited limited beliefs, our not-enoughness and worthiness wounds, and shift our conditioning that no longer serves us, we literally release pain that has held generations that came before us captive for centuries. On a very deep level it recalibrates our DNA.

And while we are healing and transforming the wounds we carry from those who came before, we're also changing the trajectory of those who come after. Our future generations will have a different standard as the foundation for the lineage.

Thus, the entire lineage evolves.

Oftentimes in life we are presented with a choice: We can take this as a burden and decline to answer the call, ending up with a wound that keeps reproducing itself. Or we can see this as a gift and an honor, an opportunity to contribute to those you'll never see or know, those who may never know our name.

It takes courage to do the work of healing.

It means the end of denial, pretending, and avoiding. It means being radically honest with ourselves and those around us, the kind that won't necessarily win popularity contests, but it will recalibrate our DNA.

So the question is, Will you answer the call?

About Dr. Shilpa

Dr. Shilpa Wadhwa is an award-winning expert in subconscious therapy, a transformational leader, and the founder of Soul Worthy Transformations, with a worldwide network of clients. Her mission is to help every woman in the world realize, at a deep soul level, that they are worthy and deserving of everything they desire.

Since 2020, Dr. Shilpa has been transforming lives by helping people overcome inner wounds, blocks, and trauma that are holding them back and causing them to sabotage their success in life, love, and business. She is now recognized as the world's leading expert in self-worth and soulful success.

Dr. Shilpa has dedicated her life to helping female entrepreneurs heal their subconscious blocks to self-worth, wealth, and success, enabling them to confidently charge what they deserve and show up as their authentic selves as powerful leaders in their industry. Her sharp intuitive skills allow her to quickly identify the root causes of her clients' issues and collapse timelines, helping them achieve healing and shifts in a matter of weeks, unlike traditional therapy, which takes years.

She is among the first few certified in Rapid Transformational Therapy and India's first HeartHealing™ practitioner. Dr. Shilpa is a recognized name in the well-being industry and was awarded the Women Who Lead national award presented by the Hon'ble Minister of State Women & Child Development Govt. of India in 2021 for her work in mental health. She was also listed in the top 20 women entrepreneurs disrupting their industries in 2021 and won the Indian Women Achievers award in 2022 and 2023.

Dr. Shilpa realized that the missing link to having the life you truly deserve is feeling worthy of having it all. She is determined to help as many women as possible up-level their self-worth, break the cycle, and heal generational patterns, the ripple effects of which will impact all those around them as well as future generations to come.

Dr. Shilpa is based in India, where she balances her roles as a loving wife and devoted mother to Aryaa and Avir. They are her world and her driving force in the quest to heal intergenerational wounds. In her free time she enjoys traveling to her favorite city, LA, where you can find her unwinding with a glass of prosecco, basking in the coastal vibes and ocean views. You can find her at www.drshilpawadhwa.com or on Instagram at @drshilpawadhwa.

CHAPTER 29

A LONGING TO BE SEEN

Through the Power of Storytelling, We Can Experience Healing and More of the Love We Are All Looking For

By Mattie C. Caruthers

C hristmas was always so magical when I was a kid. My oldest brother and I worked up a little dance routine we'd perform when all the relatives came over to celebrate the holiday. Dad would make a blazing fire in the fireplace, Mom made nutmeg eggnog from scratch, and everyone would applaud when we finished our piece. I remember the delight on their faces, enjoying the feelings we were able to produce in them.

Now, after more than forty years in the entertainment industry, I am convinced that artistic expression is a powerful vehicle for healing. Whenever we laugh or cry—whether at a television show or a movie, a book we read or a song—our bodies are expressing some of what we are feeling inside...and may have been keeping locked down in there for a very long time.

When we let out what is there in response to what we see or hear, we are no longer ignoring or denying our deeply held emotions. We are allowing ourselves to experience something of the love we all deserve, because love isn't just a value; it's a vibration. It may be something we feel in our hearts, but love is something we express through our bodies, in the way we act toward others.

We live in a hurting world that needs those healing moments maybe more than ever. As a writer, director, and producer, I'm inspired to provide them for people through stories that draw from my memories of love being shared in times of enjoyment like those Christmas gatherings. I think back to when our extended family members couldn't wait to get together to celebrate birthdays, holidays, and other special events with music, food, and highly contagious laughter.

The journey to where I am today, exercising and expressing that gift professionally, has been eventful. There have been plenty of challenges and setbacks, through which I have learned that realizing your dreams isn't just about daring to take risks but also being disciplined, dependable, and diligent. Talent needs to be twinned with tenacity.

The Courage to Say Yes

Despite my childhood performances, working in Hollywood was just about the furthest thing from my mind when I was young. I grew up in a rough part of Los Angeles, where my parents worked long hours to save enough to move their now four children somewhere else, somewhere safer. That left nine-year-old me in charge of the home a lot of the time, caring for my younger brother and sister, where I tried to be everything they and my parents needed me to be. I didn't have dreams of stardom, but I deeply wanted to be a superhero in my parents' eyes.

I didn't venture out much because our neighborhood was drastically becoming more dangerous every day due to drugs and gang activity—but then the sense of security I found inside my home was compromised by an incident involving a member of our family acting inappropriately toward me. I knew telling my parents was the right thing to do, but the resulting fallout in the family weighed heavily on me.

Moving out to Altadena, California, offered something of a new start, though I still didn't have a great sense of mission beyond the home. I dreamed of one day having a large family of my own, but when I married young, things didn't turn out how I'd hoped. The birth of my son was a great joy, but the marriage was troubled.

The relationship struggles between me and my husband

intensified until one day he stormed out angrily, leaving me in tears. I knew I had to leave that abusive situation, but I dared not even try to go out the front door because he would sometimes circle back after leaving to check up on me. I picked up my infant son, grabbed my purse, and left through the kitchen door, scaling a fence with my son on my back to escape safely.

Though I felt I had let them down, my parents welcomed me back home without judgment. But as I started to reestablish my life there as a young single mom, I had to go on welfare, and then I was hit with another unexpected blow: after many years together, my mom and dad divorced.

Then, an unexpected door opened for me. Through someone Dad had gotten to know through his work, I was offered a job at Little David Records, founded by comedian Flip Wilson and music producer Monte Kaye. Having been timid for so long, it took all the courage I could muster to say yes.

That decision set me on a whole new trajectory. Because the label was a small operation, I was expected to learn and take on all kinds of new responsibilities—and I found I could learn quickly and do well. In addition, I got to meet all kinds of people in the entertainment world, from actress and singer Diahann Carroll to comedian George Carlin, among other greats.

From being a jill-of-all-trades at Little David Records, I went on to work as a personal assistant and typist for a string of celebrities before landing a gig with legendary creator, screenwriter, and producer Norman Lear. That apprenticeship led to work as a script supervisor and associate director in television. Among those I got to work with were Eddie Murphy, Oprah Winfrey, Danny Glover, and Will Smith—who also became a dinner guest for me and my now-and-forever husband, pronouncing my chicken, greens, black-eyed peas, and cornbread to be the best he had eaten since his mom's. Our son and daughter couldn't believe the Fresh Prince was sitting at our dinner table, eating soul food (and neither could we!).

BEING SEEN FOR WHO WE REALLY ARE

One thing I learned in Hollywood is that people can be very talented in the realm of entertainment and clueless in terms of real life. While still a single mom, I'd been working for a successful producer for some time and wrote a letter asking for a pay raise. His response was to invite me to lunch to discuss things.

I was so nervous when we drove out to his favorite fancy restaurant. With all the gourmet food to offer, my boss ordered a plate of simple liver and onions, and even though I hated liver, I decided to follow suit, but I was too anxious to eat much. After some small talk, he pushed an envelope across the table. I opened it and read what was inside, but my mind couldn't make any sense of it. I looked at my boss, baffled.

"It's a marriage contract," he explained. He said I was beautiful and he had never met anyone like me. The letter detailed how he would send my son to the best boarding school and how much money I'd receive each month. He had never expressed any feelings toward me, and now here he was, presenting a proposal of sorts. "I know it's a lot to think about," he said before we finished the meal in silence.

Neither of us spoke on the drive back to the office, and soon after, I left to find work elsewhere. I spent time assisting artists such as Richard Pryor and Bill Cosby. I observed how other people who were highly successful in their professional lives often seemed to struggle in their personal lives in one way or another.

I believe that's because while celebrities are in the public eye, they usually aren't really seen in their fullness, not for their true selves. They are applauded and honored for their gifts on stage or the screen, but they can easily become human *doings* rather than human beings, valued for what they provide for others— from entertainment to employment—rather than for who they are when there is no audience.

So much of the craziness that goes on in the entertainment world, it seems to me, is people yearning to be known and accepted for all of who they are, not just their gift, and not knowing how to experience that.

STANDING UP AND STANDING OUT

I don't think people deliberately choose not to see others as they fully are; for the most part, it just happens. I experienced it too, even with all the doors that had opened up for me.

Having worked my way up the creative ladder from script assistant to associate director, I knew that I was finally ready to be given a full directing opportunity. But whenever I asked, I was always told not yet, not now. Eventually, I decided that I was going to move on from the position I had on a hit TV show because I was tired of being stiff-armed and stifled. But I wanted people to know what they had been overlooking.

Oddly, my opportunity came at our cast and crew Christmas party. My husband persuaded me to participate in the karaoke session, which was a big stretch for me—I was comfortable behind the scenes, not being center stage. Though I don't drink, I got the bartender to suggest something to settle my nerves and then stepped up to the microphone when my turn came. With my eyes tightly closed, I sang "I Haven't Got Anything Better to Do," a bittersweet number originally recorded by Astrud Gilberto and later by Natalie Cole.

As I came to the end, I opened my eyes. I saw everyone, including those who had ignored my requests for a directing opportunity, looking at me with surprise, as if really noticing me for the first time. Not long afterward, I got my directorial debut, for which I earned nominations for awards from the NAACP for Outstanding Director in a Comedy Series, and from BET, the Black television network. I felt vindicated.

While this success was satisfying, I felt I had more to bring to the table. I'd enjoyed being part of popular programming such as *The Fresh Prince of Bel-Air*, *A League of Their Own*, and *My Wife and Kids*, but I didn't just want to help others express their creativity. I wanted to bring my own stories to the soundstage, mining my experiences and what I had learned along the way. Because ultimately, I believe, we are at our best when we are doing our own work, not someone else's.

That led me to found MacMattie Entertainment, through which I am aiming to provide opportunities especially for those who have traditionally been underrepresented in the entertainment industry, notably people of color and women. I believe we need more productions that celebrate and accentuate the positive aspects of all cultures as a counterbalance to the negative stereotypes that Hollywood often promotes.

One of our first projects is the sitcom series *My Sisters and Me*. Centered on three vivacious middle-aged Black sisters sharing a home together while trying not to kill one another, the show draws on my memories of my mother and her siblings, whose example of determination to overcome whatever the world threw at them continues to inspire me. Mom made her own way in the world from the age of thirteen. She owned restaurants and worked as a seamstress; I recruited her to work with me on the TV comedy series *Too Close for Comfort* as the seamstress, while also assisting the costume designer.

PLAYING OUR PARTS TO THE FULL

If I got some of my creative genes from my mom, I also inherited some from Dad. He worked as a bus driver, though he had always wanted to be in the entertainment industry. At home he'd tap-dance around the kitchen and up the side of the fridge, making me laugh. Both he and Mom loved blues, jazz, and soul music, which was always playing in the house.

Like many people, my parents didn't get to express their creativity as fully as they might have liked, but they demonstrated it in other ways. Dad made a mean gumbo, and Mom could cook just about anything, so there was always food to be shared with others. It may not have been fancy, but there was always plenty of it, and it was made with lots of love. I remember extended-family mealtimes when we'd all sit around the table together and hold hands while my mom's oldest brother, a pastor, said an inspiring blessing that I still recite to my family today. I now realize how blessed I was to feel that kind of vibration of connection with all my amazing family members.

People tell me that my own unlikely journey has the makings of a movie. Right now I have many other stories I want to help tell, but maybe one day! What are some of the lessons I have learned along the way, though? That when opportunity knocks, you need to open the door and welcome it in. It's OK to be afraid about the step you may need to take, but do it scared, and trust the process. The world has more for you.

Don't focus on your mistakes. You are going to make a lot of them—it's all part of growing. Just learn from the experience and apply what you have discovered. Look ahead, not back. Seek to be of service to others whenever you can. Do your best work in whatever situation you find yourself in because you will earn a reputation for being dutiful and dependable. And if opportunity doesn't come knocking on your door, there may come a time when you need to go round and bang on its!

An important part of my journey has been forgiveness. Without diminishing in any way the impact other people's actions can have on our lives, we simply have to find a way to rise above the harm they may have caused. Otherwise, they are the offenders, and we are the ones who go to prison.

Part of forgiveness involves having some compassion for whoever may have injured us. For me, that meant letting go of the harmful feelings about my past and recognizing the person who mistreated me had their own issues and struggles. It doesn't excuse what they did, but it offers a measure of explanation. In coming to understand that, I was able to visit their grave one time and tell them that I loved them and I forgave them.

Life is too short to be held captive by the past. We all have an essential part to play in this thing called life, and I want to play mine to the fullest. We can only do that when we're filled up, our cups overflowing into other people's lives as we share our healing stories.

About Mattie

Mattie C. Caruthers is a true veteran in the entertainment industry. Her career started in music at Little David Records with cofounders Flip Wilson and Monte Kaye, where she was an assistant to Monte Kaye (founder of Birdland and manager/jazz producer to Herbie Mann, Stan Getz, Sonny Rollins, and the Modern Jazz Quartet). Mattie was part of a small team working on all aspects of the record label, including artist development, publicity, and distribution for records by Flip Wilson and George Carlin, as well as groundbreaking television shows. The company acquired two Grammys and five Gold Records.

Mattie ventured into film and television, where she eventually became a director, writer, and producer. Her credits include script supervisor and associate director with Damon Wayans on *My Wife and Kids*, with Will Smith on *The Fresh Prince of Bel-Air*, and with Jamie Foxx on *The Jamie Foxx Show*. She was associate director on *Let's Stay Together*, *Cuts*, *Kenan and Kel*, *The Parent 'Hood*, and *Sinbad*.

Mattie worked with Norman Lear as a writer's assistant and studied under the watchful eyes of some of the industry's most outstanding directors, such as James Burrows, Andy Cadiff, Joel Zwick, Andy Ackerman, Jamie Widdoes, Shelley Jensen, and Ken Whittingham. Her television directorial debut on *My Wife and Kids* earned Mattie a 2006 NAACP Image Award nomination for Outstanding Director in a Comedy Series, and a 2005 BET nomination.

Mattie has worked on a variety of hit movies, TV shows, and commercials alongside Richard Pryor, Oprah Winfrey, Eddie Murphy, Garry Marshall, Danny Glover, Bill Cosby, Esther Rolle, and Betty White, among others. Mattie is the recipient of the 2007 Award of Achievement from the African American Film Marketplace and S.E Manly Short Film Showcase.

Mattie's work as a writer-producer includes the screenplay of the full-featured films *Black Eye Motoring* and *Ring Bell Walk In*. She also created, directed, and wrote the sitcom pilot *My Sisters and Me*, produced by MacMattie Entertainment.

Mattie is executive producer to singer-songwriter Torin Floyd; she directed his *Art Rave* and *Right Now* music videos. She has also written and directed a short film about Torin, *The Interview*.

Mattie is the founder and CEO of MacMattie Entertainment. The company's mission is to produce distinctive and successful productions centered on positive depictions of people of color. She is also a member of the Directors Guild of America.

Web: https://macmattieentertainment.com
FB: facebook.com/mattie.caruthers
IG: www.instagram.com/mattiecaruthers
YouTube: @MacMattieEntertainment
LinkedIn: linkedin.com/in/mattie-caruthers

CHAPTER 30

DISCOVERING WHO YOU REALLY ARE

By Erika Greenwood

Have you ever noticed how bright the inside of an empty refrigerator is? The white is so bright, looking at it could blind you.

I remember because as a kid, I opened my mother's refrigerator door after school, only to find it empty. Except for vegetables, fruit, eggs, and cheese and crackers. My mom was a health nut, so most of the things that we had to eat needed to be cooked.

Mom would cook on Sundays, and that was supposed to last the entire week. But sometimes Sunday's meal didn't last.

My parents divorced when I was ten. My biological father wasn't around much growing up. We would mostly see him on holidays and special occasions. Without my biological dad's support, my mom was left to pay all the bills on our four-bedroom house with a full basement in South Bend, Indiana. The mortgage was always paid, but cash was sometimes short. My mother and bonus dad, whom I call Dad, got married when I was twelve. My bonus dad had a daughter, which meant I got another sister. They worked hard to raise me.

My younger sister and I were latchkey kids. Babysitters looked after us while my mom attended evening classes to complete her master's degree in counseling. Sometimes our dinner was canned corn and green beans because that was what she could afford. I remember eating a whole can of baked beans because I was so hungry, and then getting really sick. The experience taught us a lot. One of those lessons we learned was how to appreciate what we had.

Without the help of my paternal grandmother, who remained in our lives, my mother would have struggled more. My grandmother's support was complicated, though. It was highly conditional. When she and my mother were getting along, which was most of the time, she helped out with the things we needed. She bought us clothes and filled up the house with holiday surprises. My sister and I would sit around with the Sears catalog before Christmas and circle all the things we wanted.

On the off chance they were on bad terms, things were much different. She withheld support, meaning my sister and I would do without the extras. Perhaps leading to an empty refrigerator, or some Christmas wishes would go unfulfilled.

I remained a "healthy" kid. By the time I was eleven years old, I was fully developed. Hardly out of grade school, and here I was, walking around in a full-grown woman's body. This really came with challenges. Age-appropriate new clothes were hard to find. I fit into my mother's tops, and she let me wear them, as long as they weren't too mature. She had a coat that I absolutely loved, but I couldn't wear it because it was black. I wasn't allowed to wear black or red nail polish until I was fourteen.

I vowed to myself I was never going to be poor. One day I would have all the beautiful clothes that I wanted.

THE PURSUIT OF EXCELLENCE

I come from a family of educators. No matter what I did as a kid, someone was always stressing the importance of education.

That emphasis came from my grandparents who owned their own land. In their minds a good education was important because what you have in your mind no one can take away. Land plus education equals success in my family. That's what we strive for. The expectation is excellence.

I don't remember what I scored on the IQ test; I remember it being pretty high. Once my mom got my scores, she enrolled me in extracurricular activities: piano lessons, art, swimming, and summer camps. The school administrators told her to keep me busy, and she did. I took collegiate-level Spanish in the third grade. While my mom took master's classes, I took Spanish at the same university.

We moved from South Bend, where I spent my early years in a very progressive class, to Indianapolis after I completed the seventh grade. I was writing term papers in the seventh grade. Advanced writing may seem tough—it provided a challenge that prepared me for what was to come.

I did well academically in eighth grade at my new school. I felt challenged, and I had the opportunity to enroll in honors-level classes.

Receiving good grades opened doors for me. I won certificates and trophies for my academic achievements. For a while I had the chance to work as a peer counselor. Excellence wasn't just an idea; it was something I learned to live.

My senior year I got the unique opportunity to work in a school-organized accounting lab. This was a once-in-a-lifetime situation. I had already completed most of the classes I needed to graduate. The project operated like a real accountant's office. Students were expected to dress the part and do the work. It was amazing. I was in my happy place. It was like I was born to be an accountant.

As a career-minded teenager, I had a choice to make: either I was going to school to become an accountant, a career I had already tasted, or go into engineering. I thought long and hard. When it came down to it, though, I wanted a career that would always be in demand. I also thought about what they always say about the certainty in death and taxes: they are certainties.

With scholarships rolling in, I chose accounting. There was never a question of where I would go to college. My parents said we pay taxes in Indiana, so that's where you're going to school. It proved to be a wise choice: majoring in accounting at Indiana University.

HARD WORK

I reflected often on the promise I made to myself never to be poor. I could never quite forget the dispirited feeling of that empty refrigerator. I had already gone without during my early years, and it was time for something new.

To keep that promise, I needed to start earning money. I started working the summer before my junior year in my bonus dad's office, making fifty dollars a week. It was enough to buy what I wanted from my favorite catalog—Spiegel.

That old adage about death and taxes ultimately proved correct. Accountants, especially good ones who were good at solving problems, were always in high demand. Straight out of college I felt ready for my first real taste of corporate America. I worked all over the Midwest United States, from big cities like Chicago and Cleveland to small towns like Midland and Benton Harbor, Michigan. After completing my undergrad, I went to work for Dow Chemical Co. Midland was a small town that reminded me of Mayberry from *The Andy Griffith Show*. The city planted flowers in the medians in the street. It was really cute but slow. I left town most weekends. I was in Midland for two years, eight months, three days, and six hours before I was transferred to Indianapolis.

Eventually, I went to graduate school, where I earned an MBA in marketing. I wanted to pursue what I thought would be a more creative career path. I went to work for a pharmaceutical company as a marketing associate. My recruiter suggested that I start my career with an assignment as a short-term sales rep because after all, the best marketers had sales experience.

Sales calls? I had never even liked selling candy for school fundraisers.

My sales territory was in West Cleveland, Ohio. I had family there, but they were forty-five minutes away. Each day, I had to see eight or nine doctors. Anyone who knows me understands that I don't like to drive. Yet here I was, on the road all day, delivering complimentary lunches and samples to doctors and their staff as a strategy to explain that our product was the best for their patients.

I cried every day for the first month. I had to drive in the snow, rain, whatever weather came. Many doctors didn't want to see sales reps. They often asked why I was doing sales if I had an MBA, which was on my name tag. Most of them were nice enough, but that job wasn't fulfilling. I'm glad I did it, and I learned a lot, but I never want to do it again.

Once I completed my sales assignment, I joined a marketing team. I was so excited to enter the world of marketing...at first. It wasn't the world of coupons and commercials that I imagined. The job was a lot more scientifically technical than I expected. I thought if I wanted to be a doctor, I would have been a doctor.

My mentors were a bit frustrated with me, as I had what some would call a coveted job, but I was miserable. I wasn't interested in the responsibilities that were part of the job. My mentors cautioned me that if I left that job, then I would never get another one in marketing again. To which I thought, "You promise?"

Then one of the sales managers thought it might be a good idea to send me back into the field to do more sales. Nope. I was out.

After leaving my marketing position, I went back to my roots and got an accounting job at the same company. This was a much better fit. It had lots of deadlines, but I got to use my SAP and accounting skills and felt more at home in what I was doing.

I was comfortable. Was I happy, though? I don't really know.

As an MBA hire, I was expected to have management potential. Career discussions focused on what I needed to do to achieve that position. My supervisors didn't support me in that path, though. After several jobs, some of which I really liked, I had the opportunity to supervise a team. I was finally a manager, and it was the hardest job I have ever had. I used to have to take a deep breath each day as I walked off the elevator. I'm not a person who likes drama or conflict, but there was a lot of it in that group.

How could this happen? This job was definitely not for me. This was supposed to be my dream job. But success wasn't supposed to feel like this. I was living in a nightmare, so, I quit again. Luckily my boss's boss asked me what I wanted to do and told me not to do anything drastic. Just having the conversation was a big relief. He helped me stay with the same company I had been with most of my career working on SAP implementations and accounting. As terrible as that job was, I learned a lot, and it put me in a position for my next role, which I loved. In that role I got to design processes and solve problems…my happy place.

I learned that so many managers in corporate America try to push you where they think you belong when they aren't aware of what you are passionate about or what fuels you. I don't remember one manager ever asking me whether I was happy.

I hated that.

As I thought about my career, I realized something: no one was looking out for my happiness or my peace of mind.

No one except for me.

My happiness, my life was worth more than a paycheck. I had to define my own career. I had to pursue the kinds of jobs that made me happy, pursue those and ignore the noise of what others thought I should be.

MY OWN DEFINITION OF PROSPERITY

I came out of that experience as a manager wiser. I knew that I didn't want to be poor. But I also learned an invaluable truth: Being poor wasn't just about a lack of food or money. It was about not having the necessary freedom to make your own choices.

My mom and dad would drive us around. Mostly on Sundays, we'd wind our way through beautiful neighborhoods, looking at the open houses.

My mom was a dreamer. She grew up on a farm and dreamed of moving to the city. She wanted her kids to dream too. By showing us those beautiful houses, she was teaching us how to picture what we were striving for.

Making my own money and saving whatever I could has proved

empowering. I don't do gourmet drinks and meals. I have this saying: "Five dolla' full and fifty dolla' full feels the same." It's not my priority. How much I pay for a meal out at a restaurant doesn't impact my value.

Over my career I have been blessed to earn a salary that allows me to save. I have also been able to invest and live in my own home for almost thirty years. Although those things are nice, I really enjoy the peace of mind that comes with being able to pay for my lifestyle with ease.

EMBRACING THE INNER GEEK

I've been blessed. I set out on a mission to give myself a life of options. I never wanted to feel like I did as a kid, and for the most part, I've been successful.

True wealth, I have discovered, is defined by peace of mind. It's being able to go to sleep at night and not worry about the bills. I get to spend time with the people I love and go on great tropical vacations.

By that definition I may not be rich, but I am truly wealthy.

A sense of gratitude for the things we do have is very important. Even though I struggled as a kid, looking at how hard my mom and dad worked, I'm grateful.

I'm also blessed to be a natural-born accountant. I'm a true geek at heart, what can I say?

That term *geek* is interesting. It used to come with a lot of negativity attached to it. But now that I'm older, I want to own it.

Not only am I blessed to call myself a geek; I happily embrace it.

Look at the world as it is now—geeks have invented the things that make our lives great. I look at people like Mark Zuckerberg, Bill Gates, and Steve Jobs. They're innovators, creating the kinds of things that make the world go around. Look to the not-too-distant future with phenomena like artificial intelligence and space travel, and all of that is fueled by a geek's hard work and imagination. That's something to celebrate. Go geeks!

I have many stories to tell. Lessons I share with others so they don't make the same mistakes. The ones about finding yourself, defining your own success, and embracing it.

Being uniquely me, quirks and all, has brought me true peace of mind.

I'd like to invite you to be who you are too.

About Erika

Erika Greenwood, a seasoned certified public accountant in Indiana, brings an incredible wealth of financial expertise and industry knowledge to the table. Equipped with a Bachelor of Science degree in accounting and an MBA in marketing from Indiana University, she embodies a powerful blend of technical skills and strategic acumen.

Experienced as a financial consultant for a Fortune 200 company, Erika has managed gigantic budgets exceeding three billion dollars, demonstrating her capacity to handle financial complexities on a grand scale. Additionally, she led an accounts payable team, showcasing strong leadership skills and team-management capabilities.

Erika's professional journey extends beyond these roles. She has a strong background in designing financial business processes, including processes for lease accounting, sales and use taxes, and purchasing. These experiences have honed her ability to streamline processes and optimize results.

With over twenty-five extraordinary years in finance and IT roles in corporate America, Erika's insights and skills are invaluable. Not only did she learn crucial financial information, but also she leveraged it to build a resilient financial portfolio. Her journey reflects her critical thinking, strategic planning, and financial-management prowess.

In 2018 Erika embarked on a personal-development journey. She won a ticket at a corporate event to what she thought was a speaking conference, but it turned out to be so much more. Doing personal-development work changed Erika's perspective on life, helped her heal important relationships, and brought her invaluable peace of mind. In 2022 Erika became a Lisa Nichols Certified Transformational Trainer.

Erika has now embarked on a mission to share her knowledge, life experiences, and learnings with you. She wants to help you navigate the often complex world of finance and empower you to take control of your financial future. She aims to arm you with the tools necessary to create your own robust financial portfolio. With Erika you gain the advantage of learning from someone who not only talks the talk but also walks the walk.

In Erika's downtime she likes to spend quality time with her family and friends and also enjoys attending concerts and plays. Erika loves to walk and enjoy the sunshine, which led her to complete nineteen half-marathons.

Learn more at www.myeducatedmoney.com.
Email: erika@myeducatedmoney.com
Instagram: @ecgreenwood
Facebook: @ecgreenwood

CHAPTER 31

HEALING OUR HURTS

By Joleen Crook Frideres, LMHC, NCC, MPA, CYI

How did this happen? I was caught in a cluster of professional chaos as the newly appointed executive director of a mental health agency. A day before I was given the reins, the board finally informed me that the prior director had been fired amid fraud allegations and program mismanagement. Little did I know the board would break my trust a second time. I was now encumbered with being a change agent, which would be more taxing. With the wisdom of a wrecking ball, their first orders were to fire two remaining staff. That went over well!

The board was made up primarily of farmers—good people but with little knowledge of running an agency. Managing was like trying to do a ballroom dance with my partner wearing big, muddy boots and constantly stepping on my toes. Navigating this uncharted territory as a young professional, I was in a relentless battle to salvage an agency in shambles. I lived, breathed, and slept the rebuild. But we did it!

A year into the struggle whispers reached me that the board planned to oust me. "What? This can't be happening!" The impending guillotine hung over my head as I braced myself for the inevitable. Sitting in the brightly lit boardroom, resignation letter in one sweaty palm, I clung to the flimsy chair, dreading my impending doom. "We're letting you go," they said. The disconnect between our astonishing accomplishments and their cluelessness was dumbfounding. They had no idea. I was in an emotional landslide but kept repeating to myself, "I trust you, God." I was crushed. I was dispensable! I could feel my heartbeat in my head, while I was able to keep myself calm. Professional.

With the help of a few key staff, we rebuilt our agency. I had worked tirelessly to become a therapist and an administrator, to be and become my best self. I was the first in my family to put myself through college. I plowed through ten years of university study while working dual jobs to reach this pinnacle, to become an executive director. Now, in an instant, they pulled the ground out from underneath me. Bam!

My life felt crushed into rubble. "They did this to me!" I climbed to the top, only to be cast to the bottom. Vengeful thoughts pummeled my brain, of tearing the board members apart, wishing them to be damned. I wanted them to hurt, to feel my pain.

When we are attacked, we instinctively want to fight back and retaliate. Our minds become "hell on earth." Horrid thoughts that haunt us, tossing and turning, while we try to escape them at 3 a.m. The "wheel of suffering"—attack and defend a relentless cycle! How could they?! It's so unjust! I found myself wishing damnation upon all those responsible! Yet spiritually, I was aware when I drop the "sword" of damnation on my brother's head, spiritually, I'm the one that feels the agony. Not them! Re-sentment is feeling the same pain over and over, blow by blow. And we do this to ourselves!

I had no legal recourse in a state supporting "fire at will" laws. I could commiserate with my staff who were left in disbelief, but nothing would change my harsh reality. I felt better when I prayed for the board. Momentarily, I could break out of my vengeful hate while sending prayers and positive energy to those who hurt me. In those instances I could feel peace.

Oscillating from vengeful, angry thoughts to prayerful well wishes for everybody involved, I chose to fortify my spiritual resolve. The path of soulful self-preservation became a light against the darkness threatening to consume me. "I will not let them destroy me." I refused to carry a grievance. I knew wholeheartedly that I could have a grievance, or I could have a miracle, but I couldn't have both. I chose the miracle.

Listening to my still, small voice, I prayed and asked for guidance. Wisdom arose, "What if I have not hit bottom? Instead, I have landed on my launchpad?" I grabbed the reins of my life. "I'm going to do my dream," I inwardly elated. "I'm going to Vail." I decided to sell my home and everything I owned to fulfill my dream.

We grow flowers out of manure; heck, in our lives manure is necessary. I would take this horrid-smelling compost I was left with to produce something breathtaking. My friends thought I was crazy. Of course, my parents thought I was hasty. But they also knew I was a strong woman, and they could not persuade me not to follow my intuition. They taught me to do just that: "to thine own self be true!"

It took me about sixty days to sell nearly everything I owned. Releasing each item was like an out-of-body experience. Fear can be paralyzing. I remember the daunting moment when I realized, "I ride out at dawn." It's etched in my memory forever, me lying alone on the floor in my barren home, with nothing but a candle's lonely flicker. I had already shut the electricity off and said goodbye to my friends. Talk about the moment of truth. Now I know why we all dread and desperately try to avoid change. Often, not choosing is easier than this. Outside of our comfort zone, ahead of us stretches the unknown, devoid of anything to grasp on to—vast open nothingness—perhaps just our faith to cling to.

Driving west on I-80 in the frigid November air, I deliberately rolled my windows down to confront my stark, cold reality. "What on earth have I done?" In my little white Mitsubishi Eclipse, I sang every spiritual song I knew, including one I didn't know the meaning of—"shalom-shalom, shalom-shalom." Why not! I was frantically pulling from every ounce of divine strength I could. I adored Omaha. I cherished my friends. I loved my family. This is madness. I was forsaking all of this to heed my gut, a prompting from God guiding me down this never-ending interstate?! I had no job lined up and no livelihood. Yet as I summited the Rockies, scared out of my mind, I felt like a spiritual warrior!

A new chapter began, overflowing with miracles and profound personal growth, a transformation exclusive to those courageous enough to break free. My healing journey ascended at 8,160 feet above sea level. Transcendence was mine. The first miracle? A mentor emerged into my life. Horst, a worldly and wise leader in his sixties, helped me take ownership. I had to grapple with my naivety and guilt for firing employees without due consideration for situations I mishandled. God guided me through my anguish and helped me forgive. Did I deserve to be fired? What lessons did this ordeal hold for me? Like a child on Christmas morning, I anticipated the miracles. Through my faith I understood that when we heal, let go of grievances and forgive, miracles await. Their actions were unjust. Yet I refused to let my pain metastasize into lifelong suffering.

The miracles poured in! I was paid to lead hikes through the Rockies. Pinch me! I healed with every single prayerful hike. Surrounded by the grandeur of God, I was lifted to new spiritual heights. I was hired as a counselor, and then as director of the Mental Health Agency. I found a home at Unity of the Mountains, a spiritual group, where I grew my spiritual foundation. And it gets better! I made lifelong friendships and was blessed to house-sit a multimillion-dollar home with a spectacular view of Vail. Wow. After three glorious years in Colorado, I was beckoned home to Iowa.

A Path Toward Healing: An Emotional, Mental, and Spiritual Guide

Pain and suffering are woven into the fabric of our lives. Just notice, as we succeed in one area of life, another seems to fail: when our work life takes a hit, our relationships may flourish; when our relationship is rocky, financially, we feel secure; when we're spiritually healthy, our health may plunge. Life is suffering.

We are not alone. People can be thoughtless or cruel. What can we do? We can limit our suffering. We can choose the grievance or the miracle. We can choose to forgive or not.

Emotionally

Let's not squander our hour of pain. Instead, embrace it. "I'm hurt, angry, embarrassed," we validate our emotions. There's no rushing through this. Instead, we hold ourselves with compassion and understanding. In a world that prefers quick fixes for every ailment, there is wisdom in allowing ourselves to feel the depth of our pain. We must sit with it and embrace our hurt. We sense that within the pain lie valuable lessons for us.

Healing is a process that unfolds gently, and there are no arbitrary deadlines. We can't simply mark a calendar date and expect our pain to be done. Our culture often pressures us to return to life by Monday morning, as if our pain can be neatly packaged and stored away. How sad. Healing takes weeks or years and may surge momentarily for a lifetime. It's about tuning in to our inner voice, pondering tough questions: Have I allowed myself enough time to cry? Am I ready to release this? Can I forgive myself, if needed, or open my heart to forgive others?

Mentally

When life kicks us in the teeth and we are spiraling into the abyss of anxiety, do this: Draw a line down the middle of a page, or imagine this in your mind. List on one side specifically what "I do *not* have control over." Acknowledge the long list of what you can do nothing about, everything outside yourself. On the other side list "What I *can* control." Let's feel empowered to put our energy here: What might I say, how may I react, or choose not to react? I control my thoughts and feelings and the meaning I apply to this. Anxiety overwhelms us when we focus on outer circumstances and what others should do. This is the Serenity Prayer put into action. Powerful.

We can embody serenity by first clarifying what is beyond our control. I like to imagine Christ on the boat, just chillin', while all his friends are freaking out about the storms. Yet Christ remains calm. *Acceptance* becomes the only sane option when life whirls out of control. What?! Acceptance? We *accept* gifts with lovely bows. Right? No one easily *accepts* wrongful termination, cancer, divorce, or death. Not just no, but heck no! For our own sanity, serenity, we can embark upon an all-out street fight, which I call "sucky surrender." I hate this, I don't want this…and yet this is mine.

A new mindset: If I believe this is happening *to* me, I will immediately feel rendered powerless. What if I have the courage to change the things I can? What if this is happening *for* me, not *to* me? Is this an opportunity to learn from and grow from? Am I being guided elsewhere in my life? With a curious, creative mind, I can see my options. My goal is happiness. It does me no good to stay stuck. Are there other ways I can purposefully choose to look at this? We hold firm, "This situation will not define me." What they did does not dictate who I am. Oh, hell no.

Spiritually—Is there something bigger than us?

Who can look toward the heavens witnessing perfect synchronicity or hold a newborn baby and not have a sense that there is an entity shaping and choreographing all of this? My greatest hope is that each of us seeks to foster our faith. Spirituality is not the same as religion. Each of us blossoms when we find our own path, a relationship with the Creator, Spirit, God, which inevitably elevates hope, happiness, and security. We are not a lone wave, adrift at sea, and we are the ocean; we are the sunbeams of the sun. According to *A Course in Miracles* and many spiritual sources, we each have a "highly individualized curriculum." What truly matters is that "all is well with my soul." "This is a spiritual journey. None of us get out of here alive."

As I drove up the majestic mountains, I felt the embrace of the Rockies. This adventure could not have been gifted to me without the painful life event I had endured—being fired. I courageously grabbed hold of what I could control and accepted what I could not.

The f-word?

"Wait! What? Forgive them? Are you kidding me?! Yes, forgiveness may very well be the most selfish act we can do for ourselves. Forgiveness is in our control. What they did was absolutely wrong. What they did hurt me. But I'll be damned (literally) if I'm going to carry this pain and agony around because of them. At the heart of healing lies the often dreaded forgiveness. We may need to keep them out of our lives, true. And…we can also purposefully let go and forgive them for our own sake. What that board did was awful. In an instant they struck me down. But I refuse to let their hurt continue to hurt me. Instead, let's never attribute to malice what we can to cluelessness. What's within my grasp is how I choose to perceive those who may have wronged me. As the Bible quote goes, "Forgive them, Father, for they know not what they do."

Behavior is either an expression of love or a desperate plea for love (a nugget of wisdom from *A Course in Miracles*). When we reflect on moments when *we* fell short of our best selves, isn't there an inner recognition that "I'm not a bad person…I was just (fill in the blank) upset, hangry, triggered, etc."? This intentional perspective on human nature embodies profound, unwavering compassion. Since there's only one of us spiritually here, "one bread, one body," the more we consciously practice compassion and forgiveness toward others, the more effortless it becomes to extend that love to ourselves.

There's light and dark energy. Love and fear. Dark energy embodies fear, ego, and a right/wrong, good/bad mindset. Decisions rooted in this energy yield poor outcomes. In contrast, a mindset fostered by light and love emanates from fertile soil where good can bloom. Miracles can happen. Lean in to the light!

I get to celebrate. All is well with my soul. I am honored as a psychotherapist and coach to help people heal their hurts. Like all of us, we go through struggles. Our souls can shine bright, free from being tainted by unforgiveness or anger that can put a stranglehold on us. Have you been there? Are past hurts still hurting? Some say that forgiveness is hard. No way. What is horribly hard? Going through life carrying that yuck and muck of resentment. Let's summit together and rise above…against all odds! Choose the miracle.

About Joleen

Joleen's clients grow and blossom into more than they ever dreamed of. After coming to her with hurts, clients heal, get in touch with how they really feel. As you come to truly know yourself, you learn to love yourself. Clients experience heartfelt compassion and care with Joleen. Isn't that a real rarity these days? You'll know she cares...because counseling is her calling.

Joleen offers what you uniquely need. How? She has invested her entire life honing her skills to best offer you a plethora of clinical knowledge, techniques, and holistic healing tools. She has dozens of mental health certifications; you can find these, testimonials, and upcoming events at CourageousLifeCounseling.org. As a psychotherapist and elite coach she is passionate about helping you live your most fantastic life.

As a transformational healer, Joleen offers life-changing retreats, workshops, and online group "care-apy." Think outside of the box? *What* box!? Joleen is best at guiding you to fight fear, find your authentic self, and foster the you, you were meant to be.

As a career woman dedicated to her craft, she had her daughter late in life and was a stay-at-home mom. During this time, she had her own spiritual radio segment and authored inspirational magazine articles.

With enthusiasm she celebrates: "Let's choose to live life to the fullest, together." Sixty is the new forty. Joleen practices and encourages aging actively through dancing, boot-camp workouts, cycling, pickleball, and more. She recently became a certified yoga instructor. Join her upcoming events to enrich your life, to live life to the fullest.